D0354457

DATE DUE

Books by Enrique Hank Lopez

MY BROTHER LYNDON *by Sam Houston Johnson with Enrique Hank Lopez*

AFRO-6

LA BALSA *by Vital Alsar with Enrique Hank Lopez*

THE SEVEN WIVES OF WESTLAKE

THE HIGHEST HELL

EROS AND ETHOS

THE HARVARD MYSTIQUE

THE HIDDEN MAGIC OF UXMAL

THE THIRTEENTH JUROR

CONVERSATIONS WITH KATHERINE ANNE PORTER
Refugee from Indian Creek

Conversations with Katherine Anne Porter

REFUGEE FROM INDIAN CREEK

Conversations with Katherine Anne Porter

REFUGEE FROM INDIAN CREEK

by ENRIQUE HANK LOPEZ

LITTLE, BROWN AND COMPANY · BOSTON · TORONTO

FIRST EDITION

The author is grateful to the following publishers and agents for permission to reprint the material noted below:

Excerpts from *Voyager: A Life of Hart Crane* by John Un-terecker. Copyright © 1969 by John Unterecker. Reprinted by permission of Farrar, Straus & Giroux, Inc.

Excerpts from "The Eye of the Storm" by Eudora Welty. Copyright © 1965 by Eudora Welty. Reprinted by permission of Russell & Volkening as agents for the author.

Excerpts from "Treason's Strange Fruit" by Robert Hillyer. Copyright © 1949 by Saturday Review. Reprinted by permission of Saturday Review.

Excerpts from "The Red Hot Vacuum" by Theodore Solo-taroff. Copyright © 1962, 1970 by Theodore Solotaroff. Ap-peared originally in *Commentary*. Reprinted by permission of Atheneum Publishers.

Lines from "The Love Song of J. Alfred Prufrock" and from "Gerontion" in *Collected Poems 1909–1962* by T. S. Eliot. Copy-right, 1936, by Harcourt Brace Jovanovich, Inc.; Copyright © 1963, 1964 by T. S. Eliot. Reprinted by permission of the pub-lishers.

Unless otherwise noted, the photographs in this book are from Katherine Anne Porter's personal collection.

LIBRARY OF CONGRESS CATALOGUING IN PUBLICATION DATA

Lopez, Enrique Hank.
  Katherine Anne Porter, refugee from Indian Creek.

  Bibliography: p.
  1. Porter, Katherine Anne, 1890–1980—Biography.
  2. Authors, American—20th century—Biography.
  I. Title.
  PS3531.O752Z76 1981   813'.52   80-28331
  ISBN 0-316-53199-5

MV
*Published simultaneously in Canada
by Little, Brown & Company (Canada) Limited*

PRINTED IN THE UNITED STATES OF AMERICA

To Miranda,
my first grandchild
and the first of her generation

Time for you and time for me,
And time yet for a hundred indecisions
And for a hundred visions and revisions.
                    —T. S. Eliot
                    "The Love Song of J. Alfred Prufrock"

Author's Note

WHEN Katherine Anne Porter and I undertook the conversations that form a significant portion of this book, it was with the understanding that this would be, in part, an autobiographical recollection that would have to stand for her life. Miss Porter never intended to write an autobiography. But rarely did she tell some stories the same way twice. It was part of her charm, of course. She sitting there, attractive still, wide-eyed, that wonderfully gentle and somewhat childlike voice singsonging the story for you and the tape recorder.

The tape recorder, however, is both a miracle and a mirage. It sits there ready to take the speaker's every word, to be noncensorious, to make available, *for all time,* each of the speaker's sacred words. The speaker becomes the center of a universe, for a time. Then one listens and yes, it is true, it was as spoken. It all sounds so *right.* And so it must have been for Katherine Anne Porter.

Miss Porter was an extraordinary writer and woman. In her fiction she wrote with a crystal vision of the world, but in her life she often confused the romantic desires of the past and the fancies of the moment with realities that were too sharp for her, too much to recognize in the harsh light of day. Perhaps that was the prerogative of the Southern lady, the apple of the father's stern eye. To embroider a bit, to change the facts to fit the storyteller's mood of the hearer's fancy.

This, then, is the story of a life as its holder perceived it. Here is the life, as she recalled it, of a great writer of fiction, of *Ship of Fools,* of "Leaning Tower," of the miraculous Miranda stories.

Her fiction came so much from her life, from her observations, from her insecurities, fears and obsessions, that sometimes it is difficult to find the line between the fiction and the life. It was apparently so for her as well, as is clear in the Miranda stories and in her autobiographical recollections of her mother's death (see page 3). The lines between the life of the imagination and the life of Katherine Anne Porter blurred and melded.

The result is in your hands. It is not unlike the notebooks of a psychoanalyst, I presume, in that there is here the revelation of the life perceived by the subject, not always the life that was led. In any event, I hope this presents a balanced view of the world of Katherine Anne Porter.

Preface

IN January of 1974, just a few months before her eighty-fourth birthday, Katherine Anne Porter bought her own coffin from a mail-order cabinet shop in Arizona.

She had once asked me to buy her a plain simple Mexican coffin with rope handles, the kind she had often seen at peasant funerals in rural Mexico. "I'm bound to die fairly soon," she told me. "And I don't want to be buried in one of those garish overpriced caskets that funeral directors get rich on. So I'd be much obliged if you'd get me a plain wooden box with some good strong rope for handles."

When I resisted her suggestion, she smilingly accused me of being excessively squeamish and later asked her nephew to buy the coffin. When he also declined, she somehow located an advertisement in a mail-order catalogue and forthwith ordered a fairly satisfactory coffin. Although it wasn't as plain and simple as she hoped it would be — the joints were too smoothly sanded and the long brass hinges were a bit too ornate — the six-foot pine box was ready to be painted Mexican style. Having provided the coffin with a winding sheet of fine Belgian linen, which she had bought while teaching in Liège, she propped it against the rear wall of her closet and calmly turned her attention to more immediate concerns.

Most people would say this was a ghoulish thing to do, but it was actually quite logical and uniquely sane. Her entire life was unique to the rarest degree, unique and suspenseful. Indeed, as one follows the often incredible twists and turns of a long career filled with heartbreak and triumph, high drama and low comedy, one is inevitably reminded of Mme. Du Barry's final words as she was led to the guillotine: "My life is incredible. I don't believe a word of it!"

During our first conversation in the lobby of a Mexico City hotel, Katherine Anne Porter told me about a Nicaraguan poet she had met in the early twenties. "He was one of the most evil men I've ever known," she said. "An absolute scoundrel, who thought nothing of seducing the teenage daughter of his best friend and then bragging about it. Yet there was something strangely compelling about Salomón de la Selva, a certain sinister magnetism that made him hard to resist. He was one of three such men that I've known in my life. . . ."

But just as I was about to ask her the names of the other two scoundrels, someone interrupted our conversation, and she didn't tell me about them until nine months later.

Miss Porter made several such elliptical remarks that first afternoon — tantalizing half-finished references to marijuana, revolution, sex, literary vendettas in New York, the trials of Ezra Pound, political intrigues in Mexico, and the horrible nightmare tragedy of Hart Crane — touching upon each subject with just enough personal involvement to pique the interest of even the most detached listener. Consequently, since I had instantly become a very "attached" listener, I came away from the initial interview feeling intensely frustrated, each of my carefully-prepared questions having provoked a chain reaction of numerous other questions that (most probably) would never be answered. She herself, in a disturbingly speculative and self-mocking manner, had posed most of the queries, as if she regarded her own life as a perpetual enigma.

"There are no limits to this woman," I told one of my colleagues. "She's known everyone from Diego Rivera to Ernest Hemingway, and there's very little she has not experienced."

But there was something strangely sad and lonely in the way she lived. She had been so restless and so chronically dissatisfied. She had lived in at least fifty different places — in barren rented rooms, half-furnished apartments, a rented house now and then — moving at least once a year, sometimes two or three times in a single year, always in wistful pursuit of something permanent and stable. And in her restless wandering, she had been married three times and lived with four or five lovers, perhaps unable or at least unwilling to form any permanent attachments. Yet she had a profound and deeply personal commitment to her career as an artist, a commitment that was never abandoned.

I first met Miss Porter at a coffee-or-rum reception following her lecture at the Instituto Cultural Norteamericano in the winter of 1964. In fact, the rum was the first thing we talked about.

Holding a rum-and-Coke someone had given her, she took one sip and said, "This is much too sweet. Don't they have any bourbon and plain branch water around here?"

"Whiskey is too expensive in Mexico," I said. "This *instituto* is sponsored by the U.S. Embassy, and they always economize at these cultural functions."

"Now, isn't that typical of our State Department," she said with a wry smile. "They'll spend millions to back some stupid dictator, but when it comes to something like this, they give you cheap rum instead of good bourbon."

Setting aside her highball, she took coffee instead. It was then that I introduced myself as co-editor of *Diálogos*, a Mexican literary magazine, and promptly asked if I might interview her for our special issue on American writers.

"I'll do anything for Mexico," she said. "I've always considered this my second home."

The following afternoon we met in a remote corner of the mausoleumlike lobby of the Hotel del Prado, my bulky tape recorder snuggled under a long narrow coffee table in front of a leather couch, where we sat almost shoulder to shoulder. I had partially concealed the microphone behind a bulbous red vase filled with colorful paper flowers.

"I'm glad you've got all that machinery out of sight," she said. "I always get a bit self-conscious when I see a tape spinning round and round."

"I feel the same way," I said, reaching down to adjust the volume so as to catch the full resonance of her soft, mellow, slightly accented voice.

She was wearing a stylish pale green dress and a single strand of pearls; and, although her hair was chalk-white and wispy as gossamer, she looked more like sixty than seventy-four. Her clear blue eyes were especially youthful, now gently amused by some human foible, then coolly analytical a few moments later.

"Where shall we start?" I asked.

"Why not start at the middle — and go backwards and forwards," she said. "I guess the middle happened right here in Mexico."

So we talked for nearly four hours, my questions ranging from her adventures in revolutionary Mexico to her early childhood in Texas, to Germany as the Nazis were coming to power, to Paris, "where Gertrude Stein was throwing her weight around," to the Greenwich Village of the frail Edna St. Vincent Millay and "grumpy" Edmund Wilson, to the many other places where she lived during what she later called "the restless pilgrimage of my soul." But every morsel of remembrance was but a mere hint of her come-what-may life-style, her perpetual face-to-face exposure to all kinds of direct experience. That was her phrase: direct experience. "I didn't want my life filtered through other people. I had to see and feel for myself."

About nine months later a small portion of that interview — written by me and cross-checked by her — was published simultaneously in two magazines, the English version in *Harper's* and the Spanish version in *Diálogos*. Subsequently, while in New York negotiating certain matters for my Mexican law firm, I phoned her home in Washington, and she immediately invited me to dinner. "I'll fix you the best Mexican meal you've ever had." Then an hour later she called me back and said, "It's silly for you to fly down just for dinner. Why don't you come before noon, so that I can serve you a perfectly mediocre lunch. Then you'll be sure to appreciate the *chiles rellenos* and *mole poblano* that I'm planning for dinner."

Needless to say, I accepted without a moment's hesitation, and we had a marvelous twelve-hour conversation interspersed with excellent food (it was clam chowder for lunch) and a fine sour-mash bourbon "with just a smidgen of branch water." She was one of the most engaging raconteurs I'd ever known, wickedly humorous at times and then profoundly philosophical. She seemed so alive and expressive, it was difficult to believe she was fast approaching eighty.

But I also learned that she was no longer writing, that she had not published any fiction since *Ship of Fools*, not even a brief short story. Keenly aware of the writer's block which had always plagued her, I was soon convinced she would never write an autobiography, that no one would ever read of the incredible people and events she had been telling me about in such vivid detail. Several later visits, all of them replete with often-hilarious personal anecdotes and remarkably candid self-analysis, further confirmed my impression that she was "talking" her autobiography rather than writing it. To say the least, that was a disheartening thought.

Then one evening, as we were having an after-dinner brandy with Barbara and Norbert Schlei at the Rive Gauche restaurant, she turned to Norbert and said, "I want you to know that Hank is relieving me of the responsibility of ever having to write again."

Flattered but also puzzled by her remark, I later asked her, "What exactly did you mean, Katherine Anne?"

"Well," she said, pursing her lips and frowning slightly, "I've hesitated to ask you, Hank, because I know how busy you've been with your international law practice — but I'm going to be selfish anyway. As you no doubt realize, I won't be able to write my autobiography. I'm too old and too tired. But I'd like you to write a biography about me."

"Of course," I said without a moment's hesitation. "But I'll have to tape record some additional interviews."

"We can talk as much as you want," she said. "But let's keep the recording machine out of sight."

Happily accepting that condition, I then somewhat hesitantly said that I preferred not to write an "approved" or "official" biography. "From what you've already told me, you've been involved in considerable controversy," I said. "So I'd like to explore — as freely as possible — what others have said about you and your involvement in those controversies."

"Fair enough," she said, an amused glint in her eyes. "I wouldn't want you to write one of those mushy worshipful biographies, which no one would believe anyway — certainly no one who's really known me. But there is one favor I'd like to ask. . . . I'd prefer that you not publish your book 'til after my death. It's bound to be controversial, and I'm just too old and weary to deal with any more conflicts."

Quite obviously, I readily agreed. And within six weeks I abandoned my office in Mexico City and temporarily moved to Washington, D.C., to undertake a series of daily interviews that lasted more than a month, later supplementing them with additional weekend sessions after I had permanently established a new home in New York City. Most of our talks took place in the comfortable tastefully furnished living room of her two-story brick house in one of the more fashionable areas of the capital. But for reasons I could never fathom, she seemed to save some of her choicest stories for the dinner hour, which naturally enhanced the flavor of the superb dinners she had prepared. I've never eaten better food, nor enjoyed more fascinating conversation.

"I'm telling you things I've never told anyone — not even to myself," she said one afternoon. "But I guess there's no point in holding back at this late stage."

Upon terminating our interviews, I started writing long passages for the projected book, organizing the free-flowing random talks into a more-or-less chronological order. Then I would read them to her, adding new details she would suddenly remember and correcting a few minor errors in spelling or time sequence.

But during the latter phase of our conversations, Miss Porter suffered a physical setback that required hospitalization on several occasions. Consequently, since she never fully recovered, I eventually realized that I would have to write the book without any further interviews. Fortunately, I had already acquired far more information than I had ever hoped for.

There were, as one might expect, certain contradictions in what she told me about herself and about others. Some of these contradictions merely reflected different perspectives at various periods in her life, changes in attitudes that quite commonly occur; but there were other contradictions less easy to explain. Moreover, there were a number of self-serving statements and serious charges (some relating to personal controversies involving Gertrude Stein, Hart Crane, Diego Rivera, Christopher Isherwood, Ezra Pound, D. H. Lawrence, various college professors, and some of the critics who accused her of being a protofascist and a misanthrope when she wrote *Ship of Fools*) which I have tried to explore and analyze from various angles, often with the aid of personal interviews with some of the people who differed with Miss Porter.

Here, then, is the world of Katherine Anne Porter as seen through her eyes.

ENRIQUE LOPEZ

Conversations with
Katherine Anne Porter

REFUGEE FROM INDIAN CREEK

1

Birth of a Rebel

"My mother died less than six weeks after I was born, and it was my birth that caused her death. Though I have never known the exact terminology of the medical complications which afflicted her as a result of my birth, I was subsequently told that she suffered extreme and prolonged pain. My father prayed desperately for her survival, attending her every need and desire during those last few days, and I am convinced that her death was the saddest experience of his life."

That is what Katherine Anne Porter told me during one of our early discussions; but when I repeated her statement a week later as a preface to asking for more details, she expressed complete surprise.

"Now, where on earth did you get that notion?" she asked. "People are always saying that, Hank. I guess some reporter got it all wrong a long time ago, and now everyone keeps retelling the same mistake. But it simply isn't true. My mother died two years after I was born, and my birth had no bearing on her death — none whatever."

I simply nodded when she made that "correction," but a few hours later I replayed the tape recording of our earlier conversation, and I heard her voice clearly saying, "My mother died less than six weeks after I was born, and it was my birth that caused her death. . . ."*

There were tears in her eyes the first time she told me about her mother, but there was a rush of compulsion in her voice, a

---

* Miss Porter was born in Indian Creek, Texas, on May 15, 1890.

sense of urgency, as if she needed to unburden herself of a long-suppressed anguish. With her fingers slowly shredding the stem of a rose she had previously cut from the vine in her back garden, pressing it so tightly that the chlorophyll stained her thumb, Miss Porter seemed especially distressed when she talked about her father's prolonged depression after his wife's death. "He was so overwhelmed with grief that for many years thereafter he couldn't bear to have anyone mention her name in his presence. That was of course a terrible burden for my two older brothers and my sister. And later on it was equally difficult for me."

Sometimes they would be sitting at the supper table, chattering away as children will, and if one of them should start to mention their mother — even in the most indirect way — their father would stiffen visibly, and his cold gray eyes would command them to change the subject. "But the more he tried to shut her out of our lives the more we thought about her: she was with us everywhere and at all times. Oh, how I yearned to say her name, to touch the dresses she had once worn, to hear the same bedtime stories she had told my brothers and sister, to know all about her in the most exacting detail."

But she wouldn't have dared ask her father about her mother, and she would have remained a complete cipher in Katherine Anne's life had it not been for her aunt and her grandmother, who, as she grew older, began to tell her all the things a half-orphaned child has to know about a parent who has died during the child's infancy.

"Was she beautiful? Did she ever spank my sister? How did she meet my father? And how did she wear her hair? I had to know everything. Somehow I had to recreate all of her in my mind and in my heart. I had to fill every inch of that painful vacuum my father had willed upon us. It must have been sheer anguish for him."

Most Freudians would assume that her father probably resented her from the very day she was born, but Miss Porter later insisted that "he certainly managed to submerge such resentment (if indeed there were any) in the deepest recess of his being."

Nevertheless, she frankly admitted (in a letter to her nephew) that the children's father had once told them, "If your mother had listened to me, none of you would have been born."

Harrison Boone Porter, born in the backwoods of Kentucky and a great-great-grandnephew of Daniel Boone, had always been taciturn, aloof and frequently impatient with children; while his wife (the former Mary Alice Jones) was easygoing and gentle. Consequently, when Mrs. Porter died at such an early age, Katherine Anne, her brothers and sister were inevitably drawn to their maternal grandmother, who took charge of her son-in-law's household and reared his young brood. Their father, however, remained the dominant figure at home.

When he was stern he was stern with all of them in equal measure, but Miss Porter felt he was especially gentle with her on certain occasions — perhaps because she was his youngest child and always rather small for her age. Since they were both strong-willed and quite independent in their nature, there were undeniable tensions that later developed between them, certain abrasions that eventually drove her into a foolish "spite marriage" when she was merely sixteen years old, "but I certainly wouldn't attribute these difficulties to any grudge related to my mother's death."

Nevertheless, she did confess to certain inchoate feelings of guilt with respect to her obviously innocent involvement in her mother's death, and her impulse was always to say "no" when asked if the death was caused by her birth.

Her persistent lifelong ambivalence regarding the date of her mother's death is clearly shown in two of her short stories, in which Miranda (obviously Katherine Anne Porter herself) is the principal protagonist. In "The Old Order," the mother dies at Miranda's birth; in "Old Mortality," the mother dies when Miranda is eight years old.

There was, in fact, nothing unusual about her mother having died in childbirth, especially when one considers that it happened in a frontier community in the year 1890, when most pregnant women were still having considerable difficulties even in the more advanced Eastern cities. She died at the age of thirty-two; but even in this respect she seemed to follow a family pattern. Every one of Miss Porter's grandmother's four daughters died before she was thirty-three, although Granny herself was well past seventy when she passed away. They all lived on cattle ranches or farms and led very hard lives, struggling with only the barest necessities to feed and clothe oversized families which no one had tried to limit. "They used to say of that part of Texas that it was heaven for men and cattle but hell on women and horses." Birth control (assuming they had known about it) would have been the last thing in the world they would have practiced. It would have been considered indecent to trifle with nature. Her grandmother had eleven children, one child every fifteen months, for a total of seven boys and four girls, and her family was not regarded as unusually large.

Miss Porter's mother had only four children, but her rather frail condition would have probably precluded a larger family even if she had managed to survive her last illness. "I have mentioned her poor health because it was so frequently talked about in our family, and yet my own personal impression of her was far different from theirs. I have always thought of her as a vibrant beautiful woman with a lively sense of humor, because those are precisely the qualities that were emphasized in the stories I most wanted to remember."

Her grandmother described her as tall and slender, with clear gray eyes, smooth white skin and copper-colored hair that glowed with a deep vitality. Her teeth were small but quite regular and her mouth was soft and sensitively mobile, always on the verge of a smile. She was especially humorous in matters relating to her husband, who was apparently quite stuffy when he was younger and much given to lecturing her on household management, the rearing of children and even her personal attire, solemnly stressing his views with stern gestures and self-conscious intonations that clearly invited mimicry. And that's exactly what happened. Katherine Anne's mother was soon able to mimic every phrase and posture and would later give her comic imitations at family gatherings, all of it light and frothy but piquant enough to make its point: he eventually eased up on his domestic sermons.

Her talent for mimicry also served her well in the telling of bedtime stories to Katherine Anne's older brothers, who were frequently held in utter thralldom by her amusing flights of fancy and her obvious delight in imitating some of the people in the neighborhood. "Having heard about this wonderfully impish quality in my mother, I have for many years conjured an image of her that can never be found in the family photographs I have kept for more than sixty years."

There was one old yellowing picture which she kept in an antique silver frame, a partially faded photograph in which her mother appeared in a dark silk dress with a little fur neckpiece and a matching sealskin hat that tilted to one side. The picture was taken during her parents' last trip to New Orleans. They used to travel in a family carriage loaded with luggage from their farm near Indian Creek (where Katherine Anne was born) and would ride into town to catch a horse-drawn bus that would take them to San Antonio. That portion of the trip would require thirty-six hours. Then they would board a train for New Orleans, another thirty-six-hour journey, for a total of three days from farm to city. But New Orleans was such an exotic and exciting place no one seemed to mind the long uncomfortable trip, certainly not her mother, who was in her element in the fine shops and elegant French restaurants. Then, as if to capture permanently some sweet moment of those infrequent holidays, her father would ask her to pose for another picture, and their favorite photographer would snap her image with his cumbersome tintype equipment. "I rather suspect she was always a bit apprehensive about the flash powder they used in those days, because her facial expression in the photo I have is rather stiff and wary."

After his wife's death, Harrison Porter took the original tintype to a local photographer and asked him to reproduce it on paper. Well, it wasn't a very good reproduction. One of her eyes was so blurred that it seemed to lack a pupil, and years later Miss Porter tried to draw in the missing pupil with ordinary black ink and botched it beyond repair. "She now has a slightly cross-eyed stare," she later commented, "but I intend to keep that photograph forever because it was taken at a most happy moment in her life."

When Porter was finally able to talk about his long-deceased wife, he told his now-adult daughters that shortly after that picture was taken they had gone dancing at their favorite ballroom near Bourbon Street. He had never known anyone who was so adroit at swinging the train of her gown as their mother was. She could waltz backward and twirl her train behind her like an elegant peacock, never once stumbling or even slightly losing her balance. They especially liked to waltz to "The Farewell of the Moorish Kings to Granada," which is more popularly known in Mexico as "La Golondrina," and that was the very last number they danced to on their final evening in New Orleans. Small wonder that her death left him so desolate.

Curiously enough — in those later days when they were allowed to discuss her — Miss Porter's father indirectly blamed her mother's inability to survive her last childbirth on the horrible aftermath of the Civil War. She and her three sisters, all of whom died at an early age, had been born and raised in the ravaged impoverished South and were permanently affected by the near-starvation which afflicted vast numbers of dislocated men, women and children, regardless of race. All of their family property and worldly goods had been suddenly snatched away. Even basic foods were scarce. On more than one occasion Miss Porter alluded to the grim privations caused by that needlessly cruel war, and yet there were moments of leavening humor that poignantly illustrated the same point. She especially recalled an incident involving her grandfather which she later turned into fiction:

"He was riding along on a country road, probably going somewhere to join his regiment in the Confederate Army, when he spied a large hunk of raw bacon lying on the ground. In a split second he jumped off his horse, grabbed the bacon off the muddy ground, wiped it off on the seat of his pants, got back in his saddle and hungrily devoured it as he jogged on down the road. He later told my grandmother that it was the best piece of raw bacon he had ever eaten."*

Having heard her grandmother tell this and many other anec-

---

* This incident appears in "The Old Order."

dotes, Miss Porter always felt a strange but ineluctable involvement with the Civil War, a truly tenacious involvement which
sometimes manifested itself in the most unexpected ways. In the
summer of 1947, for example, she started rereading certain favorite books about the war, and one afternoon she got totally immersed in a genuinely heartrending passage on the fall of Richmond.

"Quite suddenly I felt myself cornered inside that lovely besieged city and actually imagined the walls crumbling around me
as the huge guns of the Union Army shelled everything in sight,
and I felt all the anguish and frustration of its loyal defenders as
their women and children fell wounded or fled in terror. The
tears welled in my eyes and deep sobs wracked my body. Finally
I threw myself on the bed and delivered myself to the full luxury
of my grief. I was still lying there in the half-light of the gradual
sundown, gently crying, when my husband [Albert Erskine]
came home and called to me from the patio. Getting no response,
he searched for me in the kitchen and then the living room, and
finally realized I was in the bedroom. As he entered the shadowy
room I rose to one elbow and cried (perhaps merely whimpered),
'Oh, Albert, Richmond has fallen!' I was absolutely heartsick."

Thinking back on that tearful afternoon, Miss Porter burst into
laughter and nearly spilled the tea she was drinking.

"And what was his reaction?" I asked when I was finally able
to control my own belly laugh.

"Well, I must say this for Albert: he somehow managed not to
laugh at me. He was, in fact, wonderfully tender and sweet about
my lavish grief. He simply took me into his arms and cradled me
in a most soothing manner, softly whispering, 'I'm just as miserable about the fall of Richmond as you are, Katherine Anne.'
What's more, he never once teased me about that strange outburst. He also was a Southerner, incidentally, and perhaps that
explains his spontaneous empathy."

It was precisely this kind of manly tenderness ("and I've always maintained that only strong and secure men can be
tender") which she associated with her father, particularly in her
early childhood. Since he never again remarried after his wife's

death, he frequently tried in his own taciturn way to fill in the vacuum of maternal care and affection which he realized every child had to have. At times he was a pleasant everyday sort of father, who would proudly hold Katherine Anne on his knee if she were prettily dressed and well behaved; but if her hair was not freshly combed or her fingernails not properly scrubbed or the seams of her long stockings slightly crooked, he would curtly send her away to "straighten out."

What she remembered most clearly about his onerous hygienic whims was the revolting mixture of prepared chalk, powdered charcoal and salt that he made them use for tooth powder. Just as old-fashioned but far more palatable were the delicious hot toddies he concocted for them when they were snively with colds.

They all dimly understood that he was genuinely concerned about their well-being, both physical and spiritual, that he simply wanted them to be reasonably intelligent and civilized when they grew up. Yet they couldn't help resenting his impatience with their customary chitchat and his disconcerting habit of asking, "How do you *know?*" whenever anyone made a dogmatic statement about the most nonessential matters. "It was nearly always embarrassingly clear that we didn't know, that we were merely repeating something we had heard." Naturally, this perpetual "How do you know?" made it very difficult for them to sustain any lengthy conversation with him, since none of them wished to appear foolish in his presence. Nor did they care to cross his path when he lost his temper. Whenever they noticed signs of an impending outburst they simply scattered out of sight, for they knew the roof was going to come off any minute. Then quite suddenly he would calm down and actually seem apologetic.

His explosive temper had once led him into temporary exile in Mexico many years before Katherine Anne was born. He had hotheadedly shot at a man with whom his sister flirted at a dance. "This, of course, was very wrong of him," Miss Porter told me quite matter-of-factly, "because he should have challenged the man to a duel, as her fiancé had done. Instead, he just took a wild potshot at the imagined offender, and that was considered the lowest sort of manners in their community."

Her grandparents, undoubtedly more worried than they ought to have been, whisked him across the border into Mexico, where he remained for more than a year, spending most of his sojourn in the capital. This entire incident was blown out of all proportion by everyone concerned, the aunt almost losing her fiancé, who stubbornly insisted that the young man had actually kissed her. She just as firmly insisted that he had merely paid her a compliment on her hair. Miss Porter wrote about this now-amusing *affaire d'honneur* in *Old Mortality*, and it had a rather touching sequel in another episode which nearly exploded her father's chivalric wrath thirty years after the fuse was lit and put out.

One afternoon, when Katherine Anne was about seven years old and her sister close to ten, they were playing near a neighbor's barn on the outskirts of Indian Creek. Having nearly exhausted themselves running in and out of the chicken shed, they were taking a short rest on a bale of hay when a freckled ten-year-old boy approached them and suggested that they play one of those silly doctor games. "Neither of us knew what he was talking about, and we were particularly puzzled when this child physician bluntly offered to pull off his trousers if we would take off our bloomers." And to show his willingness he started to loosen his suspenders as they pushed past him and scampered out of the barn. Somehow sensing what his reaction would be, they never told their father about that strange proposal — nor did they dare tell anyone else. It remained a dark secret between them for about thirty years.

Then one cheerful morning (Miss Porter had just returned to Texas after a long absence) she and her sister, accompanied by their eighty-year-old father on a nostalgic journey through some of their old haunts, suddenly spotted a familiar figure driving past them in a "rather spiffy" car. It was that same doctor-boy, now a grown man and obviously a pillar of the community.

"It's him!" shouted her sister. "It's the little doctor with freckles."

And they both broke out into wild laughter.

Somewhat annoyed by their sudden unexplained mirth, their father naturally wanted to know what in God's name they were laughing about; and they simply couldn't resist telling him the whole story. Well, that was a very large mistake. Quickly coming to a boil (almost as fast as in those far-gone days), he threatened to go back and thrash that blankety-blank sex offender who had insulted his little daughters thirty years before. He was undoubtedly the angriest octogenarian they had ever seen, and it took them quite a while to calm him down.

Miss Porter had kept a photograph of him which was taken on that very same day and he certainly looked strong and feisty enough to defend any female's honor, no matter how ancient the offense. He had clear gray eyes, finely chiseled features that one might even call hawklike, and a ramrod posture which clearly evidenced his early military training. Unlike her sister and two brothers who resembled their mother, Miss Porter acquired her father's coloring — crisp black hair and fair skin — and even her hands were shaped like his. He once took her hands, held them beside his, and shook his head in mock surprise. "Could you ever believe," he said to no one in particular, "that a little girl's hands could be such replicas of a grown man's hands? They even have the same lines."

Too young to realize that girls were expected to have beautiful slender hands, she simply blushed with pride. "I would have liked to resemble him in every respect, and I suspect he was well aware of this, because he sometimes seemed to favor me."

But she always insisted that he never coddled her, nor did he coddle any of his children. He let them run wild as they wanted to on the farm, permitting and even encouraging them to ride bareback. In what she called "this summer country of my childhood," the landscapes shimmered in light and color, mourning doves cooed in the live oaks, parrots chattered on every back porch in the little town, flocks of buzzards hovered in the high blue sky over the soft blackland farming country, full of fruits and flowers and birds, with plenty of water from tiny streams and big rivers called the San Antonio, the San Marcos, the Trinity, the Nueces, the Rio Grande, and a small clear branch of the Colorado. And there, full of colored pebbles, was Indian Creek, bearing the same name as the town where she was born.

She particularly remembered that "the colors and tastes all had their smells, as the sounds have now their echoes: the bitter whiff of air over a sprawl of animal skeleton after the buzzards were gone; the smells and flavors of roses and melons, and peach bloom and ripe peaches, of cape jasmine in hedges blooming like popcorn, and the sickly sweetness of chinaberry florets; of honeysuckle in great swags on a trellised gallery; heavy tomatoes dead ripe and warm with the midday sun, eaten there, at the vine; the delicious milky green corn, and savory hot cornbread eaten with still-warm milk; and the clinging brackish smell of the muddy little ponds where we caught and boiled crawfish — in a discarded lard can — and ate them, then and there, we children, in the company of an old Negro who had once been my grandparents' slave, as I have told in another story. He was by our time only a servant, and a cantankerous old cuss very sure of his place in the household."

Yet there was an ominous hint of violence in that flowery sweet-smelling country. There were heavy-bearded men clomping around with rough boots, spurs clanking, and carrying loaded pistols on their hips or inside their shirts when they went to church. Bedroom closets accommodated extra rifles and shotguns when there was no more room in the "gun closet." And little Katherine Anne, along with her older brothers, spent many long afternoons on a range, shooting at fixed targets or clay pigeons with pistols and rifles of several calibers. "I never fired a shotgun," she once wrote. "But I knew the sounds and could name any round of fire I heard, even at great distance."

In their idle moments, many of these gun-toting ranchers and farmers perched on fences with their heels caught on a rail, or squatted on their toes, gossiping about women, frequently chewing tobacco or whittling wood for several hours at a time. Every now and then, they would take out their razor-sharp knives and slice a "chew" with delicate precision. These knives were so keen that young Katherine Anne often watched her father, when shelling pecans for her, cut off the ends of the hard shells in a slow circular single motion, then split them down the sides in four neat strips to bring out the whole nut. Though fascinated by his skillful use of the sharp pocketknife, she never considered handling it herself. Indeed, she carefully avoided the vast variety of sharpened blades around the farm — hatchets, axes, plowshares, shears, carving knives, bowie knives, straight razors, scythes. Living as they did among loaded guns and dangerous cutting instruments, the four wildly adventurous Porter children somehow managed to escape any serious injury.

They had complete freedom around the farm, often riding bareback on frisky horses, with their father's permission and encouragement. They would loop a rope around the horse's nose and gallop off like careless breezes, now and then jumping over hedges or fences, or even a small ditch. He knew they were doing it and never tried to stop them, yet he was always nearby to help if they should ever need him. None of them ever suffered a major fall, although Miss Porter's older sister once fell off a fence while they were watching two old bulls having a fight in the field next to the farm.

When they first noticed the bulls bellowing at each other and pawing the ground, they raced toward a nearby wooden fence — it was no more than fifty feet away from them — and hastily perched themselves on the top rail. "We couldn't have had a better ringside seat." (Years later, when she became an ardent aficionada of the more conventional kind of bullfighting, she had to pay fifty pesos for a seat like that.) This, of course, was a bull-to-bull fracas with no need for matadors or fancy music. It seemed to be a special performance just for them. Well, the bulls never really injured each other in spite of their fierce grunts and an occasional locking of horns, but they certainly appeared angry enough, especially when the smaller one suddenly lunged beneath the other one's huge belly and knocked him off balance.

"That's when my sister, in a spasm of nervous excitement, fell off her perch and onto the ground. (She actually suffered a slight fracture of the collarbone, but we didn't realize that until the next day.)" By strange coincidence the two bulls stopped fighting at the very same moment and galloped off in different directions, thereby giving her sister the illusion that her scream had frightened them off. "I scared them away," she later told her older brothers, and Katherine Anne could find no reason to dispute her.

Having run all the way home to tell everyone about the great bullfight, they were naturally out of breath and terribly thirsty, for it was a hot steamy afternoon. As on other occasions, they hurried to the faucet and started to drink huge gulps of wonderfully refreshing spring water which had been cooled by several chunks of ice. But their father managed to stop them before the second swig. "Wait a minute until you cool off," he said. Then, with his inimitable dry drawl, he quoted a line that was soon to become a standard warning for all of them: "Many a man has gone to his sarcophagus from pouring cold water down his warm esophagus."

She never knew where her father dug up that particular quotation, but she did remember his quoting any number of writers, from the nameless lesser ones to Shakespeare himself. He was especially fond of *Hamlet, The Taming of the Shrew* and *Richard III*, and he took her to see those plays when they were performed in San Antonio by the wonderful theatrical troupes which used to make annual circuits of all the principal cities outside of New York. "When we attended the long sad drama about Mary, Queen of Scots, I thought the magnificent lady in black velvet was truly the Queen of Scots and was terribly disappointed to learn that the real Queen had died long ago — not at all on the night we were present."

She loved the theatre, that other world of gods and goddesses who ruled a universe quite beyond her own, whose more than human voices matched their broad elegant gestures. Her grandmother, who had heard the great Jenny Lind and Nellie Melba, would occasionally criticize the "less impressive" performances of the people they saw, and her father would compare them unfavorably to Sarah Bernhardt and Mme. Modjeska.

"But I, for one, simply couldn't imagine anyone more impressive than the actors who came to San Antonio in 1900, when I was ten years old. I can't remember their names — not a single one — because I so completely identified each actor with the role he played. No one *acted* the part of Hamlet: he *was* Hamlet, so that his real name was of no consequence to me. I sometimes experienced this same feeling when my father read poetry to us. Quite suddenly he seemed to be someone else, some sad, tormented stranger who would almost move me to tears. I have in mind his recitation of Edgar Allan Poe:

> *Her tantalized spirit now blandly reposes*
> *Forgetting or never regretting its roses.*

Even now those words evoke a most unquiet emotion. And he would also read us the *Vita Nuova*, the Sonnets of Shakespeare and the 'Wedding Song' of Spenser."

2

An Early Scribbler

ASIDE from being an unusually literate man (particularly unusual for someone lacking a formal education), Harrison Porter was a gifted raconteur on those rare occasions when he chose to abandon his customary taciturn manner. He was "almost loquacious" when he took ten-year-old Katherine Anne on a short visit to Mexico City at the very turn of the century, January 1900. As they walked along the beautiful tree-lined Paseo de la Reforma, her small fist snuggled into his strong work-chafed hand, he told her about his exile in Mexico many years before, about his family's migrations from Kentucky to Louisiana and finally Texas, and how his mother had insisted on removing his father's grave from one place to another because she couldn't bear to leave him behind. His reminiscence of the Civil War and its aftermath, often bitter but leavened with poignant humor, held her in thrall and aroused a more-than-childish curiosity about her grandparents and all the people who came before them. She was full of questions about how they looked and what they said, how they dressed and where they lived, each one of his anecdotes provoking still more questions.

But she was also curious about the present, the immediate present. As they reached the entrance to Chapultepec Park, where Presidente Porfirio Díaz went past them in his luxurious gilded coach drawn by two black horses wearing the fanciest harness she had ever seen, the wide-eyed Katherine Anne had to know what kind of man could own such finery. (Many years later she would acquire a belt with a buckle fashioned from a silver decoration from the bridle of the dictator's favorite horse.) Her father apparently disapproved of Díaz, but she was too young to comprehend his reasons.

Somewhere in the park they stopped at an open bookstall, and he browsed through several volumes written in Spanish. "He couldn't read them," she later told me, "but he enjoyed handling them, staring at the printed pages as if to absorb their meaning through sheer osmosis. He had a passion for books."

Indeed, the whole family shared that passion. Recalling her early reading, in a *Paris Review* interview Miss Porter said she had read Shakespeare's sonnets when she was thirteen, "and I'm perfectly certain that they made the most profound impression upon me of anything I ever read. For a time I knew the whole sequence by heart." She also read Dante, in the huge volume illustrated by Gustave Doré, and the poetry of Homer and Ronsard, and the translations of several other old French poets. She was also "incredibly influenced" by Montaigne in her early teenage years. And one day when she was about fourteen, her father led her to a shelf of maroon-colored books and said, "Why don't you read this? Perhaps it'll knock some of the nonsense out of you!" It happened to be the entire set of Voltaire's philosophical dictionary with annotations by Smollett. Apparently taking his suggestion as a command, she plowed through the set, but it took her about five years. Meanwhile, she read Jane Austen, Turgenev, Thomas Hardy, Dickens, Thackeray, Henry James and several other novelists. But her favorite book was *Wuthering Heights*, which she read once a year for at least fifteen years.

She was also writing short stories and poetry, having started when she was six or seven years old.* But she had such a multiplicity of half-talents, too: she wanted to dance, she wanted to play the piano, she sang, she drew. "It wasn't really dabbling — I was investigating everything, experimenting in everything." Sometime at that tender age she wrote a letter to her sister saying that she wanted *glory*. Many years later she said, "I don't know

---

*Her first book, which she herself hand-printed and bound, was titled "A Nobbel — The Hermit of Halifax Cave."

quite what I meant by that, but it was something different from fame or success or wealth."

She might have heard the word "glory" from her grandmother, who often read to them by lamplight, pausing occasionally to pinpoint a moral in a particular passage by Dickens or to offer negative judgments on writers like Thackeray, whom she considered trivial.

Afterward, her sister and she would lie flat on their stomachs and leaf through the book she had just read or some other book that might catch their fancy. There were hundreds of volumes to choose from in their house. In that particular part of the country most people were so migratory and transient that they seldom hauled books around with them; but the Porter family had accumulated a fine collection, which had been toted along from one state to another, wherever the clan chose to move. Some of those books had been in one or another branch of the family for two hundred fifty years, their pages yellowed and brittle and often margin-marked by a half-dozen hands. "We were a genuinely literate family straight on back to David Rittenhouse Porter, one of the first experimental biologists in this country, who wrote a textbook that was widely used for a long time. He wasn't the only Porter who scribbled. O. Henry was my father's second cousin, but he was considered a disgrace to the family and maybe they'll think the same about me some day."

Nobody forced the children to read; the books were just lying there waiting to be read. There was hardly a chair arm in the house that didn't have a book draped over it, and the real unforgivable crime was to lose somebody's place in the book. Aside from that, there were no strictures upon them, no one telling them that such-and-such book was too adult or improper for women and children. They had Homer, Chaucer, the eighteenth-century novels and all the classical poets, a wonderful mixture of styles and eras.

But there was one book they didn't have, something Katherine Anne had heard and read about and which she felt compelled to read if only to satisfy her curiosity. So at the age of fourteen (her grandmother had died and they had moved to San Antonio) she went to the public library and checked out Rabelais's *Gargantua and Pantagruel.* "Clutching it to my breast as if to prevent a possible escape, I rushed home and commenced reading it immediately. What a strange and expansive world it opened for me. I thought it was like Homer and Dante and Shakespeare, that I had been lifted into that upper air far beyond this grubby earth and the silly little rules of family life I had to live under."

Twenty years later, when she was well past thirty, she again read Dr. Rabelais and was astonished at what she had missed on that first go-around. None of his graphically sexual and bawdy passages had made the slightest dent on her mind. "I simply hadn't understood a word of it, except that something grand and noble did come through. He ran the gamut, you know; he went right from the bowl rotting under the earth to the beatific nation. There *was* something for me in *Pantagruel* even at the age of fourteen, and I dare say there would have been even if I had read it at the age of ten."

Miss Porter was quick to explain that Rabelais was part of her *vacation* reading, for during the school year her literary diet was far more restricted. Her sister and she received most of their formal schooling at the Convent of the Child Jesus, in New Orleans, a very dull and noneducational establishment that differed considerably from the fictional convents she read about during her carefree summers. "There were gruesome fables about lovely but unfortunate girls who had been trapped by nuns and priests who were forever immuring these young ladies in convents and forcing them to take the veil. The rites were shockingly painful and caused the victims to shriek in horror. Later on they were locked in chains and confined to dark cells, or they were forced to help other nuns to bury murdered infants in scummy dungeons infested with rats."

There were, of course, no dungeons in that humdrum convent in New Orleans, nor did she ever hear a single scream in those cloistered halls. Though they were in fact confined, their confinement was eased by a beautiful garden with huge shade trees and a lovely stone grotto. At night they were locked into a long barren dormitory, chilled by cross drafts from wide-open windows. Two watchful nuns occupied beds at either end. The students' narrow cots were curtained with thin muslin, and small night lamps were so arranged that the sisters could see through the curtains "without our being able to see them."

On occasional wakeful nights (there weren't many, for she was usually a sound sleeper), Katherine Anne would pull aside her curtain and watch one of the nuns stealthily creeping down the aisle like a phantom apparition on a strange and secret mission. But in the final analysis there was nothing very mysterious about any of them. They were dull commonplace women, some blessed with a sweet nature, who had a special talent for making everything around them seem dull. "Their only other talent was a distressing ability to spot the spiritual deficiencies of their young charges, which enabled them to quickly discourage those of us who erroneously felt a calling to become nuns."

She often wondered if any of the nuns ever found out that her sister and she liked to attend the horse races on their free Saturdays and that they were sometimes allowed to bet a dollar. ("I have always had a penchant for long odds and black horses with poetic names, no matter what their past records indicated.") Her uncle was the one who took them to the races, but they were not permitted to leave the convent if they had made bad marks, which of course made them a bit more diligent in their studies during the racing season.

"Had we lacked this unorthodox incentive, I'm sure the convent's uninspired curriculum would have proved a deadly bore."

Their reading was circumscribed and the teaching was unimaginative. Having later learned that he himself was an agnostic, she often wondered why her Daddy sent them to that faraway convent. Perhaps he felt they needed the discipline; no other reason occurred to her. There was, in fact, a remarkable degree of laissez-faire in her family with respect to religion. Her Protestant grandmother had seven sons and four of them married "perfectly lovely Catholic girls, all of whom joined the clan with a proselytizing zeal that would have thrilled the Pope." In no time at all they hauled in converts from all branches of the family. One of her aunts proselytized Katherine Anne before she was five, and she was ready to go. But they weren't totally successful, because she clearly still remembered seeing four different people go out the front gate and take off in four different directions to four different churches — Episcopalian, Presbyterian, Catholic and Methodist — while her agnostic father sat on the porch reading the *Dialogues* of Plato.

His somewhat austere skepticism was bound to affect her as she grew older, but in her early years she was greatly drawn to Catholicism. Its physical grandeur and intriguing rituals were a constant source of wonder. How she loved the stained-glass windows, brilliantly diffusing the brightness of the late morning sun, the candle-lit altar with its elegant lace ornaments and glistening chalice, and the beautifully garbed priests sonorously chanting their mysterious Latin liturgy as they moved from one level of the altar steps to another with great solemnity, pausing now and then to perfume the air with burnt incense. Even during her long estrangement from the Church (it lasted many years) she was still attracted to the esthetic aspects of Catholicism. "And now that I am back in the fold again I strongly object to this recent modernization of church ritual. Old rituals ought to be as severe as they possibly can be. I am frankly appalled by the prospect of hearing High Mass in low English, no matter how much more communicative it may seem to some people. Though I don't profess to be a regular churchgoer, High Mass has always been a joy for me, and I am one of the best Easter and Christmas Catholics you can possibly find."

What really moved her most, however, was the confessional. "You get so burdened in this world and there are things you can hardly tell even to yourself. You wouldn't tell God if He didn't already know. Nevertheless, you simply have to talk to someone, and you've got to find someone you can trust, which is not as easy as it sounds. Anyone who has been betrayed by a friend will know what I mean."

Nevertheless, she had one unhappy incident in the confessional, and that was when she told a priest that she had missed mass during a retreat shortly before Lent. He turned on her very bitterly and said, "Why do you trouble to come to church at all;

why don't you just leave? We have too many Catholics like you."

And that's exactly what she did. She just got up and backed out of the cubicle and never went back to church for fifteen years. She clearly remembered thinking to herself, "Oh, how right you are, Father," then rushing away without even waiting to be blessed or anything, not even pausing to put a nickel in the charity box. (She was seventeen or eighteen years old at that time.)

For a long time she refused to examine her feelings about it. Then, through some undefined process of introspection, she finally decided that she didn't have any true faith, that she really couldn't be a good Catholic. Although she had always considered herself a truly religious person, she found it impossible to be dogmatically religious. "I have reference, of course, to some of the dogmas which you are expected to believe literally. I could believe almost anything mystically but not literally."

Well, that attitude kept her out of the Church for more than a decade, but then she gradually decided that she had been giving too much importance to her personal views, to her inability to accept dogma.

"Moreover, I realized that I needed the warmth of feeling that the Church has for you. There is great comfort in a religion that has an infinite capacity for forgiveness, that seems especially ready to pardon even those who question its very essence. The minute you want to come back and make some act of reparation and say that you are willing to return to the fold, they take you right back. Even when you have been ostracized or excommunicated, you simply confess your error as to whatever caused your excommunication, and back you go. They can't stop you."

Though she was sure many people cling to their religion (or come back to it if they have strayed away) because there is at least a symbolic promise of a pleasant hereafter, she told me she frankly didn't care whether there is an afterlife or not, "but I do think it is one of the most charming ideas that man ever invented and it would be perfectly wonderful if it were true."

Whenever her friends or relatives speculated about such matters she was frequently reminded of a character in Flannery O'Connor's *Wise Blood*. It's a self-ordained preacher named

Haze Motes, who says: "Where you came from is gone, where you thought you were going to never was there, and where you are is no good unless you can get away from it."

Miss O'Connor, according to Miss Porter, was a deeply religious Catholic, who had a sort of self-challenging tendency to create godless people with fiendishly persuasive tongues. But she wasn't concerned about people like Haze Motes disavowing a hereafter, "and the prospect of a hereafter certainly doesn't have a thing in the world to do with my belonging to the Catholic Church here on earth."

Aside from their flexibility in matters relating to Church dogma, Miss Porter was convinced that the Jesuits have always been comfortably flexible about almost any human activity. Consider, for example, their rather easy attitude about drinking. In her part of the country, where many people were hard-shell Baptists, you would never hear of a minister taking a friendly social drink with members of his flock. Neither he nor they were permitted to consume alcohol since they saw no difference between drinking, dancing, cardplaying and adultery.

But in the Porter home, liquor was a regular household item. Her father would always take his two shots of bourbon every morning before breakfast. He had a flask on the sideboard, next to the slender crystal decanter usually filled with home-made wine. Just before dinner he would give all his children a couple of tablespoonsful of that red wine in their water, so Miss Porter always had great faith in a bit of diluted wine for growing children — but only at mealtimes.

Her grandmother was also partial to bourbon, except that she laced it with rock candy. She used to keep a quart bottle next to her bed, in a cabinet, one of those great marble-top washstands with a long mahogany cabinet on top. Inside the bottle was a generous portion of bourbon mixed with pieces of crystalline candy that would jiggle around whenever she poured herself a nip. Several times a day she would go to her room for a quick refresher, and everybody said that was probably what kept her going.

"All her life she kept that family together, working day and night in all kinds of weather, and when she finally died we all seemed to fall apart. We have never been a real family since then — just a half-dozen branches with no single core."

Miss Porter talked frequently about her maternal and paternal grandmothers, using them as models in many of her stories, but she often merged them into one person as if they were interchangeable. Both of them were bridges to an "old South" that was extremely important to her and which she tended to romanticize. In fact, she sometimes felt compelled to boast about her "good family" and the wealth they had once enjoyed. In a highly personal memoir which she wrote in 1944, she proudly recalled a letter from a ninety-five-year-old woman who had been a flower girl at her grandparents' Kentucky wedding around 1850.

"She couldn't remember whether the bride's skirt had been twenty-five feet or twenty-five yards around, but she inclined to the latter figure; it was of white satin brocade with slippers to match. . . ."

She further described the table set for the bridal banquet, with silver branched candlesticks everywhere, each holding seven white candles, and a crystal chandelier holding fifty candles. There was also a floor-length white lace tablecloth spread over white satin; a wedding cake tall as the flower girl, festooned with white sugar roses and actual live rose leaves. The room itself was a perfect bower of southern smilax and white dogwood. The flower girl also remembered an enormous silver butler dish, with feet, and with cupids and some sort of fruit around the rim. It held at least ten pounds of butter molded or carved to resemble a set piece of roses and lilies, each petal and leaf clearly delineated and natural as life.

Commenting on the old lady's amazingly detailed recollection, Miss Porter wrote: "That butter. She couldn't get over it, and neither can I. It seems as late-Roman and decadent as anything ever thought up in Hollywood."

Aside from the fancy butter, there were Kentucky ham, roast turkey, partridges in wine jelly, fried chicken, dove pie, half a dozen sweet and hot sauces, peach pickle, watermelon pickle, spiced mangoes, a dozen different fruits, four kinds of cake, and chilled custard served in tall glasses with whipped cream capped by a brandied cherry.

Although the old lady's letter referred to an event at least eighty years past, Miss Porter seemed only too happy to accept it as verified evidence, perhaps because it squared with her own inward vision of a proud family history. On other occasions, she expressed profound disillusionment — indeed bitterness — whenever she recalled the crushing reversal of her grandparents' fortunes following the Civil War. ("I am the grandchild of a lost War, and I have blood-knowledge of what life can be in a defeated country on the bare bones of privation.") Yet she spoke with pride about her grandmother's ability to "make do" in the most dire circumstances. When faced with a chronic scarcity of coffee, she parched a mixture of sweet potato and dried corn until it was black, then ground it up and boiled it, so that her family could have a dark hot drink on cold mornings. "But she would never allow them to call it coffee. It was known as That Brew."

That famous brocaded wedding gown was cut up and made over to the last scrap for a dozen later brides from the same clan; fine old linen was worn thin and mended over and over again; a collection of thin old silver and bone-handled knives gradually disappeared; and the elegant silver candlesticks were long gone by the time Katherine Anne was born. As for the ornate silver butter dish, it was replaced by a modest opal-glass hen seated on a woven nest, "rearing aloft her scarlet comb and beady eyes."

Judging from Miss Porter's later impressions, when she herself was fifty-four years old, it would seem that neither she nor her grandmother was ever reconciled with the family's lesser state — that both of them yearned for that world of antebellum splendor:

Grandmother was by nature lavish; she loved leisure and calm, she loved luxury, she loved dress and adornment, she loved to sit and talk with friends or listen to music; she did not in the least like pinching or saving and mending and making things do, and she had no patience with the kind of slackness that tried to say second-best was best, or half good enough. . . .

Though we had no money and no prospects of any, and were land-poor in the most typical way, we never really faced this fact as long as our grandmother lived because she would not hear of such a thing. We had been a good old family of solid wealth and property in Kentucky, Louisiana and Virginia, and we remained that way in Texas, even though due to a temporary decline for the most honorable reasons, appearances were entirely to the contrary. . . .

This accounted for our fragmentary, but strangely useless and ornamental education, appropriate to our history and our station in life, neither of which could be in the least altered by the accident of straitened circumstances. . . .

She also remembered that her grandmother's mind ran in flashes of perception, and that she had a sharp, impatient way of talking to people who couldn't keep up with her. She was also a stern methodical disciplinarian, who trained the children as she herself had been trained, forbidding them to cross their knees, or to touch the backs of the chairs they sat on, or to speak until they were spoken to.

Young Katherine Anne and her sister loved the smell of her face powder and the light orange-flavor perfume she wore, the crinkled waves of her hair, the round knot speared through with an elegant Spanish comb. Her once "delicate hands" had long since been ruined by hard work, but she was proud of her narrow feet with their high insteps, especially when she wore her favorite smooth black kid boots with spool-shaped heels.

She loved to have her grandchildren say their prayers before bedtime, clustered around her knees like cubs. But quite frequently, in their jealousy "to be nearest and first," they would start shoving each other and eventually fighting, "the holy hour having quite literally gone to hell." Pulling them apart like an angry referee, Grandmother would accuse them of being vulgar — "and for her, that word connoted a peculiarly detestable form of immorality, that is to say, bad manners."

Yet, in spite of her gentility, she rode horseback at a gallop until the year she died. She also smoked cubeb cigarettes ("for my throat," she would say) and often remarked that she most probably would have enjoyed the taste of real tobacco.

"In a family full of willful eccentrics and headstrong characters and unpredictable histories, her presence was singularly free from peaks and edges and the kind of color that leaves a trail of family anecdotes. She left the lingering perfume and the airy shimmer of grace about her memory. . . ."

Musing on that essay about twenty-five years after she had written it, Miss Porter seemed a hint less charitable about her grandmother: "She was indeed a strong matriarchal type, a terribly typical Southern phenomenon, which I wouldn't want to be for anything in the world. I run like hell from that kind of woman."

This same ambivalence is reflected by her ubiquitous protagonist, Miranda, who remembers that her grandmother "relied with perfect acquiescence on the dogma that children were conceived in sin and brought forth in iniquity," yet she and her brother and sister "loved their grandmother; she was the only reality to them in a world that seemed otherwise without fixed authority . . . just the same they felt that Grandmother was a tyrant, and they wished to be free of her."

But for all her inchoate resentments, Miss Porter was genuinely fond of her grandmother and would always follow her around the house like a pampered puppy. She especially remembered how grandma would reach into that liquor cabinet, take out the bottle and give it a good shake, causing the rock candies to jounce and twirl like swimming butterflies. Then, as the candy began to settle, she would pour the sweetened bourbon into a little collapsible jigger made of silver. It had a top on it and she carried it in her purse. She also carried the liquor in her suitcase when she traveled. Whenever she got tired and exhausted she simply took a good swig and was good for another three or four hours.

Once in a great while she would let Katherine Anne taste that bourbonized rock candy, which she found immensely enjoyable, but she wouldn't allow the child to sip the liquid portion of her mixture. ("Now that I have some of the same ailments that plagued Grandma, I find that bourbon can be most helpful; but you really don't need that rock candy.")

In mentioning her grandmother's and her father's daily consumption of bourbon, Miss Porter hastily assured me that she didn't want to leave the impression that they were excessive drinkers. As a matter of fact, she insisted she never once saw either one of them drunk or even slightly out of control. They were both hardworking, well-disciplined human beings who were in always firm control of their household and of themselves, and they demanded a considerable degree of discipline from all the children. Though the grandchildren enjoyed a normal range of recreational activities, they had certain set chores around the farm and pity the poor child who sloughed off the work. One of Katherine Anne's principal duties was the care and feeding of the horses and all the other animals and pets they kept in or outside the house. But the grandfather particularly insisted that they take personal responsibility for the care of their own pets.

Katherine Anne's favorite household animal was a slinky female cat which was quite pregnant on the first summer she spent at the farm. Shortly after Tabby had her four kittens, Katherine Anne found one of them lying under the old-fashioned summer house, one of those clapboard houses perched on stilts, with a wooden lattice around the bottom. The kitten was slumped over on its side, one of its legs stiffly held out and its tiny sliver of a tongue drooping from the side of its mouth. Although she had never seen a sick cat before, she could tell instantly that he was in poor shape and probably starving. So she grabbed the mother cat, who seemed disturbingly unconcerned, and held her over the limp kitten so that her teats were close to its face; and she kept holding her there, hoping the kitten would nurse itself. But it never moved a stitch — it simply lay there as limp as a wet rag. Well, then she knew something was terribly wrong and began to cry at the top of her voice, not knowing what in the world to do. Her older sister heard her and came running full speed. And when Katherine Anne tried to explain what had happened (explanations were really unnecessary for her sister could clearly see for herself), huge sobs made it impossible for her to say more than a few words. Many years later, when they had both grown into middle life, her sister told her that she had never seen such despair in a child's eyes: "I stared at you and thought, 'How in God's world can any child that young feel so anguished?' "

(Even as Miss Porter told me seventy years later, she evoked the same feeling, the utter total grief that had swept over her.) Fortunately, her sister had more self-control. She dashed back to the main house and got a medicine dropper filled with milk and tried to force it into the kitten's sagging mouth. But it was a dying kitten, far past any help they could give it, and it died right there before them. They buried it within the hour under the chinaberry tree which shaded the summer house.

That wasn't the only burial Katherine Anne shared in. Indeed, she seems to have spent a good many hours of her childhood digging graves for all kinds of creatures, even grasshoppers. Whenever she found a dead animal (it had to be small, of course) or insect, she would bury it in a little grave with flowers on top and a smooth stone at the head. Anyone who has read "The Fig Tree" will quickly recognize her as Miranda, the little girl who has buried a chicken and thereafter imagines that she hears it crying out of the ground. Having been rushed away on a family trip before she can rescue the supposedly live chicken, Miranda suffers a most frustrating anxiety until she finally learns that the "weep weep" she heard above the chicken's grave is the same noise that tree frogs make when it's going to rain.

"Such things have always happened to children, and we never seem to forget them," Miss Porter mused with a deep sigh as she told me about her childhood trauma. "My grandmother somehow managed to comfort us on those heartrending occasions. She was always there when we needed her."

But she wouldn't always be there. Just after Katherine Anne had celebrated her seventh birthday, her grandmother died following a brief siege of pneumonia. She was seventy-six years old and had been quite active until a month before her death. Benumbed and grief-stricken, Katherine Anne and her sister rushed home from the convent school in New Orleans on the first available train. It was a long sad journey, with the usual delays occasioned by engine trouble or stray cattle crossing the tracks. And as they approached a river near the Texas border, all the passengers had to get off and walk across a wooden trestle which was considered "possibly unsafe," once again boarding the train on the other side.

The sun was shining on the day of the funeral, but there was only gloom and depression in the Porter household, a profound sense of irrevocable loss. "From that moment on we started drifting apart," Miss Porter later commented. "We had lost our core, we had lost our cohesion as a family and never got it back."

As so frequently happens in the wake of such traumatic events, the Porters pulled up stakes and moved to San Antonio soon thereafter. Hoping to fill the sudden void in his children's lives (probably trying too hard), Harrison Porter went from one extreme to another, now coddling them as if they were fragile as butterfly wings, then suddenly becoming as stern as a martinet, only occasionally striking a happy medium. Most of the time, during the next few years, his two daughters were away at school and were thus happily free of his erratic discipline; but summer vacations were "a continuing war of attrition between parent and child." Being headstrong as her father and with no gift for guile, young Katherine Anne had more problems with him than her more conciliatory older sister did. As she grew older she was more apt to argue with him, protesting against what she considered willful restrictions on her freedom of action. Like most young teenagers, she was beginning to show an interest in boys, sometimes engaging in "perfectly innocent" flirtations, which he regarded with deep suspicion. Thus, when she occasionally disappeared for hours at a time, most of which were spent at the public library (her real love), he would cross-examine her with all the diligence of an angry prosecutor, quite often goading her into a stubborn refusal to answer any of his questions. Then there would be long silences between the two recalcitrant souls each waiting for the other to speak first, until one or both of them suddenly would yield to the anxious mediation of her sister or her brothers.

Ultimately, the pressures of her convent-to-home-to-convent

existence began to build up at frightening pace. Had her mother or grandmother been alive to serve as a buffer between them, things might have turned out differently. In any event, her tight little world began closing in on her from all angles, and she searched desperately for a way out. So at the age of sixteen she married a young man whom she had met through her sister at a Christmas party.

"When he saw me standing near an alcove he took me by the hand, pulled me toward him and tried to kiss me, barely grazing my cheek as I twisted away. How I managed to marry him I'll never know, for I scarcely knew him. Moreover, I married him without my father's blessing, and consequently had to lie about my age."

Confused and tormented by the instant realization that she was totally unprepared for marriage, she was a miserable bride and absolutely refused to consummate the marriage. "I don't like to talk about it, and I never mention it. But it was twenty-six years before I married again. For a long while I couldn't stand anything to do with sex. I was frigid as a cucumber and never did really get over it altogether."

On several occasions during our many day-long conversations I attempted to elicit more facts about that brief first marriage, but Miss Porter would quickly turn the conversation to something else. She even refused to tell me her young husband's name. Since they were probably married by a justice of the peace in some small town between New Orleans and San Antonio, where records were seldom kept after four or five years (if at all), the nameless bridegroom will probably remain a mystery. Perhaps that name will surface in an official biography.

However abortive her marriage may have been, young Katherine Anne had reached a new plateau in her life, and like her fictional Miranda — who also eloped to spite her father — she must now reassess all that had gone before, try to free herself of past illusions and make room for new ones.

Ah but there is my own life to come yet, she thought, my own life and beyond. I don't want any promises, I won't have any false hopes, I won't be romantic about myself. I can't live in their world any longer, she told herself, listening to the voices back of her. Let them tell their stories to each other. Let them go on explaining how things happened. I don't care. At least I can know the truth about what happens to me, she assured herself silently, making a promise to herself, in her hopefulness, her ignorance.

3

Escape from Home

MISS PORTER and her forever-nameless first husband never lived together, and they were divorced about three or four years later.* Since court records are always listed by surname (*Katherine Anne Doe vs. John Doe*), it has been impossible to verify the date or place of the presumed divorce, she always having remained resolutely mute as to the identity of her spouse.

In any event, she dropped out of the convent school and moved back to San Antonio, back to the "perpetual war of attrition" with her stern father, though there were times when they genuinely enjoyed each other's company. He, of course, wanted her to continue her schooling, hoping that she would eventually become a teacher. But she had always been an erratic student, making excellent marks in history, literature and composition, but "D" in everything else except deportment, which was frequently lower. Nevertheless, she resumed her voracious reading, often "consuming" ten or twelve books a week, meanwhile writing scores of poems, character sketches, plots and subplots of projected short stories and novels.

Her reading of classic literature and philosophy inevitably provoked a profound discontent with the parochial confines of the rural South. "They acted," she later wrote, "as if the final word had gone out long ago on manners, morality, religion, even politics: nothing was ever to change, they said, and even as they spoke, everything was changing, shifting, disappearing." Yet

_____
* On certain occasions she said that the divorce was granted six or seven years later.

Miss Porter in "an elegant dress from New Orleans," 1913

Miss Porter (right) with a friend from Corpus Christi, Texas,
on Christmas Day, 1913

Miss Porter with several fellow patients whom she taught while confined in the county tuberculosis hospital in Dallas, Texas, 1915

At the age of twenty-nine, while living in Greenwich Village

there were times when she longed for the security of her earlier childhood, especially during the first few years after her grandmother's death, when they kept moving from one house to another within the San Antonio area. "We were like a band of gypsies," she once told me with a hint of bitterness in her husky voice. "We couldn't seem to settle down." Having sold his farm, her father had a temporary financial cushion, but he was eventually engaged in trading cattle, working in a produce market as a buyer, and dabbling in real estate.

Torn between a need to find a home and a compulsion to break away from the family, Miss Porter ultimately "ran off" to Chicago just after her twenty-first birthday. Her suitcase was loaded with half-finished manuscripts and only a minimal supply of clothing. "I had to leave Texas because I didn't want to be regarded as a freak. That's what they all thought about women who wanted to write. So I had to revolt and rebel; there was no other way. And I guess they were dead sure I was going to live an immoral life. How could they think otherwise?"

(While discussing this phase of her life some twenty-five years later, she told a reporter she had written about that provincial society in "Legend and Memory," the first part of an ongoing novel tentatively titled "Many Redeemers"; but this work was never published — at least not under those titles — having been lost or perhaps deliberately destroyed by Miss Porter herself.)

Not long after she got to Chicago, having first rented the cheapest room she could find in a run-down boarding house, she found a job on a newspaper which apparently specialized in the more sensational aspects of the news. It was a huge brawling city, seething with surface excitements, particularly so for a young convent-bred girl from "back yonder." But the articles she wrote had nothing to do with that aspect of Chicago; her assignments were those generally given to female reporters — wedding notices, obituaries and cultural activities, plus filling in as a coffee-maker and sandwich-getter for the editorial staff. Crime stories and political scandals were the exclusive province of male reporters.

Overworked, bored and poorly paid, she spent most evenings cooped up in her small, airless room, munching crackers and stale cheese as she read a novel or listlessly tried to write short stories, none of which got beyond the first few pages. Perpetually short of cash but determined not to ask her father for help, she often went to bed hungry and bone-tired. There were undoubtedly many men who would have enjoyed taking her to dinner, for she was quite attractive, but she almost always refused their invitations, no matter how much she yearned for a good steak. "I simply didn't want to get compromised, and I lacked the guile that came so easily for some of the other women at the office." Consequently, she continued her meager diet and probably endangered her health.

Then, just as she was about to despair and return to Texas, there was a sudden twist in her career which seemed as unlikely as any plot ever concocted by a Hollywood screenwriter. The city editor sent her to the S & A Movie Studios to write a story about a film which had just gone into production. Hovering around the edge of the brightly lit set, now and then elbowing her way between some extras to get a closer view, she was suddenly grabbed by a man and pulled out of the waiting crowd. "Right over this way, Little Boy Blue," he said, probably referring to the dark blue middie blouse she was wearing, as he placed her in the front row of spectators in a courtroom scene. Too timid to say anything and overwhelmed by the bellowing voice of the director ordering silence, she meekly accepted her new role and tried to look as nonchalant as the middle-aged man sitting beside her.

But she temporarily lost her poise, gasping momentarily, when Francis X. Bushman himself — the first matinee idol of film — stepped in front of the whirring cameras and began emoting with a rumbling breast-heaving passion that instantly mesmerized the jury.

Equally taken in by Bushman's relentless passion — and thrilled to learn she would actually be paid five dollars per day as an extra — Miss Porter simply forgot that she was supposed to be a reporter and stayed on until the courtroom sequence was finished. When she finally went back to the newspaper after a five-day absence, she was paid eighteen dollars and summarily fired. But a few days later she was hired again at the movie studios, where she continued working as an extra in several different productions for seven or eight months, finally earning an astronomical ten dollars a day as a bit player. (When subsequently asked if she had been one of Mack Sennett's somewhat notorious "bathing beauties," she put off the question with an ambiguous smile and a vague "How could I possibly remember that far back?")

During this period the producers decided to move their ever-expanding operations to California, but she declined their offer to take her along.

"Don't you want to be a movie actress?" one of them asked, not quite believing she was serious.

"Oh, no!" she insisted. "I have more serious things to do."

Without bothering to ask what "serious things" she had in mind, the producer merely shrugged and mumbled, "Well, be a fool if that's how you feel."

And that was the end of her movie career.

The sequence of events thereafter remains unclear. Indeed, the entire chronology of her sojourn in Chicago has been muddled by Miss Porter's subsequent faulty recollection, undoubtedly prompted by a desire to conceal her age. (Her long-time friend Glenway Wescott once observed that Miss Porter tended to "simplify" when asked about her background, "and therefore I [and other friends], instead of concentrating on ascertaining all the realities, the dates and the names and the locations and so on, have always interested ourselves in what might be called story-material about her, somehow more characteristic than her mere biography.") One version had her arriving at the age of twenty-one (1911), while another version marks her arrival as 1913, still presumably the same twenty-one years of age. Having thus been in Chicago either one or three years, she finally went back to Texas in 1914, soon after the outbreak of World War I. Just a few days before her departure she saw the original Abbey Players in John M. Synge's memorable *Playboy of the Western World*, which so deeply impressed her that fifty years later she could still remember that Frank Fay was The Boy, Sara Allgood was the

Widow Quinn, and Maire O'Neill (the playwright's lovely affianced bride) starred in the role of Pegeen Mike.

Apparently still stagestruck, despite her refusal to go to Hollywood, Miss Porter made a brief theatrical tour of small towns and cities in Texas and Louisiana, singing old Scottish ballads in a costume she herself had designed and stitched together. But the hoped-for charm of this gypsy life was soon dissipated. Once again penniless, malnourished and inutterably weary of the day-to-day drudgery of packing and unpacking two bulging suitcases mostly filled with unfinished manuscripts and notes, lugging them to and from distant railroad stations where she was always waiting for much-delayed milk trains, she finally decided to go home.

Within a few weeks, however, she became quite ill and was told she was probably suffering from tuberculosis. "They wanted me to go to a big sanatorium in Carlsbad, where most of the wealthy Texans used to go. But I didn't have any money — I couldn't have afforded a big expensive place like that — so they got me into a county hospital near Dallas."

The poorest of the poor were there, many of them dying from tuberculosis or some other disease resulting from malnutrition and chronic neglect. Most of them were older people, but there were several children hobbling around on crutches or slumped listlessly in wheelchairs and narrow uncomfortable cots, ravaged by tuberculosis of the bone or "just plain old t.b." Ignoring her own weakened condition, Miss Porter asked an attending doctor if she could possibly help them in some way — amuse them, read to them or teach them how to read and write. Needless to say, he was happy to accept her offer, but nevertheless cautioned her that there were no funds available for books, toys, phonograph records or anything else that might amuse them. "Then I'll tell them some stories," she told him. "I'll invent a few of my own."

Still, she knew that picture books and records would be helpful, so she herself approached several county officials, literally begging them for just a few books, at least a few secondhand books. "But I might just as well have talked to a stone wall. They simply didn't care." Angry, frustrated and driven to desperation, she finally got in touch with an editor at the *Dallas News,* who assigned a reporter and photographer to do a feature article on the afflicted children.

The response was instantaneous when the newspaper broke the story. Hundreds of people sent crates of oranges, packages of candy, wool socks and sweaters, boxes of books and records, packages of crayons, paints, writing tablets and pencils. "It was just wonderful, the best Christmas they ever had." And now she was able to teach them how to read and write, how to use paints and crayons, how to play records on a donated Victrola with a cone-shaped speaker. Hour after hour, from early morning to sunset, she read to them, taught some of them a few simple ballads, answered all kinds of questions. But some of the youngsters were too sick to sing, were barely able to talk above a whisper, having now come to the terminal stage of their illness. "They, of course, required my special attention." She was later photographed with seventeen of her student-patients, all of whom died within two years.

Eventually, her doctor warned her to ease up, to take care of her own health. Then quite suddenly, after six months in that county hospital, she was told there had been a misdiagnosis in her case, that she didn't have tuberculosis after all. "You've got some kind of bronchial trouble," he said. "So you can't stay here any longer. We'll have to send you to Carlsbad."

Though still without funds, she was admitted a few days later. (Perhaps in those pre–malpractice-suit days, certain doctors would voluntarily pay for their mistakes; someone must have footed the bill, for it was certainly not a charitable institution.) In any event, she remained in that sanatorium about twelve months, eight of them flat on her back. "Yet nothing could convince me that I was in danger, that I had any serious disease at all, even though I ran this high fever every day along with the rest of them. But of course I did have t.b. My lungs were scarred and always remained scarred. Still, they never found a germ, they never got anything on the slides."

But she stayed there and was a good patient, carefully following all the instructions given her. She entered weighing one hundred and two pounds and was released thirteen pounds heavier, "with my hind-end as broad as I was long."

She considered Carlsbad a rather pleasant place, with awfully nice men and women leisurely strolling on well-manicured lawns between widely spaced buildings. There was a big fountain near the main dormitory, where everyone would gather on sunny afternoons, some of the younger bachelors courting pretty young women who would teasingly splash water on them, presumably to cool their ardor. Miss Porter later learned that several marriages resulted from these round-the-fountain flirtations, and she frankly wondered why they would chance it. "I wouldn't have gotten married under the best of circumstances, certainly not as an invalid."

She herself would have been a poor candidate for sustained romance. Confined in bed for eight long months, she was forbidden to read, write letters, or receive any visitors because any such activity would overexcite her. And the doctor further ordered that her upper face be covered with a dark green cloth several hours a day to make sure her "restless eyes" wouldn't cause a sudden rise in bodily temperature. Accepting these restrictions with a spartan stoicism, she gradually improved and eventually was able to rejoin her fellow patients for afternoon promenades around the fountain.

On her release from Carlsbad in 1917 she was advised to live for a while in the high dry climate of New Mexico or Colorado. She chose instead to settle in nearby Fort Worth, Texas, where she was immediately employed as a reporter on *The Critic*, a weekly tabloid devoted to politics, drama, business, and local events. Once again she found herself writing vapid society columns ("The music club is organizing Sing Songs, where our soldier boys may harmonize together quite chummily"), fashion news, and drama reviews which were ill-disguised plugs for a local vaudeville house: "We can't have too much good vaudeville for the soldier boys, and the Byyers management is giving us the best — clean, original, with plenty of comedy. A commendable eveness of quality is maintained from week to week, and the bills are well balanced."

Although the publisher of *The Critic* had confidently announced that Miss Porter would "devote her life" to his modest
weekly, she stayed only a few months. Feeling queasy and weak,
she had belatedly decided to follow the advice of the doctor who
had suggested clean mountain air. Accompanied by an old friend,
whose husband was a news editor, she moved into a rented cabin
on the side of Cheyenne Mountain near Colorado Springs. The
air was indeed cool, crisp and invigorating, so "treacherously exhilarating" that she instantly decided to climb to the very top of
the mountain. With no previous experience in climbing, she
blithely started up the steep incline in a flimsy linen dress and
soft-soled Indian moccasins through which she could feel every
sharp rock and pebble. Somewhere near the top she suddenly
slumped down on a narrow ledge, her limbs trembling with fa-
tigue, her chest aching as she gasped for air. Then just as she was
beginning to breathe more easily, a loud menacing growl came
from a cave less than twenty feet away.

"Oh, my God!" she thought. "That's a bear — at least a bear!"

Scrambling to her feet in a split second, she rushed away from
the cave and scampered down the mountain like a frightened doe,
snagging her skirt on several thorny bushes, almost losing a moc-
casin when she stumbled into a hidden ravine, never once looking
back to see if the bear was in fact chasing her. Temples throb-
bing, lungs almost bursting, her body drenched with sweat, she
ran like fury all the way back to the cabin, where she plunged
through the half-open door and fell to the floor.

Fortunately, her friend had just returned from the general
store, and she carried Miss Porter (half-dragged would be more
accurate) to a couch near the fireplace. Unable to move without
help, Miss Porter felt almost totally crippled for several days. But
some of the local natives came by and assured her it wasn't a serious or permanent condition. "That's what we call 'muscle poi-
soning,' ma'am," one of them said, "and you'll get over it right
soon."

Sure enough, on the fourth or fifth day she was out of bed and
feeling much better, though not well enough to climb another
mountain. The rest of her month-long vacation was calm and

restful, with casual flower-picking expeditions, wading in cool crystalline streams, sitting in shady glens and reading poetry or jotting notes for stories she had thought about during her long confinement, and just loafing around the cabin. She would have liked to stay at Cheyenne Mountain until winter, but she was "flatter than flat broke" and realized she would have to find a job somewhere or go back home to live with her father, not a very inviting prospect for a twenty-eight-year-old woman who prized her freedom and independence. So she packed her two battered suitcases, still bulging with more manuscripts than clothing, and went down the mountain to Denver, where she rented a cheap second-floor room in a gloomy old mansion that had been converted into a rooming house. Two days later she was hired as a reporter by the *Rocky Mountain News*, her male predecessor having just joined the infantry after reading the latest batch of atrocity stories from the western front.

No longer relegated to the society page, she reviewed books, plays and concerts, interviewed visiting celebrities and did rewrites on a few crime stories. And still not disposed to write the silly sycophantic blurbs she had written in Dallas, she was now writing drama reviews with bite and humor and occasional hints of sarcasm. Some of her critiques apparently annoyed certain senior editors, which prompted her to comment on their annoyance in a subsequent column: "A play once ran forty-seven — or seventy-four weeks in New York. It was an unusually awful play, and therefore was unusually popular. Backed by these weeks — 47 or 74 — it started a career of crime across the country and finally arrived in the West. Here in a certain city in the foothills it struck a snag in the form of a lowly critic who hadn't noticed, or didn't care, if the play ran all those months in New York . . . she up and said the play was inadequate; and, as a result, the actors, actors' friends, and her own friends acted as if all the hyenas of the Rockies had broken loose."

Quite obviously, she had deliberately chosen an incorruptible tell-it-like-it-is attitude which was later adopted by Miranda in *Pale Horse, Pale Rider*, when she also ignores the cautionary advice of a senior editor, who tells her: "All you have to do is play up the headliners, and you needn't even mention the also-rans. Try to keep in mind that Rypinsky has got show business cornered in this town; please Rypinsky and you'll please the advertising department, please them and you'll get a raise. Hand-in-glove, my poor dumb child, will you never learn?"

But, of course, no one considered Miss Porter a poor dumb child. Some of her fellow reporters thought she was "glamorous and intriguing," with violet eyes, smooth ivory skin, curly dark hair, and a slim body usually clothed in soft gray dresses. She was undoubtedly pursued by many young men, who took her dancing at the open-air ballrooms of Elitch Gardens or Lakeside Park; but the one who caught her fancy was a handsome army lieutenant from nearby Fort Logan. They met at the Tabor Grand Opera House during the intermission of a concert she was covering for the *News*. Sidling toward her as she scribbled a few notes, he asked what she was writing about with such intense concentration, and his low resonant voice instantly attracted her attention.

"There was an immediate mutual attraction between us," she later told me. "But Adam and I were very young,* so we never went to bed together. I guess we were rather afraid of each other, as people are who go into an important thing seriously. We would take one step forward then two back. We advanced and retreated just like a mating dance."

But their brief ever-so-cautious courtship came to an abrupt end when both of them were suddenly stricken by an influenza epidemic that swept through Denver and several other cities in the late autumn of 1918. Adam died within a few days, and she came perilously close to death. With an illness that she called "a medieval sweating sickness," she lost all the beautiful black hair of which she had been understandably vain. And when it came out again, it was all white and (according to her doctor) would remain white for the rest of her life. She came out of the hospital crippled and bald, one leg still swollen from phlebitis, and with a partially healed fractured elbow which the doctors thought would never be normal again. How it was broken, she couldn't

---

* She was actually twenty-eight years old, and he was probably three or four years younger.

explain for she had been only semiconscious and delirious for several weeks.

"In my delirium I had seen my heavenly vision and the world was pretty dull after that. My mood for several years thereafter was that it was not a world worth living in. And yet one has faith, one has the inner core of strength that comes from somewhere, probably inherited from someone. Throughout my life there have been times during the same day when I have both an intense wish to die and later an eagerness that can't wait to see the next day. In fact, if I hadn't been as tough as an alley cat, I wouldn't be here today."

This tragic phase of her life was the basis of her memorable *Pale Horse, Pale Rider*, which she wrote much later, using many of the same scenes and characters. Not surprisingly, she was a changed woman when she came back to work at the *Rocky Mountain News* in the early months of 1919. Now she wore a gray hood to conceal her baldness and became somewhat of a recluse, often lunching alone and going straight home after work. One conscientious researcher went through the musty files of the *News* and found eighty-one signed articles which Miss Porter wrote between February 18 and August 17, 1919, most of which were movie and drama reviews, musical criticism and a few interviews, some reflecting her profound disenchantment with most of her fellow human beings.

Commenting on this metamorphic development in Miss Porter's character, one of her close friends from that period had said, "She doesn't wait for death to effect transmigration. Every now and then she stops being what she is and becomes something else. In some secluded corner of the world, she spins a cocoon, and presently comes out more brilliantly colored, with longer, swifter wings. She leaves her old life there in a tree, dry and forgotten and dead, something she has put forever behind her."

She most probably would have been amused by that description, might have cautioned her old friend to "block that metaphor." But in her frequent and sudden moves from one place to another, she did indeed resemble an errant butterfly — for just as everyone thought she might settle down for good in mile-high Denver, she abruptly served notice to the editor that she was leaving for New York. Once again packing her half-finished manuscripts and minimal wardrobe, discarding the gray dress that had become too much like a uniform, she lugged her suitcases into a taxi and went down to the railroad station, where she boarded the Union Pacific for Chicago. There, after a brief layover, she took the New York Central to Manhattan, occasionally remembering the wide-open spaces of Texas as the train chugged through smoky factory towns and increasingly cluttered cities.

Having never been in New York, she was initially overwhelmed by the dense traffic and nerve-wracking noise outside the railroad station, and was somewhat horrified to realize she was actually shouting for instructions from a beer-faced policeman: "Where is Greenwich Village? And how do I get there?"

Not fully sure she could understand his strange voice, she impulsively hailed a cab and asked the driver to take her to the main street of Greenwich Village. "And he must have known I was a yokel from back yonder, because he charged me fifty cents for a ride that would have cost me a quarter in Denver." He let her off near a coffee shop, where she sat at the counter and hastily scanned the classified ads of the *New York Times* in search of a room that wouldn't cost too much. Scribbling four or five listings on a napkin, she took another cab and asked to be taken to 17 Grove Street, where she found a small, sparsely furnished room that she nonetheless felt was quite adequate. It was on the second floor of a little house that had been built for the gravedigger of a paupers' cemetery that had subsequently become Washington Square.

Most of her fellow tenants and neighbors were (or hoped to be) writers, painters, dancers or simply devotees of the arts, some of them outlanders like herself, others equally exiled from such places as Brooklyn, Queens, the Bronx and Staten Island. Since most of them were short of money and were desperately grabbing any job they could get, Miss Porter soon realized she was unlikely

to find the most sought-after work on a newspaper or at a publishing house. Consequently, she had to accept the first job that
came along — ghostwriting a book which was published in 1921
as *My Chinese Marriage* by M. T. F. The author was an American woman whose identity was only vaguely covered by the initials she chose. She would talk her story to Miss Porter, who
would then organize and write it. While Miss Porter was never
quite certain of the veracity of the teller's tale, *My Chinese Marriage* kept her writing and her rent paid.

Though she often said that it seemed unbelievable that anyone
would want to sign a book written by someone else, she ghosted
several other works during periods of great financial need. But
she later asked the editor of *A Critical Biography* to exclude the
ghosted books, insisting they "should have no place in the list of
my works."

Psychologically drained by such hack writing, she had little
time or energy for her own perpetually gestating fiction, and occasionally vented her frustration at some of the night-after-night
parties which had become the sine qua non of Village life. There
were many pretty and talented women at these usually spontaneous gatherings (women of various sizes, shapes and racial ori-
gins), but Katherine Anne Porter generally got more than her
share of attentive admirers. No longer wearing a hood to conceal
her prior baldness, she had silken silvery-white hair, deep-set
violet eyes, finely molded features, and unblemished ivory skin
that made her seem much younger than twenty-nine. Her gently
husky, well-modulated Southern drawl seemed to soften an astringent, compulsive irony that frequently verged on sarcasm,
which might not have been tolerated from someone less attractive
or more shrill. As so frequently happens with beautiful Southern
women, many would-be suitors were so charmed by her voice
they paid only minimal heed to what she was saying, consequently ignoring or failing to appreciate the bite in her humor,
which inevitably convinced her that "it's often difficult to insult a
fool."

There were, however, certain men who apparently *did* appreciate her subtle irony, who respected her intelligence and clearly

enjoyed talking with her all night long. One of them was a bear-sized young editor whom she met at a Christmas party. They talked about poetry at first, then philosophy, finally switching to classical music, but as he consumed more and more bathtub gin, the editor became less intellectual and more amorous. Suddenly he put his arm around her shoulder, and she quickly squirmed away.

"I've got to go," she said. "It's awfully late."

"Okay," he slurred. "I'll walk you home."

"You needn't bother, Harold. I'm just around the corner, only a minute away."

"Need some air, Katherine Anne. Go with you soon as I get my coat. Snowing out."

Realizing she couldn't dissuade him, she got her coat and met him at the door, where he drunkenly fumbled with the knob for several seconds before he got it open.

"Let's go to my place," he half-shouted. "Have a little night-cap."

"Thank you, no, Harold. I'm awfully tired and need my sleep. I really do."

"Have it your way, honey bun," he said, once again flopping his arm around her shoulder; she no longer resisted, for she would soon be home.

Staggering and slipping on the trampled snow, he tightened his hold and nearly caused her to topple over, but they somehow managed to reach her house without incident. Then just as she was about to open the outside door, he grabbed her with both arms and tried to kiss her, crushing her in a tight bear-hug that got tighter and tighter as she desperately sought to free herself. Gasping for breath, she suddenly screamed as a piercing pain sliced through her lower chest.

Momentarily tightening his grip as if to stifle her scream, he abruptly dropped his hands and reared back on his heels, his mouth agape and drooling. "Sorry," he mumbled, clumsily turning to leave and nearly stumbling off the stoop. "Awful sorry."

Leaning against the door and gritting her teeth as the pain got more intense, she watched his slow lurching retreat through a film of angry tears. She stayed there three or four minutes, breathing as lightly as possible to minimize the pain, now sharply localized on her right side just below her breast. Then slowly, ever so slowly, she opened the door and carefully crept up the stairs to her room, where she eased herself into bed without bothering to take off her coat.

Next morning, after six hours of unrelieved misery, she somehow managed to check into the emergency clinic of St. Vincent's Hospital nearby, where immediate X rays revealed a fractured rib.

"Fortunately, it's merely a linear fracture," the doctor told her. "We'll just tape your chest and ask you to take it easy for a couple of weeks."

"How about this awful pain?"

"Aspirin will do," he said, reaching for a note pad. "Now tell me how it happened."

"Just an accident," she hedged. "Nothing of any importance that I can see."

"Well, you'll have to be more specific, miss. We've got to have a record."

She hesitated, wondering if he'd believe the truth, then once again tried to hedge. "Let's just say I fell and hurt myself. In the bathroom."

"Okay, lady," he said, frank suspicion in his raspy voice, "we'll call it a bathroom accident."

The fracture healed fairly quickly, and she was soon able to resume a moderately active social life, understandably avoiding men who seemed too strong or impulsive. It was during this period that she met John Peale Bishop. He had come to a rather noisy party with Edmund Wilson and Edna St. Vincent Millay, and she noticed him standing near the door, somewhat aloof and uninvolved, a cool detached look in his eyes. Sidling through the crowd ("unobtrusively, I hoped"), she moved into his range of vision and quietly joined a conversation between two painters who lived on Grove Street, now and then glancing at Bishop "until our eyes finally met in a prolonged stare that inevitably provoked smiles from both of us." And within a few short minutes they were engaged in a casual but increasingly earnest conversation about poetry and language and H. L. Mencken, whom she had recently met and instantly disliked. They disagreed as to the linguistic merits of the Baltimore curmudgeon, but no amount of disagreement could have altered her initial reaction to Bishop himself.

When she told me about him forty-seven years later (in the fall of 1967), she could still remember how she felt on first meeting Bishop. But there was an interesting preface to our conversation about him.

We had just finished dinner at a local restaurant, sipping brandy with our coffee, when Miss Porter suddenly drew a deep sigh and leaned back in her chair. "Do you realize," she said, alluding to a previous discussion on love and marriage, "that I've been married three times and lived with four lovers, and yet I've spent most of my life alone?"

"Well, now that you've mentioned numbers," I said, "who of the seven was the most satisfactory?"

She paused and pursed her lips before answering. "None of the seven," she finally said. "The one I liked most should have been number eight."

"Could you tell me his name?"

"I don't imagine you've ever heard of him, Hank. His name was John Peale Bishop."

"That was Edmund Wilson's friend, and he was a poet," I said, remembering his name from one of Wilson's collected essays.

"Then you *do* know him, you've read him!" she exclaimed. "I'm so glad someone knows his work, because he was a fine poet — much overlooked and underrated...." Then after another deep sigh: "He was also the very essence of what a man ought to be — charming, elegant, sensitive, vastly intelligent, profoundly honest — just about everything you could hope for. But we never got together — not the way we wanted."

"And why not?" I asked.

Tears misting her eyes, her voice fading to a husky whisper, she seemed to be talking to herself: "It was scruples. Every time I was free, he was married — and every time he was free, I was married. We kept missing each other all that time. And neither of us could or would deceive our spouse. We were too honest for that sort of thing, too bound by our scruples. . . . But we should have gone ahead anyway, and damn the scruples."

Then, after reflecting a moment, she leaned forward and offered a bit of advice that one would hardly expect from a gentle seventy-seven-year-old woman who looked like an ideal grandmother in a television commercial: "If that ever happens to you — and you're genuinely in love — I hope you'll make the most of it, no matter how brief your relationship may be. Just go ahead, and never mind the scruples."

Later that evening, while still reminiscing about her unfulfilled affair with Bishop, she read excerpts from a letter to her nephew in which she analyzed what she called "three schools of love." The first one was the Sex-Is-All school, which she considered the most popular, further commenting that certain extremists "practiced wallows only with total strangers, so that no slag of personal attachment could get into the pure gold of sex." Which led to liberated young women getting involved with Italian bootleggers or Brooklyn gangsters, who slapped them around occasionally — or "brash young men taking up with high-yellow girls in Harlem, getting their pockets picked and a dose of clap."

The second school, she said, still believed in True Love, where Sex was included, but only after careful preparation. "Some of these fanatics actually waited until they were married to sleep together, but this was considered very dangerous, because sometimes, when everything was perfect, sex the louse would be tried and found wanting." She further observed that the True Love advocates got divorced almost as often as those who belonged to the Foul Sex school, except that the Foul Sexers "didn't get bruised because they had known all along that nothing lasts, while the True Lovers were left holding a sackful of broken ideals."

The third was the Stroke of Lightning school, to which she

long adhered, alternately calling it the "love at first sight" and "the hell with theories" school. Noting that it could happen any place at any time, "the only fixed rule being that it must happen with absolute suddenness," she said the male object was "instantly transfigured with a light of such blinding brilliance all natural attributes disappear and are replaced by those usually associated with archangels at least." Thus they become beautiful, witty, intelligent, sensitive, courageous, charming . . . *ad infinitum.*

Then skipping a few lines, she continued reading from the letter: "It is no good going into details, for while it lasts there simply aren't any. And when it is over, it is over. And when I have recovered from the shock, and sorted out the damage and put my mangled life in order, I can then begin to remember what really happened. It's probably the silliest kind of love there is, but I'm glad I had it. . . ."

When I asked if she had experienced these same emotions with John Peale Bishop, she said, "It certainly started that way, but neither of us cut loose. We kept holding back, which was totally against my nature. But maybe I would have scared him off eventually."

"How so?" I asked.

"Well, I'm not so sure he could have stood my kind of passionate devotion."

"And why not?"

"Well, when I fall in love," she said, using the present tense as if it might happen again at any moment despite her seventy-seven years, "it's like a summer storm, when lightning transforms the most familiar landscape into something wild and strange and beautiful; and like some object catching fire, I burn right down to a little ember."

"It must be wonderful to be loved that way — though a bit unsettling."

"I guess I sort of frightened them, or spoiled them," she said with a slight chuckle. "And I was to blame. Because if you ever treat a man as if he were an archangel, he can't ever consent to being treated like a human being again."

Thinking back to that winter eve in 1919, when she first noticed Bishop standing by the door, Miss Porter musingly surmised that he wouldn't have been too comfortable with a pair of wings.

4

Revolution, Marijuana and Murder

INCREASINGLY dissatisfied with her life in New York, especially when she realized that Bishop was not likely to get a divorce, Miss Porter soon decided to move again. Europe seemed moderately enticing, but she didn't particularly care to join the popular pilgrimage to the Left Bank of Paris, where the Fitzgerald-Hemingway crowd would eventually make Jimmy's Bar more famous than the Eiffel Tower. "I would have been completely smothered — completely disgusted and revolted — by the goings-on there," she subsequently told an interviewer. "Even now when I think of the twenties and the legend that has grown up about them, I think it was a horrible time: shallow and trivial and silly. The remarkable thing is that anybody survived in such an atmosphere — in a place where they could call F. Scott Fitzgerald a great writer!"

Having thus ruled out France, she toyed with the idea of settling in Spain. But when she mentioned this possibility to a couple of Mexican expatriates who played the piano and sang in a Village cabaret, Adolfo Best-Maugard and Tata Nacho, they emphatically argued against it: "Nothing has happened in Spain for four hundred years. It's dead. But in Mexico something exciting is going to happen — is already happening. We're in a period of great revolutionary change in every aspect of our lives. So why go to a country that's already dead or on its way to dying?"

Remembering her childhood visit to Mexico City, the elegant

homes along the Paseo de la Reforma and the blind beggars and hungry children running alongside glittering coaches, begging for a mere centavo, she couldn't resist the temptation to see what social changes had taken place in the twenty years that had elapsed. Thus, in the early winter of 1920, she took a tediously slow train to El Paso, Texas, and then rode to Mexico City on a troop train jammed with soldiers of every age, rank and description, many of them accompanied by their wives (or mistresses) and their children. There were also several unattached *soldaderas* (camp followers) and prostitutes, who seemed to be doing a rather brisk business in a Pullman coach reserved for officers. Since there were not enough seats for everyone, a vast swarm of excess passengers covered the roofs of every coach — hundreds of men, women and children perilously clinging to the wooden catwalks as the train rumbled across the barren windswept desert. Some of the more resourceful women brought along their charcoal braziers and cooking utensils and somehow managed to prepare the traditional tortillas, frijoles and chile for their hungry families.

When they pulled into Chihuahua late in the evening Miss Porter stepped off the train for a breath of fresh air and casually glanced at the roof of her own coach. It looked like a militarized mobile kitchen, with bayoneted rifles silhouetted against the darkening sky, gray-white smoke oozing from the hot braziers, and all those roof-bound passengers gently smiling and joking as if there were not the slightest iota of danger. Although they probably restricted their cooking to the prolonged station stops, she was frankly amazed that no fires broke out during that tedious six-day journey to Mexico City. But, as a practical matter, how else could they have fed themselves? There was very little food available at any of the stations, and the meals on board were (as they still are) ridiculously expensive. As a matter of fact, she was sure their food was tastier than her own pallid fare; it certainly smelled better.

Compared to most of the jam-packed coaches on the train, the one in which she rode seemed almost luxurious, although such accommodations would now be regarded as less than second class. Every seat was occupied, some doubly occupied by a mother and

child, and the air grew fetid and warmer with each passing hour.
There were two American men sitting near her (they were apparently the only non-Mexicans on board), and one of them expressed a slight annoyance with all the pistols, rifles and machine
guns that were stashed on the overhead racks or casually leaned
against a window. "Having been reared on a rough Texas ranch
where the menfolk often settled their differences in duels — and
without any of that fancy Hollywood kettledrum music — I was
not in the least perturbed by the ubiquitous armament inside the
train. Even to this day, at the age of seventy-eight, I would
greatly enjoy going to a downtown shooting gallery, but most of
my gentle friends refuse to go with me. Perhaps life has become
too effete for people like me."

But there was certainly nothing effete in the ambience of Mexico when she traveled through that war-ravaged land in 1920.
There were bandit-soldiers like Pancho Villa, *campesino* (peasant) leaders like Emiliano Zapata and regular army men like Car-
ranza, and they had fought tooth and nail for ten long years in
what was the most devastating civil war in Latin American history. Over ten million people were killed and the property damage was incalculable. There was incredible disorder and needless
cruelty, but it was a genuine revolution that finally wiped out the
old order — the despotic regime of Porfirio Díaz, who ruled
thirty years with the connivance of the Catholic Church and a
deeply entrenched oligarchy of urban millionaires and even
richer *hacendados* like Don Luis Terrazas, the owner of half the
state of Chihuahua.

She could see the charred ruins of some of their immense hacienda (ranch) mansions as the troop train chugged southward
through small pueblos like Delicias and Guadalupe and then
through the larger towns of Durango and Irapuato and Celaya,
where whole buildings had been leveled by cannon fire or burned
down by angry oppressed peons. The walls of most houses and
store buildings were densely pocked with bullets or plastered
with painted slogans: *Viva la Revolución, Muerte a la Tiranía,
Pan, Tierra y Libertad* (bread, land and liberty).

During a prolonged stopover at Durango she noticed the *Pan,*

Tierra y Libertad slogan crookedly spelled out with calcimined rocks half-buried on the side of a hill.

"That's what we've been fighting for," said an old man with a much-mended rebel uniform. "And Pancho Villa will see that we get it. He's one of us — he's from Durango and he's the bravest man in Mexico."

Some people, many of them liberal Mexicans, would later tell her that Villa was more bandit than revolutionary, that he was cruel and undisciplined and not really the Robin Hood his supporters claimed him to be. However cruel he may have been, she thought it would have been interesting to know Pancho Villa; and at one time she seriously contemplated an attempt to interview him. An agent for one of the larger international news syndicates (Hearst or Scripps-Howard) had approached her in New York and suggested that she try to arrange a personal meeting with Villa, an idea that fascinated her. Later on, however, she told her Mexican friends that "this obviously anti-Villa newspaper syndicate was merely trying to use me," that they were hoping Pancho Villa would do her harm or kidnap her, thus giving them cause for demanding armed United States intervention against his rebel forces.

"Of course, one could never prove such a charge; but the project never came off anyway, because my friends in Mexico finally dissuaded me from trying. I have always regretted listening to those kind well-intentioned people, for I am sure nothing serious would have ensued."

Villa was undeniably a fascinating man to Miss Porter, whether rogue or hero. "Anyone who could arouse such adulation and hatred and fear, who could rise from untutored poverty to a position of power that changed the face of a nation, must have been a person of consequence. Moreover, he showed every sign of a truly charismatic personality, and charisma is a rare quality indeed."

The friends who finally persuaded her to abandon the notion of interviewing Pancho Villa were several artists and intellectuals she met on first arriving in Mexico City. They were comrades of the Mexican bohemians she had known in Greenwich Village, and they had been alerted to the probable date of her arrival. In fact, two of them had been at the Bellavista railroad station on three successive days, meeting each train from Chihuahua in search of the "beautiful *americana* with platinum hair and violet eyes."

Easily recognizing her as she struggled up the arrival ramp with a suitcase in each hand, they introduced themselves as friends of Adolfo, instantly relieved her of the heavy luggage and handed her a huge bouquet of flowers. Their names were Jorge and Moisés, and they were the most charming and attentive reception committee she had ever known (or would ever know).

"Adolfo tell us to get for you a nice hotel room, not expensive," said Jorge in slow, deliberate, pleasantly accented English. "But we have arrange something more better — a very nice room in a *pensión* with flower garden."

"That's so nice of you — absolutely wonderful!" she exclaimed. "As long as it's reasonable in price."

"Oh yes, we remember what Adolfo say."

Boarding a horse-drawn cab waiting at the curb, they took her to an old colonial-style house on Campos Elíseos, proudly indicating various points of interest along the way. The somewhat austere but gentle landlady showed her a large room on the top floor, which Miss Porter immediately rented after noting that it opened on an outdoor terrace overlooking a garden. Understandably pleased by her reaction, Jorge and Moisés insisted that they celebrate the occasion with a few drinks and dinner at their favorite café.

"There you will meet some of best talents and brains of our revolution," Moisés assured her.

He was right, of course. Mexico was in a state of turbulence, "a most promising chaos," and many of the young people she would meet were destined to play a large role in political and cultural revolution that altered the very fabric of Mexican life. Among them were Manuel Gamío, Jorge Enciso, Moisés Sainz and Miguel Covarrubias, young attractive and extremely learned archaeologists who were deeply involved in a sort of pro-Indian movement which emphasized the importance and vitality of Mexico's indigenous past. Until these men appeared on the scene (along with such distinguished indigenistas as José Vasconcelos and Alfonso Reyes), most Mexicans were inclined to boast of their Spanish blood and to play down or actually deny their Indian or mestizo ancestry. Many light-skinned women would refuse to shave the hair off their legs or armpits for fear of being considered half-Indian if their legs were sleek and hairless. Some of them still had hairy legs, which frankly appalled Miss Porter, especially when she considered their reasons for letting it grow.

The pro-Indian archaeologists-anthropologists were given a helping hand in their campaign by three polemical muralists, José Clemente Orozco, Diego Rivera and David Siqueiros; but the latter pair always impressed her as being more anti-Spanish than pro-Indian. She remembered spending many afternoons in Diego's studio, listening to his sometimes charming and roguish diatribes against "you degenerate gringo capitalists." When she reminded him now and then that most gringos were much poorer than he was, he would simply tell her that the "germ of your capitalism has infected all of us."

Nonetheless, as is so frequently true with talented rascals, she felt he was capable of charming even his most natural enemies. How else could one account for the Rockefeller clan paying a large fee to see themselves insulted by a self-proclaimed communist on their very own walls? "They obviously should have known what he had in mind, and he no doubt told them in advance, smiling all the while as he pocketed their handsome check. My Jewish friends would call that *chutzpah.*"

His colleague, David Siqueiros, also had a large measure of *chutzpah* and a similar knack for extracting huge sums of money from supposedly despised millionaires. One of them allegedly paid Siqueiros five million pesos (or four hundred thousand dollars) for a four-wall mural in a private Catholic chapel with a heliport on the roof. (Bear in mind that Siqueiros made no bones about being an atheist and a communist.)

Miss Porter first met Siqueiros at a party in Diego Rivera's studio, a wonderfully gay fiesta with lots of mariachi music and the tastiest food one could possibly imagine, slices of barbecued pork covered with mole verde, hot tortillas and frijoles refritos. Siqueiros's young wife was with him, a beautiful girl with a diffident manner and large brown eyes that seemed perpetually wary. Miss Porter and she were drawn to each other immediately, probably because they both felt a bit alienated in that crowd of confident brilliant artists and intellectuals. Apparently Siqueiros sensed there was a certain natural empathy between them, because he thereafter took the liberty of depositing his young wife ("I use the word 'deposit' to indicate his frame of mind rather than mine") at Katherine Anne's home while he wandered off on one of his *macho* escapades. Most Mexican men had that exaggerated maleness which is called machismo, so she couldn't really single him out on that score; but that still did not prevent her from resenting and indeed scorning his blithe assumption that women were of a lesser species.

A year before he died I talked to Siqueiros about Miss Porter, and he remembered her quite clearly.

"Oh, sure. Everyone knew little Cati.* She was very beautiful and witty and spoke Spanish much better than most foreigners. But why would I (or any other Mexican) want to leave my wife with a woman of the world like her? Especially a wife as innocent as mine. After all, everyone knew Cati had had affairs with that Nicaraguan poet, with Felipe Carrillo, and even Diego Rivera. She was one of those pretty señoritas, mostly gringas, who supposedly mixed paints for him. That was Diego's euphemism for anyone he was having an affair with: 'She mixes my paints.' Most of us just called them models. And, you know, Cati also lived with that gringo who worked at the American Embassy, in that house in Coyoacan next door to that crazy American poet who once lent me his house."

"You must be referring to Hart Crane," I said.

"Well, I don't remember his name; someone said he wrote

---

* "Cati" is the nickname for Catalina, which is Katherine in Spanish.

pretty good poetry — but I do remember that he had a weakness for little boys."

Miss Porter subsequently affirmed that she had indeed mixed paints for Rivera "because that was the chic thing to do in those days," but she made no mention of any affair with him. She, in fact, spoke quite bitterly about Rivera, shaking the ice in her bourbonless glass to emphasize each phrase:

"As he grew richer, more famous and noisier, I came to the conclusion that he was a dishonest, treacherous charlatan on a scale commensurate with the size of his biggest murals. He had a great talent; that no one can dispute — yet one simply couldn't escape the realization that Diego was principally interested in himself rather than in the proletariat he professed to love, and there was no one who could rival his genius for autopublicity and self-aggrandizement."

Indeed, I remember thinking that her bitterness might have been prompted by something more personal than mere ideological disagreement. Since both are now dead, we shall never know what caused her sudden fury against him.

Whatever she may have thought about the *macho* attitudes of Rivera and Siqueiros, Miss Porter readily conceded that some of the men who belonged to their little group felt no need to parade a dubious masculinity. One of them was Moisés Sainz, an ardent revolutionary and intellectual who became one of her closest friends and confidants. Moisés was an experimenter in every phase of his life — his work with the government and in his personal affairs — and he was frequently apt to drag his friends into all sorts of novel activities. He was no less an innovator when he later became the Minister of Health.

It was he who persuaded Miss Porter to smoke some marijuana in the summer of 1921, enthusiastically stressing the hallucinatory wonders of what he called "this harmless weed." Although this happened forty-six years before our series of interviews, she still remembered the experience as if it had happened the day before.

There were about fifteen people at this particular marijuana party ("Why do these modern young hippies call it 'pot' when 'marijuana' sounds so much more poetic?"), which was held in an old colonial house in Cuernavaca. Seven of them drove down from Mexico City in an elegant Essex touring sedan, one of those wonderful old cars with a canvas top that shook and rattled as they sped through the mountains at a breath-taking forty miles an hour. Moisés was at the wheel, alternately humming and singing his favorite revolutionary ballad, "Adelita," as he calmly spun around the steep hairpin curves overlooking the immense always-lush valley of Cuernavaca.

His intense brown eyes glittered with anticipation as they turned into a cobblestoned heavily shaded street that ran parallel to a deep ravine. They stopped at a large house at the very end, a rambling adobe structure with a conventional vine-covered patio and a long tiled terrace facing the westerly hills. Leaning over the low terrace wall, she could see the ramshackle *jacales* of two squatter families who occupied the lowest level of the rocky arroyo at least one hundred feet directly below them. It was a precipitous drop that made her slightly dizzy at first glance, like looking straight down from a tenth-story window.

"Stay away from that wall," one of the hosts warned her. "The bricks under that cracked adobe are a bit loose and wobbly." She needed no second warning.

After a brief exchange of introductions — not many were needed, for most of them knew each other — they all gathered around the huge unlighted fireplace and made ready to smoke the marijuana reefers which had been prepared by a man named Rogelio.

"Some of you haven't smoked *la yerba encantadora* [enchanting weed]," he said. "So I'll give you a simple demonstration of how to do it."

Gently fondling the home-made cigarette between his slender fingers, he carefully placed it between his lips and lit it with a match. Then he inhaled deeply, literally sucking in the smoke with a hissing sound to make sure it penetrated to the very bottom of his lungs. When he exhaled, only a small portion of the smoke came out of his mouth. Then he took another drag, this time holding on to the reefer as if to avoid swallowing it with his hard-sucking method of inhaling. This curious process was repeated four or five times, and then the same cigarette was passed to Moisés, who took a deep drag and then passed it on to Katherine Anne.

"Though I took the reefer without any outward show of concern, I felt a cold shiver run through me like a skeleton running his finger down my spine. But I was determined not to back down at this crucial moment. First exhaling to make more room for the marijuana fumes, I put the reefer between my imperceptibly trembling lips and drew in the smoke with the same sucking intensity Rogelio had shown us."

It burned much less than she had anticipated, and she simply allowed it to leave her lungs of its own accord, with no conscious effort on her part. The second and third puffs were much easier for her, although she was somewhat surprised not to feel any immediate reaction. When it finally came, however, she felt herself suddenly transported into another dimension.

"It was the same room, mind you, but an entirely new dimension of it, the room and all its furniture curiously detached from its normal rectangular boundaries and now freely floating within itself. Even I seemed to be floating and moving about in slow motion, not quite touching anything I reached for (my purse, a pre-Columbian artifact on the table, a red leather book), yet I must have actually grabbed and held them for a while."

Everyone appeared to be moving about in a trance, talking in a soft deliberate manner so that each syllable they spoke came forth separately and apart, and there was a muffled giggling all around her. Soon she found herself giggling without really knowing why — a slow burbling giggle that may well have been prompted by some long-forgotten humor. Moisés was sitting on a low table near the couch where she was sitting, apparently engaged in a conversation with her, although there was obviously no thread of communication between them.

"Then with no prelude whatsoever, I had the distinct impression that I could actually see his thoughts whirling around inside his skull, like little levers and springs and tiny cogwheels busily ticking away inside a glass dome. I turned and slowly looked around the room and noticed that everyone else had a clear transparent crystalline skull with mad-whirling mechanisms which went faster and then slower as their conversations ebbed and flowed. I felt slightly guilty and conspiratorial, uneasily conscious of eavesdropping on their private thoughts."

Turning back to Moisés, she saw that his little cogwheels had ground to an abrupt stop even though his lips were still moving. No longer able to bear the sight of all those frightfully exposed mechanical brains, she slowly but firmly walked out of the living room onto the long terrace and sat on a wooden bench near the door.

Her vague apprehensions gradually subsided and were finally snuffed out by a comfortable euphoria, a feeling of complete detachment from all worldly concerns. Looking far beyond the terrace wall, she could see thousands of shimmering stars caught in the sharp angular branches of a dead and leafless jacaranda tree; and she felt a strong urge to walk out into the dark sky, fully confident that she could indeed defy the laws of gravity.

"Easy as pie," she said to herself, jauntily walking across the terrace towards the far wall — the one which her host had previously warned her to stay away from. At first the wall seemed to recede from her, then suddenly she was right there and starting to climb over it when someone grabbed her from behind.

"No, no, Señorita Porter. Don't sit on that wall."

It was the same host again, gently leading her back to a safe chair. "I probably would not have climbed over the wall and into the sky, in spite of my hallucinated desire to do so, because there is always some unconscious self-prohibition that saves us from such foolishness — or so I have been led to believe."

Nevertheless, she was grateful for his concern and later, when she had recovered from the effects of the marijuana, told him so. Most of them gradually slipped back to normalcy in about two hours, though she remembered afterward that it seemed much much longer to her.

"I'm glad now that I had my experience with marijuana," she said, "especially under the care and auspices of such kind friends (two of them, according to the fixed rule of their group, would refrain from smoking in order to watch over the others); but I would not care to do it again. I was simply not meant to fool around with drugs of any kind."

Even such presumably mild pills as Benzedrine had an awful effect on her. Several years later a doctor she had never known before, who had come to treat her for a slight nervous exhaustion, gave her some pills to take just before going to bed. She couldn't recall what they were, "but I most definitely do recall the unspeakable anguish they caused me to suffer. Rather than send me into a restful sleep, those two pills tore my nerves apart and sent me into an emotional chaos. I struggled through twenty-four hours of stark terror, unable to sleep even five minutes, and the hallucinations that plagued me were like a preview of hell itself." Then, when the drug began to wear off, she fell into a deep melancholia and wrote an extremely strange note to herself that was filled with utter despair. Fortunately, she quickly recovered from the untoward effects of that nameless drug but later discovered she had bruised her leg on stumbling over a chair sometime during the night. "Believe you me, that marijuana binge in Cuernavaca was child's play compared to the nightmare caused by those pills."

Even though the pill incident had occurred some thirty years before, she shuddered as she described it for me. But when she resumed her narration of the Cuernavaca marijuana party, she was more relaxed. Long after she had regained her normalcy, she had a most engaging conversation with one of her fellow smokers. His name was Jorge Enciso, an archaeologist whom she had known for several months. They had got into a discussion of Aztec and Mayan stone carvings, and Jorge casually stated that the Indians had fully exploited "all of the seven basic designs." There are, of course, only *two* basic designs in art — the circle and the straight line — and all other supposedly basic designs are derived from these two. But when she mentioned this to Jorge, he stubbornly refused to accept her thesis and immediately began to sketch triangles, waves, rectangles and whatnot, all of which are clearly related either to a circle or straight line. Enciso was terribly annoyed when she pointed out each relationship and was even more infuriated when she told him that the *two basic designs were really an expression of sex.*

"All machinery is based upon the principle of sex," she told him. "What more proof do you need than the simple in-and-out piston motion of a train engine?"

That was too much for Jorge. "Nonsense!" he shouted. "Sex has nothing to do with machinery, Katherine Anne. You Americans want to mechanize everything."

He was actually more embarrassed than angry, and she could tell he was one of those men who prefer not to discuss sex in a frank open manner, certainly not with a woman.

"As a matter of fact," she said, glancing at him in a vaguely challenging way, "I have always felt that most men (in spite of all their dirty locker-room jokes) are essentially prudes about sex. I mean real honest-to-goodness sex, not the soiled furtive animalism which some people write about."

But aside from Jorge's disinclination to discuss the fundamentals of sex with an emancipated female, she considered him one of the more progressive young intellectuals in Mexico and also a loyal helpful friend.

Not long after they met in the spring of 1921, he introduced her to Frank Nivens, an elderly American archaeologist who had spent his whole adult life discovering and digging up buried Indian cities all over the country. Nivens's shop was on the top floor of a dilapidated and musty building near the Zócalo, a large drafty room with several dusty shelves and a long work table piled high with pre-Columbian artifacts. He had bushels of jade beads, mud-caked obsidian knives, bronze bells and black clay whistles shaped like tiny birds. There were also at least twenty skulls and four or five whole skeletons, one of which was no larger than a four-year-old child.

The following morning he invited her to go with him on "a dig" at his latest buried city not far from Mexico City, and on the way he gave her some additional data on a theory he had started to explain during their first meeting. It concerned the origin of ancient Mexicans. It was not an original theory and was, in fact, subsequently rejected by other scientists; but Nivens sincerely believed he had discovered it by himself. In any event, it was a sort of religion with him, a romantic mystical concept about a "lost continent" and how the original Mexican tribes had come from China or Mongolia in little skiffs, somehow dodging between hundreds of islands which later disappeared into the ocean.

"Just look at the faces of some of my diggers," he said as they neared the ruins. "You'll see unmistakable evidence of Oriental ancestry."

After having shown her the newest excavations, he suggested that she wander around on her own to get a genuine down-to-earth feeling of the area once ruled by Montezuma. He probably sensed her curiosity, and she was indeed grateful for a chance to poke around the partially unearthed pyramid and the small village nearby. During the next few hours she explored some of the older diggings, pausing now and then to collect dusty shards of clay pottery which may well have predated the coming of Cortés; and later on she came across a small mound of human skulls and bones bleached by years of exposure to wind and sun. One of the skulls was tilted at an angle which made it seem rather quizzical. Almost compulsively she reached down to pick it up and cradled it in the palm of both hands. Then she carefully sat down on that mound of skulls and eased her own weary bones.

Not far from her was a spread of pepper trees and a wall of organ cactus enclosing an adobe house. Just outside the open doorway there was a young woman making tortillas on a metal brazier, expertly patting the *maza* between her hands and then deftly flipping the raw dough onto the hot metal plate. Though it was manifestly impossible, she imagined the inimitable good smell of those tortillas tantalizing her senses. In no time at all she got off her throne of bones and hurried over to the house.

"*Buenas tardes,*" she said in her best Spanish. "Could I possibly buy a tortilla?"

She knew the young woman would offer one: no self-respecting Mexican would ever think of selling any kind of food under such circumstances. And, sure enough, she gave Miss Porter three tortillas and insisted that she make herself a taco with some *carnitas* she was keeping hot underneath the brazier. "Aside from her instant generosity, there was a certain natural grace in the way she offered to feed me, an inherently gentle manner that would have shamed some of the so-called ladies I have seen here and there." Moreover, she was a genuine beauty. Her brown eyes were almond-shaped and vaguely Oriental, her glistening black hair pulled severely back into a long single braid that reached her slender waist, and her finely wrought features were unbelievably classic. "Here is royalty in every sense of the word, I said to myself, the very essence of fine beauty." Several hours later Miss Porter tried to capture that impression in a rambling paragraph in her notebook but could find no words to adequately describe her.

On her next visit to the archaeological excavations Miss Porter saw her again. She had come to deliver her husband's lunch — he was Mr. Nivens's foreman — and she had also brought the old man some live fowl, which she had slung over her right shoulder. Half of them fell upon the flat of her back and the rest were dangled across her breast. The captive chickens squirmed and fluttered against her slim body, but she appeared not to notice them as she moved gracefully past the work area with an instinctive serenity. When she had finished her errands and disappeared, Miss Porter mentioned meeting her to Mr. Nivens and expressed great admiration for her gentle queenly style.

"Well, she's got a touch of royalty all right," he said, glancing in the direction she had gone. "And she's also one hell of a woman. I've never known another like her. There aren't many women who can kill another woman and still maintain their natural poise."

"She killed someone?" she asked, bewildered by what he had said. "She killed another woman?"

"Three months ago — in that little village over there," he said. Then he told her all about the young woman, whom Miss Porter was later to call María Concepción in the story which bears the same name. She had been married to Juan the previous year in a formal church ceremony, which of course gave their marriage a special distinction, since most of the marital unions in the community were common-law affairs. She was barely eighteen at the time but a fully mature woman nonetheless. Perhaps it was her unusual grown-up manner which unnerved her young husband and led him into a less demanding relationship with a fifteen-year-old chippy who lived in a neighboring village. Whatever the reason, Juan got more and more involved, finally abandoning his home and running off to join the army. His young sweetheart, probably a camp-following *soldadera* at heart, ran off with him.

They stayed away for several months, then suddenly returned to set up house in his old neighborhood, within shouting distance of the home and wife he had abandoned. The teenage "second wife" was pregnant and ready to give birth. María Concepción — "let's call her that because I simply cannot remember her real name" — coolly ignored them both and went about her daily chores without the slightest indication of strain. But shortly after the teenager's child was born, María went into action. On a bright sunny afternoon, when most of the villagers were at work or taking a siesta, she stealthily crept into her husband's second home and stabbed his young sweetheart to death. She stabbed her at least twenty times and "left her looking like a sieve," according to Mr. Nivens. Apparently no one saw the murder, but several neighbors saw María coming home with the week-old baby gently held in her arms. That evening two policemen, who had been summoned by Juan, visited every house in the village but failed to get one scintilla of evidence concerning the gruesome crime. There was a complete conspiracy of silence, a strange and eerie sense of justice well done. Juan moved back to his old home, and María Concepción accepted him without a murmur of reproach.

"There was a seeming black-and-whiteness to that episode because most Indians are puzzlingly stoic," said Miss Porter, later recalling the incident. "Yet on closer examination of those close-mouthed people, one finds deep layers of crossed emotions that are chilling to contemplate. The people I wrote about in *Flowering Judas* appeared more complex on the surface but their motives were less difficult to spot, particularly if one made an effort to understand the social and political ambience in which they operated."

And the *ambiente* — somehow the Spanish word seems more

encompassing than its English equivalent — in Mexico during the early twenties was charged with explosive tension. There were street riots almost daily, sudden middle-of-the-night deportations of foreign agitators, parades of workers carrying red flags, constant battles between Catholics and Socialists in Yucatan and Morelia, and fevered discussions in reactionary newspapers as to the best means of stamping out Bolshevism, which was the exclusive term for all forms of radical work.

It was a fascinating spectacle for Miss Porter, although singularly difficult to record because events kept overlapping and contradicting each other. On several occasions she tried to write about it but found herself hopelessly snared in a journalistic nightmare, which became even more confusing from week to week. It was impossible to write fully of the situation unless one happened to be one of those fourteen-day wonders who came dashing in to gather some quick definitive impressions, mostly at the Ritz Bar, and then quickly dashed out again to write their confident expert analyses for the large magazines.

One boozy expert once quite frankly told her that his best (probably *only*) source of information was "this fellow Pedro who tends bar at the Majestic." There were other newsmen who probably felt that Jaime at the Hotel Cortéz was a more acute observer of the Mexican scene.

Quite obviously, the true story of Mexico was not to be found in bars frequented by foreign correspondents, nor from official documents, nor from guarded talks with diplomats. Nor could it be gathered entirely from the so-called man-in-the-street. The lives of those people were too widely scattered and complex and vast; too many forces were at work, each with its own intensity of self-seeking.

Acutely aware of all the conflicting ambitions of people around her, Miss Porter wondered if any country besides Mexico had so many types of enemy within the gates: "Some of them were friends of mine (or at least associates of friends), so I had a chance to watch them at close range." There were foreigners and natives, hostile to each other by tradition, but mingling their ambitions in a common cause. Mexican capitalists joined hands with

Americans to squash their revolutionary fellow countrymen. The Catholic Church enlisted the help of Protestant strangers in the subjugation of the restless Indians, now determined to get the land promised them by agrarian reformers. Englishmen, Americans and Frenchmen maneuvered endlessly for political and financial power, oil and mines; "a splendid horde of invaders who were understandably distrustful of each other but nevertheless unable to disentangle their mutual interests." Then there was the bourgeoisie, much resembling the bourgeoisie elsewhere, who were defiantly opposed to all idea of revolution. "We want peace and more business," they chanted.*

The Catholic clergy, sensing that their great power was on the downgrade, were particularly active in the conservative campaign against what they inevitably called the Bolshevist menace. The more astute indulged in skillful political stratagems, and there were street brawls for the hotheads.

Miss Porter was particularly disturbed by a tactic she described as follows: "For the deeply religious and superstitious peons there was always the moldy infallible device: a Virgin — this time of Guadalupe — had been seen to move, to shine miraculously in a darkened room! A poor woman in Puebla had been favored by Almighty God with the sight of this miracle, just at the moment of the Church's greatest political uncertainty; and now this miraculous image was brought to Mexico City to be viewed by thousands of awed believers. The priests, of course, insisted on a 'severe investigation' to be carried out by themselves, but meanwhile placed the statue in an oratorio, where it would be living proof to the faithful that the great patroness of Mexico had set her face against reform. The peons were naturally advised by the priests that to accept the land given to them by the Agrarian Reform Laws was to be guilty of simple stealing, and everyone taking such land was to be excluded from holy commu-

---

* In 1921 Miss Porter wrote one of the most astute analyses ever written about the politics and politicians of Mexico during that turbulent era. Her essay "The Mexican Trinity," published in *Century* magazine, should be read by any student of Mexican history.

nion — a very effective threat. Consequently, the government agents who came to survey the land for purposes of partition were attacked by the very peons they had come to benefit."

As a somewhat renegade Catholic, whose faith was subsequently restored for reasons set forth elsewhere in this book, Miss Porter found these tactics most reprehensible.

Some of her revolutionary acquaintances ("I intentionally avoid the word *friends*") were also engaged in dubious tactics, but they seemed less treacherous to her because they were at least nominally allied with the poor workers and *campesinos*. The group most frequently talked about was mainly composed of discontented foreigners, lacking even the rudiments of the Russian theory. Moreover, there was not a single working revolutionist among them. "They were great sitters and talkers, who loved to intrigue but had no inclination for the dull and sometimes dangerous chores they habitually assigned to their local comrades."

Her principal character in *Flowering Judas*, Braggioni, is a composite of several would-be revolutionists who belonged to this international clique; but one of them stood out more clearly than the others. He was a self-assured, darkly handsome but chubby man who became interested in her friend Mary Doherty and started dropping by her apartment fairly often. "Now, Mary was one of those virtuous, intact, straitlaced Irish Catholic girls, the kind who had undoubtedly provoked Paul Rosenfeld's dictum that the Irish were born with the fear of sex even before Christianity. Well, this fat revolutionist suddenly increased his visits to the point of causing Mary to worry a bit about his ultimate intentions."

So Mary asked Miss Porter one day to come over to sit with her because she was expecting another visit from so-and-so. She lived alone in a small apartment which was described fairly accurately in *Flowering Judas*, including the little round fountain shaded by a judas tree in full bloom. Having been delayed somewhat, Miss Porter was hurrying past the open window and noticed Mary sitting very primly on a stiff chair, patiently listening to the furry soft voice of this corpulent man, who was fingering his guitar in a faintly insinuating manner. Quite suddenly she came to the conclusion that Mary didn't know how to take care of herself, that she certainly did need someone to stand guard.

Although Miss Porter disliked the role of a meddling chaperone, she somehow felt obligated to stay there in spite of his all-too-apparent resentment. Finally he gave the guitar an angry spank that made it twang with pain, then abruptly rose from the couch and stomped out of the house.

Months later someone told Miss Porter that he was a prominent member of an underground group with vast international connections. Moreover, he had certain loose ties with some of the Mexican revolutionaries, who later involved her in a few subversive errands, which are discussed in a subsequent chapter.

There were heroes and villains in all those rebel outfits, some of whom she would openly criticize in night-long conversations over a glass of cheap wine in some sidewalk café.

"But you mustn't say those awful things, Catalina," they would tell her. "They're part of our movement."

But she simply couldn't accept that kind of reasoning and quite emphatically told them, "It's absurd to pretend that all these people are good and courageous when some of them are self-serving rascals with their own personal intrigues." She couldn't see where she was obliged to say so-and-so was a hero when he wasn't. Even as propaganda this was no good. The Braggioni breed, whose principal contributions were long and tedious arguments about "the right kind of Marxism," would have merely bored her had she not been aware of their ability to obstruct the efforts of more sincere men.

Her Mexican friends were less talkative than the Braggionis but much more actively engaged in the real work of the revolution — people like Moisés Sainz and Manuel Gamío, who worked in government offices specifically dedicated to carrying out long-cherished reforms. During that period the Mexican cabinet was made up of intensely radical people like Calles, moderates like Huerta and extreme reactionaries like Pani, just the right elements for a brutal tug-of-war. The liberals and radicals finally won out after several years of internecine struggle. Their task would have been easier had there been a genuine demand for a social upheaval by the masses, but most of the *campesinos* were sluggishly inert, no doubt mesmerized by their long servitude. "They were a lost people," she later wrote, "who moved in the oblivion of sleepwalkers under their incredible burdens, silent and reproachful figures in rags, bowed face to face with the earth. These are not the kind of people who make revolutions."

She was convinced that most revolutions are made by less burdened individuals from the urban middle class, people like Calles and Madero and Obregón. And although he never had the opportunity to attain the status of these elder revolutionaries, Felipe Carrillo must surely be included in that good company.

She met Felipe a few weeks after her arrival in Mexico. He was then a *diputado* (congressman) from the state of Yucatán and an acknowledged leader of the radical faction in the Mexican Congress. No liberal was more hated and feared by reactionary congressmen than Felipe, and on one memorable occasion they launched a bitter attack on him that eventually exploded into a full scale riot within the chamber itself, an event she noted in a subsequent article. For three whole days the lawmakers went on a rampage of dissent, most of it concerning Felipe, who later told her it was the most hysterical comedy he had ever seen. Finally, President Obregón ordered that the riot be squelched by whatever means were necessary. Whereupon the fire department went down to the white-pillared Chamber of Deputies, turned on a high-powered hose through the open windows, and soaked the rampaging congressmen to the bone. Felipe was probably the wettest of all.

Judging from another incident which involved Miss Porter, Felipe apparently had a penchant for getting drenched. This particular episode occurred in Chapultepec Park on a pleasant summer afternoon. They were idling along in a rowboat, amiably chatting about Miss Porter's proposed trip to the Mayan ruins in Felipe's native Yucatán (he himself was a handsome distinguished-looking Mayan Indian), when it occurred to her that she ought to help with the rowing.

"Nonsense," he said, gently holding her wrists. "How can you possibly row with these thin grasshopper arms?"

He said it with great affection, so that it was really no insult, but she couldn't help feeling a bit challenged. "Well, why don't you let me try, Felipe? I'm not as fragile as you think."

Amused by her persistence, he handed her the heavy cumbersome oars and leaned back on the bow with exaggerated ease. Returning his faint smirk with a tight smile, she clutched the oars too tightly and slashed them into the water. But in her stubborn haste she dipped one oar far deeper than the other, causing the boat to lurch sidewise. Felipe instantly jumped from his relaxed position, wildly grabbed for the opposite oar, and, with the full weight of his body lunging down, tipped the boat over. They both went splashing into the shallow lake, yelling for help at first and then roaring with laughter as they waded ashore with not a stitch of dry clothing.

That evening, while dancing at the Salón México, they found themselves periodically chuckling about that wonderfully silly episode, "and I am sure the other dancers considered us slightly balmy." Incidentally, that same dance-hall was later immortalized in a musical piece by Aaron Copland. Felipe had taken her there on other occasions and had very expertly taught her all the latest dance steps, including one of those low-bending tangos which Rudolph Valentino had made so famous.

During this period Felipe Carrillo was also courting a lovely young American journalist named Alma Reed, to whom he was subsequently engaged to be married. He was killed, however, shortly before their wedding date in a vile political murder instigated by certain military officers who feared he might some day become president of Mexico. He had just been elected governor of Yucatán by a huge popular majority; but before he could take office, he and his brothers — along with several political associates — were assassinated by General Huerta's henchmen.

"That was a terrible loss for his countrymen," Miss Porter later told me with a catch in her throat, "and a bitter personal loss for those of us who cherished his friendship."

When I subsequently asked Miss Reed about Miss Porter's relationship with Felipe Carrillo, she painted a much different picture: "Well, I guess Katherine Anne tried to add Felipe to her list of conquests and has probably exaggerated whatever happened between them. But he must have been aware of her other affairs, so she was just a passing fancy to him. I was Felipe's true love — his only love. Miss Porter meant very little to him, no matter what she might have told you."

Shortly after Carrillo's death, one of his friends wrote a hauntingly beautiful ballad, "La Peregrina," which was dedicated to Alma Reed.* But Miss Porter apparently told her friend Glenway Wescott that it was written for her. In his review of *Ship of Fools*, he said: "One of the revolutionaries wrote a song about her, *La Pelerina*, which I have heard tell, has become a folk song; little companies of boy singers, like boy scouts in a dream, sing it in the streets." (Aside from misspelling the song title, Mr. Wescott was misinformed on all other counts: it's usually sung by adult trios and mariachis in saloons and nightclubs.)

Whatever their relationship might have been, Miss Porter was profoundly depressed by Felipe's death and found it difficult to resume her day-to-day chores as a teacher in one of the slum schools on the outskirts of Mexico. For several weeks she avoided her usual haunts, knowing she would be unable to engage in the kind of chitchat one has to expect even from the most serious people. Most of her close friends kindly understood her need for temporary exile; just as kindly, they decided to bring her back to her normal scope of activity.

It was Roberto Turnbull who devised a nearly perfect gambit for snapping her out of the doldrums: he made her the leading lady of a low-budget movie he was filming in Mexico City. Perhaps "leading lady" is too broad a term for what she did, because only her *legs* were used in that unique role. "Roberto wasn't interested in the rest of me."

The plot of his little comedy was about a young man working in a half-cellar, who falls in love with the legs and feet of a

---

* Miss Reed became a permanent resident of Mexico and remained single until her death in 1970. Budd Schulberg has written a screen play based on her life.

señorita passing by the narrow window above. The whole story was his pursuit of the upper part of this girl. "I had often been told that I had pretty legs and (although I never could see it myself) I couldn't help but be pleased." She was doubly flattered when Roberto decided to photograph them for his movie. What's more, they made her seventeen pairs of the most beautiful shoes she had ever seen, everything from red and gold brocade to the most exquisite black satin. She wore them all in a series of very silly scenes all over the city, sometimes hoisting her skirt just above her knees as she dashed across a cobbled street in the slums or across the wet grass in the Alameda Park.

The producers, who were poorer than the most impoverished church mice, gave her the shoes in lieu of monetary compensation, and she was totally satisfied. The movie, by the way, ended with the young man finding the elusive girl, who was portrayed by an extremely beautiful Mexican actress with dark smoldering eyes. "Unfortunately for Roberto, the cameraman wasn't quite good enough and consequently failed to get my legs matched with her body."

Several years later she met a Mexican artist who gave her that dead-fisheye look in the face and then let his gaze wander down past her knees to her feet. "Oh, I know you, I know you," he said. "I remember you now."

She never did ask him why.

5

Bullfights and Lawsuits

COMFORTABLY seated in an old wicker chair on the cool shady terrace outside her rented room, Miss Porter scribbled copious notes on all sorts of things during her first few months in Mexico City, but she wrote little if any fiction. Once in a while she would drag her "manuscript suitcase" from under the bed and browse through some partially finished short stories, editing a line here and there or scrapping an entire page, all the while mumbling to herself, "I've got to work, I've got to work, I've got to settle down and work." Yet nothing seemed to move her beyond a mere fret.

One story, however, had been germinating in her mind, insistently nagging her, almost demanding to be written. Its seed had been planted on the day she met the beautiful Indian woman at the archaeological excavation, the woman who had killed the teenage chippy who had stolen her young husband. She had been especially fascinated when she learned that the murderer had taken her victim's infant child as if it were her own, as if she herself had given it birth. Thus, Miss Porter had already named the protagonist "María Concepción," and the rest of the story had been shaping in her mind, word after word, line after line, until she finally sat down and put it on paper. But the first draft failed to satisfy her. The second was equally unsatisfactory. So she kept on writing one draft after another, refining each phrase and chipping away excess words like a finely skilled diamond cutter who demands only the best of himself. The fifteenth or sixteenth draft (she had lost the exact count) was the one she sent to *Century* magazine, which published it in 1922. It was, in fact, the first short story she had ever published.

Meanwhile, she had written several articles about Mexico, two of which revealed a profound understanding of the nation's turbulent political development: "The Mexican Trinity" and "Where Presidents Have No Friends," which also appeared in *Century* magazine. Both pieces were by-products of prolonged and passionate discussions with certain Mexican intellectuals, nightly habitues of the Café Flores, who had instantly welcomed her into their select circle. Most of the time she would be the only woman at their favorite sidewalk table, and she soon realized that many passersby considered her a loose woman, "one of those crazy gringas who probably slept with anyone." No decent Mexican señorita would have dared to be seen surrounded by bearded bohemians at a sidewalk café, especially at night. But Miss Porter could not have cared less. "I wouldn't have missed being with my brilliant charming friends for all the pesos in Mexico — certainly not to please all those prissy women, who were every bit as Victorian as the people back home."

Several artists and writers occasionally joined the group, adding their special insights and biases to the night-long discussions and incidentally providing her with material for future stories. In "The Martyr," published in *The Century* for July 1923, she made a satirical portrayal of "the greatest artist of Mexico," whose model leaves him for another artist. To ease his pain, Ruben consumes huge quantities of food and liquor and becomes ludicrously fat, finally dying of a sudden seizure at the Little Donkeys café, moaning his last words for posterity: "Tell them I am a martyr to love. I perish in a cause worthy of the sacrifice. I die of a broken heart! Isabelita, my executioner!" As one can readily see, this much-too-obvious satire was considerably inferior to "María Concepción," and Miss Porter wisely excluded it from her various subsequent collections.

An equally weak story, "Virgin Violeta,"* was fashioned after a Nicaraguan poet, Salomón de la Selva, whom she also met at the

---

* Also published in *Century* magazine, December 1924.

Café Flores. Though she apparently had an affair with Salomón, she was absolutely embittered when he freely bragged about having seduced the teenage daughter of a friend. "He was an evil man, totally without scruple," Miss Porter later declared. "I think he was beyond redemption. Yet there was something strangely compelling about Salomón, a sinister fascination that was not easily resisted. And he certainly knew how to handle women."

Fortunately, most of her Mexican friends were cut from a different cloth from Salomón. They were kind and generous and supportive — "just good close friends with whom there was no sexual involvement whatsoever." Among them was Miguel Covarrubias, who would one day become a great painter, distinguished archaeologist, and director of Mexico's world-renowned Museum of Anthropology. But when she first knew him, he was a shy seventeen-year-old artist, who spent hours and hours sketching highly amusing and devastatingly perceptive caricatures of the Café Flores's ebullient clientele. Ultimately, Miss Porter showed his sketches to the editors of *Vanity Fair* magazine, who immediately commissioned a steady flow of caricatures from young Covarrubias, thus making him one of the most successful artists in the United States during the so-called roaring twenties. But in those early days, he and all the other Mexican artists and writers with whom she consorted were scraping along on little or no income, with no expectations of bettering their condition.

On the other hand, she socialized with some people she characterized as "a most lordly gang of fashionable international hoodlums." They were French, Spanish, Italian and Polish, most of them with titles and prominent names, including a duke, a countess, two barons, a marquess and an "uncertified prince." Their money came from inherited wealth or fancy enterprises like the importation of fine cognac or custom-built sports cars for corrupt politicians. Drinking only the most expensive liquor at exclusive clubs and restaurants, they also played such fashionable games as polo, tennis and golf, drove sleek high-powered cars like maniacs, and never missed a bullfight or boxing match, always accompanied by beautiful women garbed in the latest Paris fashions. "A fast, tough, expensive, high low-life they led . . . and from time to

Miss Porter as seen through the eyes of the
Mexican cartoonist Miguel Covarrubias, 1920

*With her father
in the early 1920s*

*On a visit to a
friend's villa in Cuernavaca,
Mexico, in the late 1920s*

time, without being in any way involved or engaged, I ran with this crowd of shady characters and liked their company and ways very much. I don't like gloomy sinners, but the merry ones charm me. . . ."

It seems doubtful that such a group would have permitted her to remain "uninvolved," an aloof detached spectator, particularly as a woman whose only entrée would have been her beauty, for she certainly had no wealth, no great reputation, nor the kind of family background that would have assured her acceptance in that *haut monde*. In any event, it was through them that she met an Englishman who was to lead her into "one of the most important and lasting experiences of my life."

His name was Shelley, and he soon let her know (with an offhand modesty, of course) that he was indeed related to the great poet — was his great-great-nephew, to be more specific. Rich and self-assured, he could afford any of the expensive sports, but he had a particular passion for horses, which he bred, raced and sold with the cold merciless detachment of "the true horse lover." When she commented on his cool attitude toward his animals, his answer sent chills down her spine: "What is there to like about a horse but his good points? If he has a vice, shoot him or send him to the bullring; that is the only way to work a vice out of a breed."

He could be equally impatient with what he considered human vices, as she would eventually learn while visiting a ranch with him. Inviting them to go horseback riding across his vast hacienda, the owner gave Miss Porter a frisky stallion, who immediately took the bit in his teeth and scampered away at breakneck speed, rushing down a steep mountain path as she held on with an expertise she had learned as a child. Giving him an easy rein, she let him finally run himself to a standstill on more level ground. But her expert horsemanship made no impression on Shelley. He insisted that the stallion was not a good horse and that she should have refused to ride him. And when she asked how one could possibly refuse a horse offered by one's host, he coolly reminded her that "a lady can always excuse herself gracefully from anything she doesn't wish to do." He was, of course, even more disapproving when she told him that she had liked being run away with, that it had been positively exhilarating, particularly because it had been so unexpected.

This grumpy chronic disapprover of frivolous females was a stocky, well-muscled, red-faced man, whose bright blue eyes made him seem a shade younger than his fifty years. Like some of the landed gentry of his native England, he dressed with elegant, impeccable taste, was so superbly tailored that she confidently dubbed him "the best-dressed man in America, North or South." His highly polished shoes and boots, made of the finest leather, alone would have justified that extravagant claim. But for all his good points, she did not fall in love with him — far from it. "We struck up a hands-off, quaint, farfetched, tetchy kind of friendship which consisted largely of good advice about worldly things from him mingled with critical marginal notes on my character — a character of which I could not recognize a single trait." But when she insisted that she was not at all like what he had described, he would simply say that she *should* be — or that she was, but didn't know it.

Having assumed the task of remolding her flawed but possibly reparable character, Shelley led her through a series of educative processes which inevitably culminated with a bullfight, surely the acid test of anyone's character. Like thousands of Americans before and after her, she resisted the idea of going to a bullfight. She had always hated the slaughtering of animals for sport, even though admitting to a certain hypocrisy in her attitude. "I am carnivorous, I love all the red juicy meats and all the fishes," she later wrote. "Seeing animals killed for food on the farm in summers shocked and grieved me sincerely, but it did not cure my taste for flesh." When she was older, her father criticized her tiresome timidity and logically argued that if she cared to eat meat she should be able to kill the animal that provided it; otherwise she would be nourishing herself on the "sins" of other people. All of which forced her to ask herself if she were "just pretending to finer feelings than those of the society around me."

Shelley apparently shared her father's views, and finally pressured her into attending a bullfight. It was the first corrida of the season, Covadonga Day, in mid-April of 1922, and she particularly noticed a long procession of flower-bedecked carriages approaching the Plaza México, with elegantly dressed men and with beautiful women wearing their finest lace veils, their highest combs and the fanciest fans she had ever seen. They were, indeed, a dazzling group of aficionados, but their gaudy presence was almost forgotten when the *toreros* paraded across the ring — Ignacio Sánchez Mejías and Rodolfo Gaona. "You'll be seeing the best Spaniard against the best Mexican," she heard Shelley saying as the crowd rose to greet them. But her attention was riveted on a handsome blonde American woman riding a magnificent thoroughbred gelding just behind the bullfighters. "She'll be fighting a bull on horseback, and she's probably the finest damned rider in the world — just wait 'til you see her."

Her name was Hattie Weston, and she did not actually fight the bull. Adopting the Portuguese style, she passed the charging beast with a series of exquisitely timed maneuvers, piercing his back with two colorful banderillas but never attempting to kill him. Nevertheless, it seemed dangerous enough to Miss Porter, who was happy to see both the bull and Miss Weston leave the ring alive and well.

Then came the moment she had been dreading — when the real bullfighting would begin. With cold trembling hands and painful tinglings in her wrists and collarbone, she felt a mingling of fear and excitement, and a lump rose to her throat as a huge raging bull burst from the *toril* gate. He and the other five bulls were from the ranch of the Duke of Veragua, all of them as brave and enormous and handsome as any she would see afterward. She herself best described that first beautiful monster who charged into the sun-splashed plaza: "His hide was a fine pattern of black and white, much enhanced by the goad with fluttering green ribbons stabbed into his shoulder as he entered the ring. . . ." And she also saw a highly aesthetic effect in "an interesting design in thin rivulets of blood, the enlivening touch of scarlet in his somber color scheme. . . ."

Bellowing with rage, the bull rushed at the waiting picador's horse, blindfolded in one eye, disemboweling the defenseless horse with one vicious sweep of his sharp horns while the picador

feebly pretended to stave him off. The horse staggered in his own
entrails as Miss Porter flinched back and covered her eyes, whereupon Shelley grabbed her wrists and pulled her hands down to
her knees as inconspicuously as he could. And when she shut her
eyes and turned her face from the gory spectacle, he snapped at
her in a hoarse angry voice: "Don't you dare come here and then
do this! You must face it!"

Conceding a certain logic in what he was telling her — and also
determined to see it through at whatever emotional cost — she
somehow managed to open her eyes and to keep them open as the
matador continued fighting that first bull, gradually overcoming
her revulsion and suddenly becoming as excited as everyone
around her. And when Rodolfo Gaona sighted the magnificently
brave bull for the kill, she was straining on tiptoe to see it all, now
almost blinded with emotion as he plunged the sword deep into
the bull's pulsating hump. Exultantly yelling with the rest of the
roaring crowd, she gratefully kissed Shelley on the cheek as he
shouted like someone fully vindicated, "Didn't I tell you? Didn't
I?"

Smilingly admitting that he had indeed told her, she settled
back in her seat to watch the rest of the corrida, which confirmed
her new role as a full-fledged aficionada. But she never again attended a bullfight with Shelley, their somewhat incongruous
friendship coming to an end soon thereafter. "There was a blood
guilt between us," she later surmised. "We shared an evil secret, a
hateful revelation. He hated what he had revealed in me to himself, and I hated what he had revealed to me about myself."

Nevertheless, she continued going to the bullfights with her
Mexican and Indian friends, attending more than a hundred cor-
ridas, in which six hundred bulls were killed; and quite often she
would attend a *sorteo** in the corral back of the ring several hours
before a corrida, a ritual for only the truly dedicated fan. She and
her friends also went to cafés frequented by bullfighters and
would engage in endless discussions about this or that breed of
bull or about some new *novillero* climbing the ranks into full sta-

---

*The process of sorting and matching the bulls into presumably equitable pairs.

tus as matador. But, as a sensitive, poetic artist who had always considered herself deeply compassionate, she was troubled by her sudden and enduring passion for a blood sport which people like herself had always condemned:

"There was something deeply, irreparably wrong with my being there at all, something against the grain of my life; except for this (and here was the falseness I had finally to uncover): I loved the spectacle of the bullfights, I was drunk on it, I was in a strange, wild dream from which I did not want to be awakened. I was now drawn irresistibly to the bullring as before I had been drawn to the racetracks and the polo fields at home. But this had death in it, and it was the death in it that I loved ... and I was bitterly ashamed of this evil in me, and believed it to be in me only — no one had fallen so far into cruelty as this! ... How could I face the cold fact that at heart I was just a killer, like any other, that some deep corner of my soul consented not just willingly but with rapture?"

Aside from her addiction to bullfighting, Miss Porter was favorably disposed to almost all aspects of Mexico — the music, the architecture, the literature, the revolutionaries, and (most definitely) the food. She had eaten plenty of hot spicy dishes in San Antonio, which had always been more Mexican than American, so it was easy to accept hotter and spicier foods in Mexico City itself. She was particularly fond of the food prepared in private homes by maids and cooks who followed no set recipes but simply improvised with whatever meats, fowl or vegetables were at hand, often using leftovers to concoct delectable variations of standard fare. They were particularly skillful with soups and hot sauces, some of which were so delicious that she finally decided to make some herself. Having first asked her landlady's permission, she spent several mornings in the kitchen, carefully watching Petra, the cook, casually preparing a wide variety of meals; and she was especially attentive when Petra started making her favorite *salsa picante*. She used seven or eight kinds of peppers (chiles): long slender red peppers of varying degrees of hotness; medium-sized peppers that were even hotter; and small peppers about an inch long, which were piercingly hot. (Miss Porter had seen these different kinds of peppers strung up along the walls of little neighborhood stores, where they had been allowed to dry until they were brittle and almost black, like dried blood.) The various peppers were then steamed until they were soft — still whole, but limp as wet rags. Then Petra deftly pulled off the stems, scraped out the seeds, and ground them in a bowl made from lava stone, grinding them into a "roaring red-hot pulp," while adding pinches of cumin, oregano, chocolate perhaps, and several other ingredients.

In no time at all, Miss Porter learned to make her own special sauce, changing the ingredients and varying the ratios of little and big peppers. And many years later she added different kinds of liquor to the basic pulp — black Jamaican rum, perfumed Spanish sherry, and Rémy Martin cognac, adding a dash of monosodium glutamate. But, unlike Petra, she would have to protect her eyes against the hot fumes with goggles and her hands with rubber gloves whenever she cooked a batch for herself and her friends. For many years she sent bottles of that super-hot sauce as Christmas presents to her closest friends. Finally, Eudora Welty gave it a name that stuck forever: "KAP's Hell-Fire Sauce." One of her friends suggested that she make huge quantities of it and sell it in fancy bottles and probably make tons of money like Colonel Sanders. To which she smilingly answered, "I should spend my whole life trying to be a writer, only to be remembered for my hell-fire sauce?"

Gentle old Petra would have been dismayed to hear that Señorita Porter had diluted her sauce with liquor; and Miss Welty's quaint name for it might have troubled her. Like most working-class Mexican women, she was devoutly religious and highly superstitious, so that any reference to hell or the devil was not taken lightly. It was she who encouraged Miss Porter to attend the Fiesta de Guadalupe, the holiest of all holy days in Mexico. But when Miss Porter asked some of her avant-garde atheist friends to accompany her, they flatly refused to go. "I wouldn't go to that kind of fiesta for love or money," one of them said. "It's all superstitious nonsense that's been foisted on poor ignorant people by the goddamned church. It's a sickening spectacle."

So she went alone to the cathedral known as "La Basílica," where she joined a crowd of tired heavily burdened pilgrims who had come miles and miles to worship at the feet of the Virgen de Guadalupe, patron saint of Mexico. Their clothes were dusty and their dark faces streaked with sweat. Some of them, anxious to show complete devotion, had crawled the last few miles on their knees, and their already soiled white trousers were clotted with drying blood. Less devoted pilgrims stared at the crawling worshippers with awe and admiration, perhaps wondering if their own faith lacked sufficient fervor. "Those are the true believers," someone whispered to no one in particular.

Momentarily wondering how the Church could encourage (or even tolerate) such excessive reasonless zealotry, Miss Porter picked her way through clusters of women and children sitting outside the cathedral, some of them munching tacos or fruit purchased from rickety stalls lined along the curb. Though it was still early, the stench of rotting garbage was almost unbearable. Passing through two stalls which displayed mounds of rosaries, scapulars, brass medals and painted plaster images of the Virgin Mary (Mexican Virgins with brown faces), she nearly tripped on a half-naked baby who had crawled away from his mother. Further on, near the main gate, she saw a group of Indians, dressed in fantastic costumes, solemnly dancing to a jangle of bells and tambourines, each one carrying an arch of flowers that kept losing petals with each jerky movement. Their bronzed sweating faces were like masks, their eyes unblinkingly blank, as they danced a slow, monotonous step, advancing and retreating from each other, then turning and bowing in a joyless saraband that seemed endless.

Inside the massive cathedral, she saw hundreds of Indians kneeling on the flagged floors in front of the magnificent white altar, their solemn faces dimly lighted by scores of flickering candles. Scarcely breathing in the rapt stillness that seemed empty even of silence, they were staring at the Holy Tilma, the simple peasant garment of Juan Diego, on which there was a picture of the Virgen de Guadalupe. They had been told and firmly believed — the Church fathers having verified the miracle — that the Virgin's image had suddenly appeared on Diego's garment on the twelfth day of December, 1531, ten years after Cortés had brought Christianity to the heathen followers of Montezuma. Thereafter, the Church had easily converted a whole nation of people who had just as fervently worshipped the Aztec, Mayan and Toltec deities.

"And why not?" she thought to herself. "Was this miracle any less believable than the resurrection of Christ? And was Juan Diego's much-revered tilma any less idolatrous than the crucifix upon which Christ had been nailed?"

Bemused by the basic similarity of all such miracles, she followed another silent group of Indians as they climbed the nearby Hill of Tepeyac (once an Aztec *teocali*) to the small chapel that contained the reclining image of the beloved Virgen de Guadalupe. The pilgrims quietly, reverently crowded around the glass case that protected the life-size plaster image, touching the soiled glass, crossing themselves, then rubbing their anointed fingers on the afflicted parts of their bodies. One man reached up and touched the glass, then solemnly rubbed the forehead of his sick and emaciated wife, who apparently had been unable to break through the dense crowd around the case.

Several months later, still unable to erase that pitiful scene from her mind, she summarized her reactions in these words: ". . . I see the awful hands of faith, the credulous and worn hands of believers; the humble and beseeching hands of the millions and millions who have only the anodyne of credulity. In my dreams I shall see those groping insatiable hands reaching, reaching, reaching. . . ."

When she expressed these feelings to Jorge Enciso and Manuel Gamío, they merely shrugged and said, "And what would you expect from a church that feeds on fear and superstition?"

Out of kindness and discretion, she didn't mention how they themselves had become devotees of Aztec and Mayan cultures which had also been nourished on fear and superstition and idolatry. Going back to the indigenous roots of Mexican civilization, they were active participants in the *indigenista* movement that was fostering a deep awareness and pride in their country's "glorious pre-Hispanic past." Numerous teams of anthropologists and archaeologists were busily excavating the ruins of buried cities, extracting thousands of artifacts — beautifully carved idols, exquisite vases, household implements, agricultural tools, codices carved on walls, an immense Aztec calendar based on highly sophisticated astronomical calculations, various types of musical instruments, and huge stone gods that would have mesmerized even the most determined skeptic.

Her friends were immensely proud of this vast archaeological treasure, and she shared their pride. "I sure wish all these wonderful things could be seen in the United States," she once told them. "It would certainly change their minds about Mexicans."

"And why not?" asked Gamío. "We could arrange a big exhibit and take it to New York or Washington."

It was an offhand suggestion, which no one seemed to take seriously — except for Adolfo Best-Maugard, who had a penchant for making idle dreams come true. It was Adolfo who had persuaded the Museo Nacional de Antropología to build exact replicas of the Mayan ruins from which certain artifacts had been excavated, thus creating what he called "a living history," an idea which had been called too quixotic by his colleagues. He was the most practical idealist Katherine Anne Porter had ever met. Consequently, when he accepted Gamío's suggestion at face value and later announced he was organizing a traveling exhibit of Aztec-Mayan-Toltec treasures, his friends immediately joined him. In less than six months they selected about eight thousand objects of the most beautiful work ever made in Mexico, including the enormous Chac Mool statue that was known as the Mayan Bacchus.

It was a young people's project all the way: Best-Maugard was twenty-seven, Covarrubias was seventeen, Lozano and Merida were twenty-two, and their senior technical advisers, Gamío and Enciso, were in their early thirties. Miss Porter, who wrote the monograph for the exhibit, was the oldest person in the group, having now reached the age of thirty-three. She was also designated — by an official proclamation of President Obregón himself — as the North American representative and organizer.

Confident and full of enthusiasm, she went back to the United States to arrange shows in various galleries, but she ran into snags from the very outset. She tried galleries in New York, the Corcoran in Washington, two museums in Chicago and St. Louis, and the story was always the same: "It looks like a fascinating exhibit, but we can't handle it." Just vague, evasive refusals, with no concrete reasons. But she soon found out that all of them had been pressured from Washington. The United States government, which had refused to recognize Obregón's revolutionary regime, would not allow the exhibit to come into the country because certain officials considered it "political propaganda"!

"I could tell you one of the most appalling stories about our active political enemies who really stopped us," she later commented. "You can't imagine the number of powerful men who were determined that President Obregón was not going to be recognized. And they attacked that show; they wouldn't let us take it into this country."

Finally, someone told her that he "could arrange something" if the exhibit could be brought to California. So they hauled the whole trainload of artifacts to Mexicali, but they still couldn't get permission to get it across the border. They were told it would be impossible *unless* it was declared as a commercial enterprise on which import duties would have to be paid. "It was the hardest thing that ever happened to us. They kept us on the railroad siding for nearly two months. We tried everything in the world. But you know you can't fight international politics, at least we couldn't. So there was a dealer from Los Angeles who came and said that he would buy the whole show."

Frustrated and disheartened, Best-Maugard got official permission to accept the offer, and the subsequent show-and-sale in Los Angeles was an enormous success. Museum curators, gallery owners and private collectors poured in from all over the country, some of them later reselling their objects in Europe. Consequently, the original collection was soon scattered all over the world, "and all of us were really heartbroken."

More than thirty years later Miguel Covarrubias recalled that sorry episode with a gentle irony: "Poor, poor Cati — I've never seen anyone so angry, so sick at heart. She had always been lovely and kind and generous, but she could erupt like a volcano when anyone crossed her like those gringos did at the border. She was angrier than all the rest of us put together."

And she vented some of that bitter anger in long hurriedly scribbled passages in one of her notebooks, hoping some day to incorporate them in a short story or novel about the revolution.* Now, more than ever, she was a wholehearted partisan of Obregón's radical programs for reshaping the sociopolitical structure of Mexico. She had felt that fervor from the very first day she was exposed to the revolution, when she witnessed a violent street battle between some Maderistas and Federal troops. Crouching next to an old woman, she had seen the fighting from the window of a nearby cathedral, with a heavy grapevine providing a convenient screen. When the shooting stopped and the dead bodies were being piled for burning, the old lady solemnly declared, "This is a great trouble now, but it's for the sake of happiness to come, señorita."

Since she had crossed herself as she said it, Miss Porter mistook her meaning and asked, "In heaven?"

"Oh, no," she answered with outright scorn. "I mean here on *earth*. Happiness for men — not for angels!"

That simple phrase seemed to catch the whole meaning of the revolution, and Miss Porter often recalled the incident whenever one of her American friends asked what all the fighting was about.

But her partisanship was bound to cause trouble sooner than later. About six months after *Century* magazine published her article, "Where Presidents Have No Friends," she was informed by the editor that the Doheny Oil Company had threatened to sue her and the magazine for one million dollars. She happened to be in New York at that particular time, having moved back and forth from Mexico at least once a year during the early twenties, so she was able to meet several times with the worried editor and

---

* She was later to write a catalogue for a traveling exhibit of Mexican craft, but this earlier "exhibit" had fired her passion and imagination.

publisher during the week after they learned of the impending suit.

"You needn't worry," she confidently told them in their initial conference. "I can easily prove that the Doheny people have been conniving against Obregón's government. Besides, I don't have a million dollars — not even a hundred dollars."

"Neither do we," said the publisher. "But they can sure put us out of business, Katherine Anne. Anyway, their lawyers want to see you right away, for some kind of deposition. So you'd better put on your best hat and get down there."

"I'll also wear my best gloves," she said with a certain cockiness.

She rather welcomed the chance to get out of her small cluttered room in Mme. Blanchard's old rooming house at 61 Washington Square South, where she had just finished writing a short story on a roaring hot night in July (1923). Carefully placing the manuscript into her suitcase, she put on her lightest summer dress, a floppy hat with a saucy blue ribbon, and immaculate white gloves, "a perfect outfit for legal combat."

But after a brief discussion, during which she expressed a great desire to air "this whole stinking mess" in a wide-open court trial, the oil company's lawyers apparently decided the lawsuit would be a useless exercise.

When she got back to Mexico a few weeks later, she could hardly wait to tell her friends how the Doheny "gang" had backed away from a head-on confrontation. It was an admittedly minor triumph, but they all reveled in it with their customary enthusiasm, toasting their beloved "Cati" with several tequilas at the Café Flores. (When Doheny and Secretary of Interior Fall were later convicted in the famous Teapot Dome scandal, she could gloat with even greater satisfaction.)

Soon thereafter most of them left the city for archaeological digs in Yucatán and Oaxaca, and she resumed her job teaching English and ballet dancing (which she had studied in Texas shortly before her bout with tuberculosis) at a public school in a poor *barrio* near the railroad station. Though she enjoyed her eager bright-eyed pupils (one of them wrote, "We lov ar ticher" on the blackboard), teaching them drained most of her psychic energy, making it almost impossible for her to write anything.

"But I needed the money — it was only a few pesos — to pay for my room and board. I was forever living on the barest of margins."

6

Seven Days in a Boston Jail

D URING the next three years Miss Porter seemed to be on a constant shuttle between Mexico City and Greenwich Village, renting a different room each time she moved. While in the Village she lived in low-cost rooming houses on Gay Street, Jones Street, Charles Street and Bank Street, her luggage consisting of the two well-worn suitcases she had been lugging around for at least ten years. One of them bulged with manuscripts awaiting completion; the other was slightly less crammed with dresses, blouses, skirts, underwear and shoes. Whatever other possessions she had accumulated — books, paintings, pre-Columbian artifacts and rugs — were generally stored away in the homes of accommodating friends, she knowing full well she would never reclaim most of these momentarily treasured objects.

"I've got to travel light," she would often explain to people who were curious about her transient life-style. "I simply can't afford to carry everything with me, so I don't permit myself to become obsessed by possessions."

Nor was she likely to form any close personal attachments. Her contacts with John Peale Bishop were episodic and fleeting, for he was still married and apparently faithful; and no other man seemed to arouse her to that emotional pitch which, "like lightning, makes the most familiar landscape wild, strange and beautiful."

Writing, then, was her real love, but it was a love fraught with frustration and disappointment. Her literary output was high in quality but meager in quantity, the compensation scarcely worth mentioning. Her principal publisher was *Century* magazine, which had a low circulation and therefore paid minimal fees of fifty to one hundred dollars per article or short story, and most writers were happy to get that. Her infrequent book reviews for the New York *Herald-Tribune, The New Republic*, and *The Nation* were equally low-paid but required much less effort.

Two of her essays, both based on Mexican themes, were published in 1926. The first one, "La Conquistadora," was a six-page commentary on the fascinating letters of Rosalie Caden Evans, a fellow Texan who had inherited several haciendas from her English husband, who had acquired them during the Díaz regime. Pursuant to Article 27 of the new Mexican constitution, the government had proceeded to expropriate her lands for subsequent repartition among landless Indian peasants — and she had resisted them at gunpoint, finally being shot from ambush in August 1924.

Though admittedly impressed with Mrs. Evans's physical courage, mystical exaltation, social poise, avarice, financial shrewdness, witch-wife superstition and timeless feminine coquetry, Miss Porter accurately observed that "no single glimmer of understanding of the causes of revolution or the rights of people involved ever touch her mind. . . . The demon that possessed her was by no means of so spiritual a nature as she fancied: she was ruled by a single-minded love of money and power." Yet there was frank admiration for La Conquistadora's relentless and reckless opposition to the armed and sullen Indians, particularly when she rode into their midst with her pistol drawn, singing *"Nous sommes les enfants de Gascogne!"* But Miss Porter finally had to conclude that Mrs. Evans was not a genuine heroine: "As a personality, she is worth attention, being beautiful, daring and attractive. As a human being she was avaricious, with an extraordinary hardness of heart and ruthlessness of will; and she died in a grotesque cause."

Her second piece, "Quetzalcoatl," was a devastatingly perceptive review of D. H. Lawrence's overpraised *Plumed Serpent*. Lawrence had gone to Mexico hoping to find among the Indians what he failed to find in his own people and within himself: some central core and meaning to life. He was convinced that communion between man and man, and between man and god, was based on some kind of blood-modality that only the Indians possessed — and he wanted to share that modality, to extract the "secret of second strength" that would give him certain magic powers. But, having experienced much more of Mexico than he ever would, Miss Porter knew that Lawrence "remains a stranger gazing at a mystery he cannot share, but still hopes to ravish, and his fancy dilates it to monstrous proportions."

She had heard somewhere that Lawrence was in a raging temper from the moment he crossed the border and that he blamed this on what he called vibrations of cruelty and bloodshed from the soil itself and from all the people who lived there. "He felt," said Miss Porter, "that the Mexican motive of existence is hatred. Lawrence is a good hater; he should know hate when he sees it." Further on, she observes that he had used the novel to vent all his accumulated hates: his grudge against women, for example, and his almost phobic resentment of any kind of machine. Then came this rather puzzling judgment: "His contempt for revolution and the poor is arrogant, not aristocratic: but he is plainly proud of his attitude. It is part of his curiously squeamish disgust of human contact." Which suggests that an *aristocratic contempt* might have been acceptable to her.

In any event, she finally concluded that *The Plumed Serpent* was a pretentious and presumptuous attempt by Lawrence to penetrate a mystery he couldn't possibly understand — that his Indians were merely what Indians might be if they were all like him. His three native protagonists, modern incarnations of Aztec gods, were essentially Europeans — "further variations of Lawrence's arch-type, the flayed and suffering human being in full flight from the horrors of a realistic mechanical society, and from the frustrations of sex."

As one might expect, her critique was warmly praised by her Mexican friends at the Café Flores. They had deeply resented Lawrence's facile and derogatory judgments on Mexico and were doubly annoyed when they learned that certain English and American critics now regarded him as the foremost authority on the Mexican psyche. Their *querida* Cati, on the other hand, had once again shown a profound understanding of an easily misunderstood people, and she had exposed Lawrence's shallow pretensions with great finesse. "You're as Mexican as we are," one of her friends remarked after reading her review out loud at a sidewalk table outside the café. "We'll have to make you a citizen, Cati."

But there was nothing even remotely Mexican in a short story she finally finished (after months of rewriting) shortly after the Lawrence piece was written. Set in a totally-Southern ambiance, "He"* was her first portrayal of a mentally incompetent person and how he functions within a family and in society. With cool objective irony, she explored the love-hate relationship between a simpleminded boy and his mother, who had never bothered to give him a real name. She and her husband (the Whipples) identified their son as "He" or "Him," and throughout the story Miss Porter ironically capitalized the "H" as if referring to Jesus Christ.

Announcing her love for Him to everyone she met, the mother nevertheless allowed Him to climb trees, to handle bees because He didn't seem to feel the stings, to tend a dangerous bull, to work harder than He should, to steal a pig from its obviously ferocious mother — never showing concern for His safety, yet vaguely wondering what the neighbors would say if He were injured. Eventually, after the boy suffered an accident and made a slow recovery, the family doctor advised the Whipples to send Him to the County Home. And when a neighbor drove Him and Mrs. Whipple to the home, He began to cry and she imagined He might be remembering all the mistreatment and hardship He had suffered. Crying herself, she once again insisted that "she had loved Him as much as she possibly could, there were Adna and Emly who had to be thought of too, there was nothing she could do to make up to Him for His life. Oh, what a mortal pity He was ever born."

Perhaps reflecting Miss Porter's own state of mind, "He" was a

---

* Published in *New Masses* (1927).

relentlessly pessimistic story, which revealed the corrosive effects of poverty and mental illness on poor "white trash" families, many of which she had seen firsthand while living in Texas and Louisiana.

Having returned to the Village (for the third or fourth time) in 1927, she finished another short story in which the principal characters were identified as "he" and "she" to give them a universal Everyman-Everywoman quality. Entitled "Rope,"* it was a brief sardonic portrayal of a marriage that alternated from love to festering hate. Ironically, the first and last paragraphs stressed the tranquility of the rural setting, but in the intervening passages the couple engaged in a seemingly trivial but bitter argument over a rope he had bought instead of the coffee she had asked him to buy. Finally, he returned to the store two miles away to get her coffee, her laxative and several other items, taking the rope in exchange. But he hid it instead — and later reappeared; rope in hand, his *machismo* defiantly reaffirmed. Meanwhile she had completely changed. No longer petulant, she had happily prepared his supper and smilingly awaited his return, no longer caring about the rope.

Though concise and expertly executed, "Rope" was a minor effort, somewhat akin to a concert pianist running his scales to keep his fingers limber. Her more serious work was still germinating in her mind or vaguely taking shape in bits and snatches crammed into spiral-bound notebooks which she carried everywhere, always bearing in mind Li Po's injunction that "the palest ink is better than the most retentive mind." She even carried her notebook on some of the picket lines she marched in during that militant era.

"We were always picketing about something," she later remarked, "especially our gang in the Village."

Inevitably, she got involved in the massive demonstrations protesting the murder convictions of Sacco and Vanzetti. That celebrated case first attracted her attention while she was living in Mexico in the early twenties. Her friends in New York, knowing

---

* Published a year later in *Second American Caravan.*

her sentiments in such matters, would occasionally send her form letters asking for a contribution to their defense fund, and she would send back a few dollars whenever she could scrape them up. However, her interest seemed to diminish as the case dragged on, perhaps because of her more immediate involvement in certain revolutionary activities in Mexico. But when she returned to Greenwich Village in the spring of 1927, she was instantly swept into a wide variety of protest groups. Everyone in the Village, especially her bohemian friends and the people who called themselves "the radical left" (we apparently have a new kind of "left" every twenty years) seemed to be involved in that memorable *cause célèbre.* "Though we were all passionately convinced that Sacco and Vanzetti were victims of a vicious frame-up, no one could match the angry eloquence of an artist friend who lived in a hayloft studio near MacDougal Alley. I especially remember the evening he invited me to his flat to help him concoct a new supply of bathtub gin."

He lived on the top floor of an old warehouse, usually with his current model-companion, but he was temporarily disengaged at the moment. His first name was Michael, but Miss Porter couldn't recall his surname, probably because she was never able to pronounce it. In any event, Michael met her on the top landing, having no doubt heard her clomping up the hollow unlit staircase. She had noisily stomped on each step to keep up her courage in the gloomy darkness, and the effort had pretty well exhausted her.

"Sorry about the stairs," he said. "I'll have to rig up some lighting one of these days. Two weeks ago one of my models fractured her ankle on those damned stairs."

Noticing a half-finished painting of a nude woman as she walked into the studio, Miss Porter naturally concluded that she had been the injured party; but when her eyes had adjusted to the semidarkness she could see that most of his paintings were only half-finished. Aside from those canvases, his enormous flat was nearly bare except for two easels, an army cot and a large wooden table cluttered with cans and tubes of paint. "It was all fairly typical, of course — including the faint sweet smell of burnt marijuana. Smoking the weed was a rather new fad in those days, but it wasn't particularly novel to me: I had smoked some several years before in Mexico, where it was already rather *passé* back in 1922."

Dragging an old wooden crate from under the table, Michael gave it a perfunctory swipe with a soiled rag and asked her to sit down while he prepared drinks. It was sure to be rotgut whiskey or homemade gin served in a jelly glass. As he was handing her a gin sling he commenced a long bitter tirade against the governor of Massachusetts, who several days before had refused to grant clemency to Sacco and Vanzetti. They were now scheduled to die within ten days.

"That so-called investigation by his mealymouthed blueblood committee was a farce from beginning to end," Michael told her. "The governor wasn't looking for *outside advice*—he merely wanted *inside approval* for a decision he'd already made."

Governor Fuller had appointed President A. Lawrence Lowell of Harvard University, President Samuel W. Stratton of M.I.T., and a retired judge to investigate the case and thereafter to advise him on the question of clemency. On August 3 he denied the plea and announced that his special committee had advised him against a new trial. It was this recent development that Michael was denouncing with his customary scorn and bitter humor, continuing his monologue with mounting anger even as he started to prepare a new batch of gin. It was really a simple mixture — straight alcohol and a bit of juniper juice to give it flavor — but in his frenzied wrath against "those lousy Boston bigots," Michael kept adding either too much alcohol or too much juniper juice, finally overflowing his mixing bowl, which was actually a cylindrical porcelain umbrella stand.

"Only rotgut whiskey was made in bathtubs," Miss Porter later told me with a knowing smile. "Even though people called it 'bathtub gin,' most gin was made in much smaller containers. When Michael's mixture spilled over the rim he simply mopped the liquor off the floor with his all-purpose rag and called it quits."

Having borne witness to his slapdash liquor-mixing procedures, she rather suspected it would be poor gin. And it was. In fact, it was totally undrinkable. But since he was still full of fury about the injustice to Sacco and Vanzetti, Michael drank several tumblers of it, gulping it down as he prowled through that large studio like a sullen tiger, speechifying with the most glorious eloquence and then falling into gloomy silence. It was indeed a moving performance and it was probably in the back of her mind when she decided a few days later to join the front-line protestors in Boston.

As most of her contemporaries will recall, Nicola Sacco and Bartolomeo Vanzetti were accused of murdering the paymaster and an armed guard of a shoe factory as the latter were transporting the payroll from the bank on April 5, 1920. From the very onset and during the next seven years both men insisted they were innocent, but on July 14, 1921, they were found guilty of murder after a six-week jury trial before Judge Webster Thayer. Because of repeated and irrelevant references to the defendants' radical affiliations during the course of their stormy trial, it seemed obvious to Miss Porter that those poor immigrants were being tried for their political beliefs and condemned to death for being anarchists.

"When the judge gets out on a golf course and bluntly says, 'I'm going to get those red bastards,' then you know justice will be thrown out the window," she recalled with lingering bitterness, as if she were reliving that period of her life. "Well, there were a number of decent Bostonians — people like Professor Felix Frankfurter of the Harvard Law School — who simply wouldn't accept such a monstrous perversion of the law."

They had formed several committees to appeal the case, asking for a new trial on various legal grounds but sadly failing each time. Then just as everyone was about to despair, a man named Celestino Madeiros (who was under a death sentence for another crime) voluntarily confessed he had participated in the payroll murder and declared that neither Sacco nor Vanzetti had been involved. But when the defendants' lawyers moved for a reversal or at least another trial on the basis of Madeiros's confession, Judge Thayer denied their motion and sentenced Sacco and Vanzetti to death. It was at this juncture that Governor Fuller appointed what everyone regarded as a "namby-pamby committee to back up the judge."

Needless to say, all hell broke loose. Newspapers everywhere printed critical articles and editorials on the case, mass meetings were held all over Europe and the United States, thousands of petitions were sent to Massachusetts, and finally there were long picket lines outside the courthouse and around the state capitol.

No longer content merely to sign long impersonal petitions or to attend protest meetings too far away from Boston to impress anyone in authority, Miss Porter finally accepted an invitation to join the on-the-spot demonstrators. The group which invited her was headed by Rosa Baron, an ardent and sometimes devious organizer who was forever involved in one cause or another.

"I subsequently realized what her game was and that she would use anyone from anywhere to promote her various communist causes; but in those days I was sometimes willing to march with the devil himself if the specific cause was a just and decent one."

So when Rosa's aide asked her to help the committee, she agreed to go, realizing of course that she wasn't being asked because her name would add luster to the list of notables. Except for a few close friends, nobody as yet considered her a writer, but she was a good typist, and a willing sign-carrier in all kinds of weather, and Rosa was well aware of her usefulness. She was also apparently aware of Miss Porter's financial condition, because on the following day the committee's New York representative brought her a ticket for the night boat to Boston and a five-dollar bill to tide her over the first two or three days.

Her going-away arrangements were rather simple and uncomplicated except for one problem: she couldn't decide what clothes to pack for her picketing chores. Most of her previous demonstrating had been during the autumn or winter months, when weather conditions clearly demanded sensible clothing; but since it was the hot sweltering month of August, she was tempted to take along a couple of light frilly blouses and a cool chiffon dress with soft billowy sleeves — anything to ward off the muggy heat.

Perish the wish. This would be serious business which obviously called for clothing and conduct suited to the occasion. There would be no flapper-fanny dresses there, no roaring-twenties miniskirts with tassels. Nor were they likely to be marching (as one would be these days) alongside boys with unkempt beards and open-sandaled feet.

("I think some of our young picketers today sadly betray their cause when they wear so-called psychedelic makeup and carry silly signs about free love and pot," said Miss Porter rather sadly. "No decent demonstration or mass meeting should be permitted to degenerate into a freak show for the benefit of misguided nit-wits venting any perverse idea that happens along.")

Although her speculations about proper picketing apparel were probably more restrained on that long-ago summer afternoon, she finally decided on two plain white blouses, a light gray skirt and two no-nonsense dresses.

Shortly before sunset she hailed a taxi on the corner near her flat and took the short traffic-muddled ride to Christopher Street, where the night boat was docked. It was an old travel-worn vessel, bulky and graceless as a frumpy old woman, but it was a ship nonetheless, and she had always loved anything that traveled on water. Her spirits soared the moment she set foot on board, and yet a few minutes later she felt a most awful depression when she spotted the dark headline on a discarded newspaper: ANARCHISTS DOOMED. The article obviously referred to Sacco and Vanzetti, and she couldn't bring herself to read it.

"I simply could not admit I was embarking upon a futile journey, that nothing I nor anyone else could do would save those wretched men from death. We would march, we would wave our placards and shout our protests, we might even momentarily convince ourselves our cause would triumph in the end, but deep in our miserable hearts we would know that it was all shadow play."

Had she not been alone — had there been one other person on the boat to join her in that vain hope — she most likely would have cast aside the heavy gloom which came over her as the boat pulled away. Somewhere on the upper deck a radio was turned on full blast, giving forth one of those boop-boop-a-doop songs which she had always associated with people like Clara Bow.

"Some of the more absentminded members of my generation complain of the horrible rock 'n roll lyrics we hear these days, but, although I've never really paid any attention to them, I know they can't be any sillier than the ones we sang during the twenties. The music I heard that evening as we left New York harbor was so inane I moved way over to the far side of the boat and flopped myself down on a wooden deck chair."

There she sat for several hours, letting her thoughts drift from here to yonder, yet always uneasily conscious of the approaching death of two Italian immigrants whose names had become a tandem phrase signifying political persecution: Sacco-and-Vanzetti. Their names were never separated in the public mind. You couldn't mention one without mentioning the other — no more than you could say "Laurel" without "Hardy." Since people are often flippant in times of stress, that same comparison may have crossed her mind even then. And she might have smiled — but only fleetingly. Her low mood was beyond all humor. Afterward, as she stretched out on her narrow bunk, she could hear the foghorn moaning through the darkness and imagined it was moaning for her.

In her story, "The Cracked Looking-Glass," Rosaleen has the same sensation. And like Rosaleen, she also felt the heavy engine pounding under her, the grand steady beat shaking the very marrow of her bones. When she finally dozed off, New York City seemed a thousand miles and a hundred years away.

The next morning the boat docked at Providence and everyone scurried down the gangplank like anxious bedraggled mice. Although people generally referred to it as the "night boat to Boston," it went only as far as Providence. From there Miss Porter would go to Boston by train, and on that hot summer day it was a tedious stop-and-go journey which seemed twice as long as it really was. She finally got off at South Station and lugged her suitcase to a nearby dingy hotel which apparently served as an informal headquarters for out-of-town picketers.

Several of her Village acquaintances were milling around the lobby, most of them jabbering away about the latest developments in the Sacco-Vanzetti case, while two of the less talkative ones solemnly painted slogans on large cardboard placards. One of the sign painters, a tall gawky girl with a prim yellow blouse, had underestimated her space requirements and had consequently found it necessary to squeeze and curl the "zetti" in Vanzetti down the right-hand margin of her narrow poster, each letter smaller than the preceding one. "Many years before, when I was ten years old and briefly engaged in the liquid refreshment business, I'd had the same trouble with the word *lemonade*. The 'LEMO' was always very large and the 'nade' hopelessly puny and limp."

After she had unpacked her few belongings and changed into a fresh blouse, she reported for duty at the committee office near the Boston Common. There she saw John Dos Passos, Mike Gold, Patrick McGibbon, Edna St. Vincent Millay and several other people from New York. Later on she was to meet Daisy Borden Harriman, who used to come down to the headquarters in beautiful lace dresses, huge white horsehair hats with flowers, and the loveliest long gloves Katherine Anne had ever seen. "One always had the impression that Daisy had merely stopped by on her way to a garden party or a fancy Beacon Hill wedding. Now and then she would sit down beside me and chat while I typed out some of the later-to-be-famous letters of Sacco and Vanzetti, and on one such occasion she said, 'Why are you doing all this?' "

"I'm doing it," said Miss Porter, "in the hope that the people who run this country will learn something from this experience — that they'll realize how dangerous it is to misuse the judicial process."

"Oh, people don't care," Daisy said. "Really they don't. All this will be forgotten in another five years."

But even though she felt it was all for naught, Daisy kept coming in to help, most of the time serving as an informal hostess for the committee. Rosa Baron no doubt believed that Daisy, in spite of her limited abilities as a radical worker, was nonetheless valuable because of her family background. What better front for a communist-dominated organization than a name like Borden

Harriman? Genuine double-barreled respectability and no questions asked from the person who provided it.

To a much lesser extent Miss Porter felt that her own presence was also presumed to lend a bit of respectability to Rosa's group. Though she had been drawn into a number of liberal causes, some of which had resulted in her being arrested at least ten times prior to her picketing in Boston, she had somehow managed to avoid any close identification with well-known subversive groups. There were others like her, of course — nice honest aboveboard people whose sincere desire to help the poor and oppressed often led them into associations with old pros like Rosa and her brother. "Now there was a strange pair. Though they were both theoretically devoted to Karl Marx and Lenin and generally agreed as to their overall goals, they frequently had the most violent arguments over day-to-day tactics."

Sometimes Rosa, who was clearly the stronger of the two, would threaten to turn her brother over to the police or to denounce him to the party hierarchy — surely the most curious combination of threats Miss Porter had ever heard. Meanwhile she would be sitting by her typewriter, perfectly still, feeling like an eavesdropper at a family quarrel. "It was foolish of me to have been so sensitive; they couldn't have cared less about my hearing them for there wasn't a stitch of privacy in their makeup. They would have argued and fought about anything anywhere and in the presence of anyone without the slightest hesitation."

She especially remembered the nasty row they had in front of Mrs. Sacco, who was frequently brought to headquarters to rally their spirits and sharpen their sense of urgency. She was a red-haired, brown-eyed, sweet-faced little creature who was perfectly delighted with all the friendship offered her. Her childlike gratitude and frank trust in all of them was almost unbearable. Naturally she was convinced they would succeed. It never occurred to her that they wouldn't be able to save her husband's life.

She seemed even more optimistic than usual on one particular afternoon in late August. Having first greeted the Barons, she walked over to the typists' section to chat with them about something or other, her dark eyes alive and cheerful. Then right out of nowhere they all heard a loud shriek followed by a babble of angry accusations. It was Rosa, of course, scolding her brother about a press release he had issued that morning, he meanwhile defending himself with petulant cross-accusations. The rest of them — three typists and a poster painter — merely paused for a second and shrugged knowingly, but Mrs. Sacco was terrified by their shouting anger. Her mouth slightly agape, she seemed on the verge of bolting out of the room, but their argument came to an end as abrupt as its beginning, and she stayed on for another half-hour, nervously fingering the long black rosary she usually carried and occasionally sneaking a glance at Rosa.

On the morning after her arrival in Boston, Miss Porter joined the picket line at the courthouse. They were supposed to march from the Robert Gould Shaw monument to the corner of Pemberton Square and back again, but she hadn't gone more than fifty feet when a stocky leather-colored Irish cop approached her and gently laid one of his hands on her forearm. Why he chose her rather than one of the other seventy-five marchers she never knew. She certainly didn't look like a ringleader, and her manner was definitely modest and unassuming. Whatever the reason, she knew she was being arrested and of course submitted without a whimper. He was, incidentally, a very polite officer with clean but loose-fitting white cotton gloves and a dark blue uniform which fit him like a tight corset.

"Judging from his firm confident stride as he escorted me down to the Joy Street lockup, I must assume that his shoes, at least, were a perfect fit."

They didn't talk much on the first day, but on her six subsequent arrests (she was apparently his first victim every morning) they discussed a number of things. However, the minute they walked into the police station he was all business. First of all he would "book" her with a most solemn expression on his face, each time asking her name as if he had never seen her before. Then he would take her to a large cell, known as a bull pen, where there were several other women incarcerated for various crimes ranging from dime-store theft to prostitution.

"Since my crime bore no relation to theirs (picketing must

have seemed a rather silly and fruitless activity to them), they regarded me as a somewhat suspect outsider." And their suspicions were no doubt further aroused when Miss Porter would be bailed out three or four hours later — only to be jailed again on the following morning for the same offense. "Looking at it from their viewpoint, I can well understand their disinclination to accept me as one of their gang."

The man directly responsible for getting her out of jail every afternoon was an attorney named Edward James, the son of William James and nephew of Henry James. He was always accompanied by his aide, a fat bouncy Portuguese lad who wore a little red bow tie. James was a slender stooped-over man who looked as if he had been dried on the bone. His short whiskers were gray, his face was slightly gray, his eyes cold gray, his hair ash-gray, and he wore a light gray suit and dark gray hat. From top to bottom he was like a gray thin ghost.

"And galloping along beside him was this chubby red-faced creature just full of blood and guts. His hair was jet black and oily, natural live oil pouring out of his healthy scalp. That young man was Edward James's life blood, and Lord knows he needed it."

The second time they bailed her out she asked the young man (his boss was lagging behind) the name of their organization. Everyone belonged to a committee of one kind or another. "Oh, we formed our own committee," he said. "Mr. James and I are the only members."

And that two-man organization came down to the jail every day and bailed out a whole gang of them with their own money. They certainly were dedicated to the cause; but, ironically enough, Mr. James later turned out to be a most awful fascist. First he supported Mussolini — then Hitler. Nevertheless, in the summer of 1927 he had a total sympathy for Sacco and Vanzetti, and that's all Miss Porter could have asked for at the time.

Well, after they had bailed her out she would rush back to headquarters to copy more letters, patch up torn placards or answer the telephone. There was always something to keep her busy. Her evenings were comparatively free of organized activi-

ties except for an occasional speech by someone like Felix Frankfurter or Professor Frank Taussig, both of whom were eloquent
and heartbreakingly persuasive in their condemnation of Judge
Thayer's trial conduct. Even in her later years, she found it impossible to believe any sincere right-thinking man could have
failed to accept their reasoning. "I doubt that anyone could have
been more moved than I was, and consequently I renewed my
chores with increased determination."

However, each morning the same policeman would show up
just as she was starting to march; he never let her picket for more
than seventy-five paces before arresting her. Not once was she
permitted to reach the corner. He'd simply tap her on the shoulder and off they would go to the Joy Street police station. On the
very last day, when they all knew in their hearts that their efforts
had been futile, he let her go all the way to the corner and half-
way back to the monument before pinching her. When he finally
stepped forward to arrest her, Miss Porter said, "You're late this
morning." And he gave her the most apologetic expression one
can possibly imagine — he actually blushed and stammered.
"The poor man had probably been delayed by any number of
things, so I very magnanimously forgave him."

This time, as he whisked her away to make up for lost time,
they got an unusual reception from an unruly mob near Boston
Common. They started throwing bricks and bottles at Miss Porter — also a few flowers and confetti — but no dead mice she was
happy to say, nothing like that. The sidewalk was littered with
that strange and puzzling assortment of missiles, so she turned to
her nice policeman and said, "Let's try to sort this out — who are
the roses for and who gets the bricks?"

He stared at her with his hard blue Irish eyes and said, "Lady,
I don't know and I frankly don't give a damn!"

And she said to herself, "My God, this poor harassed man must
be tired to death with all of us."

He had to arrest twenty or thirty picketers a day, and she was
probably his first customer every morning. As soon as he got rid
of her he would have to hurry back for his second one, then a
third one (always with the same weary but patient look) and so

on down the line. Repeating the same routine with the very same people day after day.

One would have expected him to become quite impersonal and bored with it all, and yet she felt that he did have a certain interest in what they were doing. On one of their strolls to jail (she thought it was the third one) he said, "What are you doing in all this — you seem like a decent person."

Though she knew she couldn't possibly convince him, she said: "Now I'm not really sure whether they're guilty or not, but I do honestly believe these men have *not* had a fair trial — that they're entitled to a new trial in some other jurisdiction, away from this inflammatory atmosphere in Boston. And if your officials will only agree to those simple conditions I'll pack my bags and you'll never hear from me again."

"I think they're guilty," he said in a flat dry voice.

"If you're so sure," she said, "why don't you give them a fair trial?"

"They had a fair trial," he muttered, "and now they're going to burn."

He was right about the burning, of course, and on the morning of the last day they all knew it was over: the hour for the execution had been definitely set by Judge Thayer. Yet they all went back to the picket lines and marched all day long. "We wouldn't quit; we went right on and picketed until sunset and finally straggled off in the darkness, exhausted both in body and spirit, no longer able to muster even the merest shadow of hope."

Sacco and Vanzetti were to be executed at midnight, a curious and rather sinister hour for one's death. It seemed so final and beyond all redemption. Feeling thus, she later joined the thousands of silent dead-faced men, women and children who were gathered outside the prison, some of them sullen and angry, others wearily resigned. The police, many of them mounted on horseback, had set up barriers to control the crowd, and most of them carried long billy clubs, tear-gas bombs and shotguns. Whenever anyone tried to breach the barrier he was pushed back with a billy club pressed crosswise against his throat. One or two push-backs were enough to convince her that she had better behave. She just stood there, chatting now and then with a friend, smoking an occasional cigarette and staring at the top floor of the building where the electrocution would take place. "I have never stared at a building with such unrelieved horror and fascination; years later I could have sketched every contour of that tower."

Finally, just a few seconds before midnight, the lights slowly dimmed like an expiring flame, signaling the deaths of Sacco and Vanzetti in the electric chair.

Heartbroken and physically numb, a small group of them went back to their hotel and later got together in Patrick McGibbon's room. Someone had managed to get a good supply of bootleg gin, lemons and ice, and they all decided to get drunk together and perhaps shed a few tears in the company of good friends. They were sitting there in dead silence, utterly crushed and not getting drunk at all, when suddenly a tall lovely Irish girl grabbed a bottle of gin and started marching up and down the crowded narrow room, singing:

> The night that Paddy Murphy died
> I never shall forget
> The Irish all got stinking drunk
> And some ain't sober yet.
> The only thing they did that night
> That filled my heart with fear —
> They took the ice right off the corpse
> And put it in the beer.
>
> Sooooo-O-O that's how they showed their respect to Paddy,
> That's how they showed their honor and their pride.
> That's how they showed their respect for Paddy Murphy —
> Respect for Paddy Murphy on the night that Paddy died.

It was a song for an Irish wake, and when she finished the second chorus she took a long swig from the bottle and then sang, "Your father was a grand old man — and to hell with him!" Then she took another swig and asked everyone to join her. And they did drink with her and also started singing and laughing with her, getting drunker and drunker with each new song.

"Then we got obscene," Miss Porter recalled with a faraway

smile. "And we began singing the most terrible bawdy lyrics, our laughter now fringed with a shade of madness."

At last, having settled into a more bearable sadness, they got into a tight little circle and started hugging and kissing each other and saying, "Good night and tomorrow's another day."

"It was a truly memorable night and I wish I could remember the names of all the people who were there. I do know that Edna Millay wasn't there: that pale wisp of a child-woman was not for this earthy group. They were mostly my old rambunctious radicals and subverters from the Village — no communists, mind you, but good oldfashioned radicals whose motives were clean and simple."

The next day as they got ready to leave (their bills had been paid by the committee), Miss Porter said to one of the organizers, "What do you mean — sending me up here with this communist crowd? You know I'm not one of them."

He told her it didn't matter who you fought with in a case like that.

"Oh, yes it does," she said. "You can't fight the devil with fire. These commies weren't concerned about Sacco and Vanzetti, they were merely using them for their own purposes."

She also told him how Rosa Baron had even threatened to turn in her own brother for saying things not strictly in accord with pure communist doctrine.

"Didn't Saint Theresa do the same with her brother?" he asked.

"That may be," said Katherine Anne. "But I choose to think Saint Theresa was merely joking."

She had of course read the famous letter where Saint Theresa threatened to turn her brother in to the Inquisition; "but she never did, you know."

Well, she got her return ticket, and this time they gave her ten dollars for expenses. Afterwards, when she had resumed her daily routine in New York, she tried to write about the Sacco-Vanzetti case, but could not. (It's interesting to note that nowhere in her short story "The Cracked Looking-Glass" does Miss Porter mention that Rosaleen — really Miss Porter — was headed for Boston to picket for Sacco-Vanzetti.) "It was all too much, too confused, too full of raw emotion. There were so many terrible aspects to the Sacco-Vanzetti campaign, such horrible self-seeking motives on the part of some of the organizers. They often seemed like vultures hovering over a carcass."*

She actually heard one of them saying to a younger comrade, "How could these political illiterates really expect us to save their lives? Of course we're not going to save their lives — they're much more valuable to us dead than alive."

According to Miss Porter, "All they cared about was a couple of handy martyrs. Poor Nicola Sacco's wife was really convinced that everyone was genuinely concerned about her husband's life. She was a sweet innocent trusting person whom they used like a rag puppet. They were equally machiavellian in their exploitation of Vanzetti's sister, Luiga. She was a tall gaunt sickly-looking woman who had been dragged through street processions in Paris by the French communists, then brought to New York for several protest rallies, and finally taken to Boston for the huge indignation meeting on the night before her brother was put to death. When she came onto the platform she saw beneath her hundreds of torches, placards and upraised fists and people shouting, 'We'll avenge you, Luiga! We'll avenge you!' That confused and miserable soul looked as if she were staring into the very pit of hell. She was absolutely horrified and frightened and seemed to be rejecting the whole thing. There was a sweaty red-faced publicity man standing next to me, and he kept saying, 'Jesus! ain't this a good show. *We* got this up, you know — *we* got this up!' " They certainly had. It was all masterfully staged from beginning to end, and it was dramatic, no doubt about it. Luiga had been the *pièce de résistance* of their campaign from the moment she was yanked out of Italy and toured through Europe and this country; but she had finally rejected them. She knew those people had abused her in a most heartless way, not caring a damn about her feelings. You could see it in her face. There was something wonderful in her reaction, yet no one has ever mentioned it."

Counterbalancing the uglier aspects of that much-publicized

---

* More than fifty years after the fact, she published in 1977 a brief book about the Sacco-Vanzetti case.

affair, Miss Porter mentioned her great fascination with the Sacco-Vanzetti letters, which some of them copied for subsequent press releases. There was a certain poetic simplicity in their writing, an intuitive dramatic flair in some of their short choppy sentences. The men declared their innocence openly and directly, without strain or guile, and she couldn't help but believe them. Certainly Felix Frankfurter, a most intelligent and perceptive man, was convinced of their innocence, and he labored long and diligently on their behalf. Of all the good sincere people on their side, she felt that Frankfurter always stood out because he was the kind of man who could bore in and take charge with great determination and efficiency.

"No one — not even the most experienced and skillful agitator — would have been able to sidetrack Professor Frankfurter into the devious bypaths of international communist politics. Some of those professional lovers of humanity undoubtedly tried to swarm all over him, hoping to use him for their own long-range purposes, but his sole nondeviating purpose was to save those two men. How that must have frustrated them!"

She was understandably leery about so-called revolutionaries, for she had recently met a whole gang of them down in Mexico. "Only a few had the malice, the cleverness, the sharpness of wit, the hardness of heart, stipulated for loving the world profitably, but each one would eventually see himself kicked out of his feeding trough by other hungry world-saviors." That's how she would later describe them in *Flowering Judas,* her fat loathsome Braggioni combining the more salient characteristics of three or four of them.

For a short while she had collaborated with one of the more charming scoundrels, running some of the errands assigned to Laura in the same story. She had visited political prisoners in their cells and brought them cigarettes, food, clothing and sometimes a few pesos, which they probably spent on their favorite narcotics. Now and then she would deliver messages disguised in equivocal phrases from the *jefe* (chief) or from friends who wouldn't have dared come near the prison, knowing full well they would be jailed instantly. Most of the prisoners called her Catalina or, in a genuinely endearing way, *gringuita* (little gringa);

and they would frequently engage her in long rambling conversations about how lonely and bored they were. One of them counted cockroaches to pass the time; Pedro Luján was writing his memoirs on scraps of wrapping paper; José Gómez spent his waking hours drafting angry manifestos, while another man furtively made plans for liquidating a comrade who had double-crossed him. Others simply lay on their hard cots complaining about the slowness of the *jefe* in getting them out of prison, trusting Señorita Porter not to repeat their insults around headquarters.

She would listen to them with great patience and sympathy although most of their talk was frankly boring and depressing. Inevitably, one of them was sure to ask her how and why a nice young gringa like her had ever gotten involved in the revolution. Then they would be so amused with her Southern-accented Spanish that she seriously doubted anyone ever listened to a thing she said. But in spite of her imperfect communication she was inclined to believe her presence was comforting, perhaps useful.

During that same period she had also smuggled letters from headquarters to certain fugitives hiding in miserable shacks along the back streets of Mexico City. Most of these trips were made after nightfall, and she was frequently amused by the exaggerated cloak-and-dagger precautions of the man she visited. They would be sitting on sleazy cots in darkened rooms, talking in unnecessarily low voices and forever glancing toward the window as if a firing squad were waiting for them just outside. Then on the following Sunday morning she would see them casually slouched on a bench in the Alameda Park, munching a taco and listening to the band concert, knowing damned well they had *never* been in danger.

But once in a while she would have to deliver a warning message to someone who was really in danger. Then, like Laura, she would knock on his door long after midnight, enter in the darkness and say to him: "They will be looking for you — seriously — tomorrow morning after six. Here is some money from Vicente. Go to Vera Cruz and wait."

She could always tell when she was dealing with a truly involved rebel — there would be no need for extraneous drama. Yet it wasn't always deadly serious. There were occasional diversions for even the most devout and dedicated radical, and the diversion which seemed to interest them most was sex. Almost without exception, the revolutionaries she met in Mexico considered themselves irresistibly attractive to women. (They weren't all Mexicans, however; some were Russian, Polish, Italian, German, Hungarian, French and Rumanian.) Many were like her protagonist in *Flowering Judas*, compulsively *macho* with any female who came near them and instantly vindictive whenever they were turned down.

"A thousand women have paid for that," says Braggioni, and he means every word.

Being young, attractive and a gringa, Miss Porter naturally got her share of unwanted and often silly attention from men who were obviously disconcerted by her coolness. One of her good non-*macho* friends once told her that certain comrades considered her a very cold *gringuita*. Selectivity was so often equated with frigidity. Nevertheless, she was useful to them and they never hesitated to ask her to run errands for them.

On several occasions they sent her all the way to the border to deliver money to exiled Mexican radicals living in Texas. In fact, one of these long trips caused her to lose her job as a ballet instructor at a school for young girls. Her sudden and unexplained absences had predictably annoyed her students' mothers, who finally complained as a group to her immediate superior and close friend, José Vasconcelos. "Poor loyal José — he tried to fend them off with all kinds of wild excuses but ultimately found himself obligated to take action."

"I'm so terribly sorry, Katherine Anne," he told her. "But you'll have to admit they're right. You can't have ballet classes without a teacher. I'll have to find someone else to take your place."

He clearly had no other choice — he had to fire her, and she should have prepared herself for that eventuality. But she wasn't prepared. She had somehow expected some guardian angel to take care of her job while she scurried from here to yonder on one of those subversive missions. Consequently, she was truly stunned when José gave her the bad news. Not only was her pride bruised, but (far more painful) her pocketbook was sorely wounded. Teaching was her only source of income, a meager one to be sure, but enough to sustain her. How was she to live now? She couldn't ask for help from her family. They, having never approved of her coming to Mexico in the first place, would have insisted that she come home immediately.

"There's nothing you can write *there* that you can't write just as well right here in Indian Creek, Texas — or in San Antonio if you insist on running off somewhere."

Having understandably ruled her family out of the picture as far as this particular crisis was concerned, she felt totally unprotected and admittedly sorry for herself. With only a mumbled word of thanks to Vasconcelos (he seemed so genuinely concerned about her), she rushed out of his office and later wandered along the beautiful tree-lined Paseo de la Reforma hoping to ease her anxiety. Long solitary walks had always served as a kind of therapy whenever she felt emotionally adrift, but on this particular day no amount of walking would have sufficed. About midafternoon she decided to share her melancholy with the person who was in charge of the underground activities in which she had been involved. Perhaps he could offer her a contact for new employment.

Luis Mendoza (that was only his "cover" name) was a shrewd well-fed radical who seemed to have his grubby fingers in more pies than one could imagine. In modern jargon he would be known as an "operator." He was also one of the most attentive listeners she had ever known; he could always manage to hear more than was said because he listened with his eyes as well as his ears. But when she started to tell him about having lost her job, he wouldn't have needed any special powers of observation: the tears gushed from her eyes from the moment she opened her mouth. She just let herself go and sobbed like a child.

"Why, Katherine Anne," he said in great surprise, "you're actually crying! We had always thought your heart was made of stone."

"But can't you see?" she said between sobs. "Can't you see that I'm all applesauce inside?"

7

An Invisible Visitor

W HEN she returned to Greenwich Village after the execution of Sacco and Vanzetti, Miss Porter was besieged by friends and neighbors who wanted firsthand reports about the final desperate campaign to save their lives. Wherever she went in the weeks that followed — the corner grocery, the local coffee-houses, bars, private homes and the park benches in Washington Square — the Sacco-Vanzetti case was virtually the only topic of conversation. There were endless recriminations and heated vows of retribution "against the system," most of which came from people she considered ineffectual would-be rebels who hadn't yet finished rebelling against their mothers and fathers. Compared to some of the serious revolutionaries she had known in Mexico, they were like children trying to impress each other with tough talk, their bravado increasing in direct proportion to the amount of gin they consumed.

She soon tired of their "petulant babble" and began to avoid her usual haunts, spending most nights alone in her room, either reading or trying to write serious fiction, her daylight hours having been spent in hack writing to make enough money for room and board. Usually too exhausted to write anything of consequence, she had to content herself with reading some of the books her friends had been recommending over the years.

One of them was *The Making of Americans* by Gertrude Stein, about whom she had heard a number of amusing stories that were fast becoming legends. Favorably impressed by Miss

Stein's singular style, she wrote a brief article in which she flatly
stated that "next to James Joyce she is the greatest influence on
the younger literary generation, who see in her the combination
of tribal wise woman and arch-priestess of aesthetic." Noting that
The Making of Americans had been written twenty years before
(1906–1908), Miss Porter found it very up-to-date, even without
such points of reference as movies, automobiles, radio or prohi-
bition. "We feel in it the vitality and hope of the first generation,
the hearty materialism of the second, the vagueness of the third."
She also perceived the book as a slow, ever-widening spiral that
unrolled itself horizontally, with all the characters appearing to
be motionless and yet each one passing through all stages of
life —from birth to death — in a single time span.

Stating that next to Jews, the Americans were the most moral-
istic people and that Gertrude Stein was an American Jew, Miss
Porter concluded her critique with high praise indeed: "She is
free of pride and humility . . . she is honest in her uncertainties. . . . People can learn only one or two fundamental facts about
each other, the rest is decoration and prejudice. She is very free
from decoration and prejudice."

But less than a year later, Miss Porter was apparently changing
her mind about Miss Stein. In what might have been intended as
a mere playful jab, she wrote a two-page parody that carried all
the impact of a slashing uppercut. Titled "Second Wind," it included the following passages: "This was not all. This was another one a younger one a sadder one a wiser one a smaller one a
darker one with gray skin being reading The Making of Americans three times all summer. It was ended then. But you say she
is wiser then why is she sadder then it is not sadder to be wiser
then. Oh, yes, but when things go dead it is different. . . . Being
stammering is being Mr. Lewis in one way and being stammering
is being Gerty in another way and it's all in the day. This way
today. Being stammering together is a chorus and a chorus being
stammering together is thinking. Thinking being stammering. . . ."

Some Stein devotees openly resented the parody and immediately characterized it as "bitchy," which led Miss Porter to won-

der what adjective they would have used if it had been written by a man. Most of her friends, however, were highly amused and encouraged her to do more of the same. "But that was a mere trifle, written on the spur of the moment," she later commented. It was the kind of thing she did when trying to avoid more serious writing — just a notch better than reading all the labels on the pantry shelves or reading every classified ad in *The New York Times*, anything to keep herself from her real work.

But in one of her more productive intervals she managed to write the final version of a story that had been "nagging" her for some time, "The Jilting of Granny Weatherall."* Based upon what she subsequently called "the usable past," the story focused on the impending death of an old lady who bore a striking resemblance to Miss Porter's own grandmother. An omniscient observer reports the stream of consciousness of eighty-year-old Ellen Weatherall on the last day of her life, as she shifts back and forth from consciousness to semiconsciousness, confusing the past and present, recalling old dreams and fears and grudges. Active, strong-willed and self-sufficient, she had reared a large family after the death of a young husband; but for sixty years she had been fretting about her first fiancé, George, who had jilted her on the very day they were supposed to be married. She had later married John Weatherall and named their first son George.

Cantankerous as ever in her last few hours, she had nonetheless lapsed into moments of wistfulness, wanting to see George so that she could tell him about her fine husband and her children: "Tell him I was given back everything he took away and more. Oh, no, oh, God, no, there was something else besides the house and the man and the children. Oh, surely they were not all? What was it? Something not given back!"

Not yet reconciled to that ancient loss, she asked God for a sign as preparations were made for administering the last rites of the Church. But there was only a priest in the house "and no bridegroom" (the absent bridegroom being the Jesus of Matthew 25:1–13), and this final jilting she could not forgive. Unable to

---

* Published several months later in *transition* (1929).

accept the ultimate affront, she willed her own death as she blew out the candle by her bed.

But as one who had always taken great pride in keeping an orderly house, she had made sure that everything was in perfect shape before she agreed to die. "Things were finished somehow when the time came; thank God there was always a little margin over for peace: then a person could spread out the plan of life and tuck in the edges orderly. It was good to have everything clean and folded away." As George Hendrick skillfully points out, Miss Porter's description reminds one of Henry James's description of May Bartram's compulsive orderliness in *The Turn of the Screw:* "The perfection of household care, of high polish and finish, always reigned in her rooms, but they now looked most as if everything had been wound up, tucked in, put away...."

She had, indeed, been heavily influenced by James, and there would be Jamesian echoes in much of her fiction; but there was a sharper edge in her perception of mankind, a tenacious refusal to gloss over human frailty, which often resulted in bitterness and a rather bleak pessimism. (She later acknowledged a lifelong debt to James in a biographical essay in which — with a hint of wistful envy — she repeatedly mentioned his financial security: "... the freedom of money is an added freedom of grace and the power of choice in many desirable ways.... It was merely a fact that they [the James family] could afford to be beyond material considerations because they were well provided.... But one of the goods, a main good, without which the others might wear a little thin, was material ease....")

And it was material ease that Miss Porter lacked, had always lacked since leaving Indian Creek. Yet, aside from her anonymous hackwork and ghostwriting, she refused to write (was no doubt emotionally incapable of writing) the kind of sob-sister fiction that was published in magazines of broad circulation. Her kind of downbeat fiction would not have got beyond a quick reading of the opening paragraphs. Consequently, she was confined to the so-called "little magazines," which paid little or nothing to their contributors. One such magazine was *transition*, which published "The Jilting of Granny Weatherall" and another story titled "Magic," apparently completed during the same period (1928). Here again she used a Jamesian narrative technique. The narrator was a black maid, once a servant in a bordello but now working for Madame Blanchard,* whose hair she was combing as the story evolved. When Madame remarked that her bed sheets wore out so quickly because they were bewitched, the maid was prompted to tell her own story of magic, which had occurred at the house of prostitution controlled by a cruel, nasty madam who habitually cheated the girls. When Ninette, the most called-for girl, eventually rebelled and said she was leaving, the madam viciously kicked her in the groin and shoved her out into the street. Then the madam's cook, a bad character "with much French blood," made a magic brew to lure Ninette back — and she did indeed come back, contrite and meekly submissive, having been forced to do so by cooperative cops and pimps.

The narrator's account of Ninette's story was not necessarily the truth, but a dramatized version of it. Simple and naïve, the narrator was oblivious to the ironies involved. She believed, for example, that the magic potion actually worked; she referred to the brothel as "the fancy house"; and she missed the irony in a male customer's "Welcome home" when Ninette returned. Moreover, she ended her story as if it were a happy-ever-after fairy tale: "And after that she lived there quietly."

Occasionally, Madame Blanchard would interrupt the maid, bringing the reader back to the narrative frame and coincidentally sharpening the cool irony.

Skillfully written and tightly compressed into five pages of complex psychological insights and bitter social criticism, "Magic" got favorable reactions from most of her friends; but she was frankly upset by an ambiguous comment from John Peale Bishop, with whom she had maintained an intimate friendship despite their "scrupulous avoidance of sex" while he was still married. "It's an interesting story though rather slight," he told her. "But you're getting there, Katherine Anne." Fortunately, the editors of *transition* had no reservations whatever and immedi-

---

*Miss Porter had once lived in a rooming house belonging to a Mme. Blanchard.

ately accepted it for the next issue, paying her a nominal twenty-five dollars, plus five complimentary copies of the magazine.

Meanwhile, she had successfully applied to the Guggenheim Foundation for a grant that would enable her to write a book on Cotton Mather and the witches of Salem, a subject that had fascinated her since early childhood and which she had been researching on and off for at least seven years. Suddenly she had more money than she had ever had before — six hundred dollars — so she hastily bade all her friends goodbye and took the first available train back to Mexico, her two battered suitcases replaced by a "brand new" secondhand steamer trunk filled with books, research notes, manuscripts-in-progress, a new lace blouse, and most of her old dresses and shoes.

But when she got to Mexico City she found it difficult to work. The rainy season had started earlier than usual, and her rented room was cold and damp most of the time. Fearing another siege of pneumonia or influenza when she developed a persistent cough that sounded like a guttural bark, she decided to look for a warmer, sunnier climate — preferably near the ocean. Her old friend Jorge Enciso suggested Acapulco (then a mere village) or Vera Cruz, but an English friend persuaded her to try Bermuda instead. "You can probably rent a house rather cheaply during the off-season," he said. "Or get a cheap hotel room somewhere."

When she finally got to Bermuda, after a long tedious journey on a small boat, she took a room in an inexpensive hotel and started looking for a house. As luck would have it, one of the first persons she asked about possible rentals told her that "the Hollys are leaving for the summer, and they'll probably want someone to look after their place." And an hour later the Hollys, who usually rented their house for five hundred dollars per month, agreed to let her have it for only fifty dollars. "They wanted me to keep it alive, to keep it fresh, and that's exactly what I did."

Located on a beautiful crescent-shaped beach, it was a large handsome house built of white coral, with twelve rooms and three baths. There was also a lovely garden that would be tended by a regular yardman, who slipped in and out like a secretive cat. (Most of the Holly family had gone from England directly to

Virginia, but this branch of the family had been shipwrecked in Bermuda and happily chose to stay there.)

At the very last minute, just as they were ready to leave, Mrs. Holly asked if she'd mind taking care of a two-month-old kitten named Rufus. "I'll be happy to," said Miss Porter. "He'll be good company." Indeed he was. Frolicking all over the place, from room to room, up and down the stairs, and under all the furniture, Rufus was the ideal companion for such a large lonely house. He would, in fact, be her only companion during the five months she stayed there.

She lived like a hermit during that entire period, allowing no one in the house except an old black woman who came to clean twice a week, and a young boy who would come by to sell her onions, pomegranates, bananas and fish. Once in a while he would bring her a live lobster from a trap he had beyond the next cove. The rest of her food would be delivered once a week by the teenage son of a local grocer, who would park his bicycle near the back porch and shove the bag inside the screen door. Occasionally, someone would come by and ask her to go riding or swimming, but she would politely decline, explaining that she had work to do.

"I never saw a single soul in that house," she later recalled with a touch of pride. "And it was terribly important for me to be alone. It changed my mode of thinking, so that I forgot about clocks and sun time, and I went back to the moon and the tides, thus finding an absolute perfect harmony in my life."

She wrote when the moon was full and kept working later and later, all night long, until the moon receded into the early dawn. "It was the most lovely thing that ever happened to me." With all her research materials close at hand, she concentrated all her thoughts and energy on the long-awaited book on Cotton Mather, "writing on moon time and tide time." It seemed to work like a charm, for eventually she finished eleven of the twenty chapters she had planned. But sometimes she would get very tired, especially when she was doing the witchcraft chapters, and she would suddenly feel terrorized, as if the evil she was writing about had come into the room. "If you knew as much about them as I did, had studied about them and thought about them, and lived with them so long, you'd know they had become palpable, had substance. Over the centuries they still have."

Feeling thus, she had a horrible impulse to get up and run, to go down the road and away from that house forever. Yet she would just sit there and shudder, forcing herself to go on writing — "but finally the time came when I knew I had to get up and walk through that evil. . . ."

On the day when Miss Porter told me about her sojourn in Bermuda, we had a prolonged and fascinating discussion on all sorts of occult phenomena, during which she revealed certain aspects of herself that I had not seen or heard of before then. In all her published work, there was nothing to indicate that this distinctly feminine side of Katherine Anne Porter ever existed. Perhaps a summary of our discussion will give the reader some notion of what I mean.

She had invited me to a Sunday brunch which consisted of *escargots bourguignonne*, freshly-baked sourdough bread, and a German champagne that had been chilled for an hour. Toward the end of the meal, as she was about to eat her last morsel of sauce-dabbed bread, she paused suddenly and stared across the table. "I wonder if Flannery O'Connor would have liked this combination of snails and champagne?" she speculated in a half whisper. "Perhaps not — too French maybe. She was an Aries, you know, an almost classical example of an Aries."

Momentarily puzzled by her sudden switch from food to astrology, perhaps missing a subtle link between them, I asked if she believed in the signs of the zodiac.

"Not re-e-e-ally," she said, slowly drawing out the word and glancing at me as if to determine whether I was a believer or skeptic. "But it's kind of fun to fool with."

Then a few minutes later, as she was preparing espresso on the mahogany credenza near the window, she suddenly produced a booklet from a top drawer. "Here's something I got years ago in

Paris," she said, with a throwaway lilt in her mellow voice. "Some English friends gave it to me on my birthday. Kind of amusing."

It was a slender thirty- or forty-page book on astrology, with a woodcut reproduction of the zodiac on the brown cover. Holding it close to my eyes, I saw that she had written numerous names in very small letters on the outer rim, four or five opposite each sign. On the fringe of the four names next to "Gemini," I saw a penciled "Hank L?" in cramped handwriting.

"How did you know I was a Gemini?" I asked, assuming it referred to me.

"I merely guessed it," she said, breaking into a pleased smile. "That's why it's still in pencil. But I just knew you were, Hank. As a matter of fact, I'll bet you're a double Gemini."

"Well, I don't know if I'm a double anything," I said, glancing at the other names. "But my birthday is May 28."

"There you are!" she exclaimed, lightly slapping the credenza in triumph. "I hit it right on the button. A double Gemini if ever I knew one. That's why we get along so well. Either that — or we'd fight like cats and dogs. No neutral ground between us, Hank."

Quickly leafing through the inside pages, a frown of deep concentration on her usually smooth brow, she finally stopped at a page with a woodcut scorpion on the upper margin. "Now here's Scorpio," she said in a dead earnest tone that belied her earlier it's-kind-of-fun-to-fool-with disclaimer. "That's Ezra Pound's sign, you know. And look what it says here. You read it for us; my glasses are in the kitchen somewhere."

Taking the booklet, which she held open at the desired page with her thumb as we walked into the living room, I read the opening sentences: "Scorpio is the sign of creative power, represented by the 'm' of primitive power with a stinging tail added, expressing the ability of all life to protect itself from undesired compulsion. Scorpio in any chart will show a person's capacity for developing and strengthening his own creative resource. . . ."

Her head slowly nodding as I read, Miss Porter interrupted my reading with a reminiscent sigh. "Oh, that's him, all right. That huge creative talent, self-directed and mostly self-educated in such esoteric things as ancient Chinese poetry. And then that terrible compulsive sting always there to cut anyone down. A true Scorpio in every sense."

Meanwhile, glancing at the next paragraph, I said, "But look at this passage that says such individuals 'have real political gifts.' How do you square that with Pound's screwy actions during the war?"

"Well, that was awfully strange," she conceded. "But, you see, he actually believed he had those political gifts that Scorpios are supposed to have. And maybe he did — but simply didn't use them right."

We then turned to the Taurus page, where she had scribbled the names of Edmund Wilson, Robert Penn Warren and Archibald MacLeish. Once again I read the opening paragraph as she leaned back with her eyes closed: "Taurus is the sign of stamina. The symbol is the bull, represented by his face and horns, expressing life's persistent exercise of its powers. A Taurus is an individual who is eager for experience, if he can have it on his own basis; who is inclined to be patient and to hold steadfast to his own ideals."

Her eyes still closed, her fingers gently rubbing the edge of the table, she seemed totally engrossed in a deeply private analysis of what she remembered about her old friends, matching their personal characteristics with the catchall abstractions she had read and reread in the slender booklet she apparently had kept at hand for more than a decade.

Finally, pursing her lips in final judgment, she delivered the not unexpected verdict in an accent that was slightly more Southern than usual. "Now that's pretty accurate, I think. Bunny, Red and Archie — yes, all of them — were about as stubborn and steadfast as anyone I knew. Real bulls, all of them. And you could rely on them no matter what. It shows in their writing, if you take the pains to look for it — that steady unwavering line of thought that won't get sidetracked by mere passing fads and silly fashion. That's why Bunny Wilson is such a successful critic: he's always had that firm base to work from. Typical Taurus."

Having thus launched an astrological analysis of many of her closest friends, skipping back and forth from one sign to another, we spent at least four hours speculating about Edna St. Vincent Millay (Pisces), Ernest Hemingway (Cancer), Caroline Gordon (Libra), Eudora Welty (Aries), Flannery O'Connor (also Aries), and many others whose names she'd jotted on the outer rim of the zodiac. It was obviously great fun for her, but there was always that hint of serious belief in her whimsy, as if part of her emotions were perpetually at odds with the cool, fiercely analytical mind that had produced the spare diamond-hard short stories which some critics had called "slightly misanthropic."

Inevitably, we dipped into matters relating to the occult, and she told me about a harrowing experience she'd had in Bermuda. She told me about the house she had rented from the Hollys. It was located on a rather isolated dune with shaggy growths of high grass that could have concealed any intruder, especially after sundown. Consequently, she had carefully double-bolted every door and window before going to sleep.

"Perhaps my uneasiness was influenced by the book I was trying to write," she told me. "I was deep into the second phase of my work on Cotton Mather and all that business about the witches of Salem."

She had, in fact, studied almost every aspect of witchcraft, black magic, voodoo, poisoned herbs, evil curses, moon madness, black masses and all kinds of strange beliefs in various countries and different cultures. Occasionally her intense probing, her stubborn determination to comprehend the demonic motivating core, the primeval rationale of certain occult phenomena — "none of which could be grasped without considerable empathy" — would lead her into baffling psychic terrains that only fools or saints could travel. Fully aware of the emotional traps on that forever-alien terrain, she couldn't resist exploring the darkest corners and most devious paths — sometimes with a curious compulsive defiance.

One afternoon, while she was scribbling a few notes on one of Cotton Mather's younger victims, bending closer to her desk as the waning sunlight gave way to dark shadows, she was nearly jolted out of her chair by a sudden chilling breeze directly behind her.

"Someone had entered that room," she told me in a whispery voice, her eyes bulging wide as if she were once again experiencing the very same sensation. "No one had opened the door, nor any of the windows, but I knew there was a new presence in that room. Almost at my elbow. And as palpable as my own hand. I couldn't see it, of course, because that kind of presence is never visible to the human eye. But it was certainly occupying a space just behind my right shoulder, standing there as motionless as a mummy but giving off subtle but distinct vibrations."

Why it was there she didn't know. Nor did she know enough about the history of that old house — what tragedies or griefs might have taken place there — to venture a quick guess. "So I felt myself saying 'Who are you? And why are you here?' I say *felt* because I could feel my lips making the words, but I couldn't hear them. There wasn't breath enough in me to give them sound.

"Yet, for all my fear, I was determined not to give in to whatever it was. Determined not to leave that room. Not even my chair. I knew that if you run away from a thing like that, if you yield even an inch, that you will never be yourself again."

So she just sat there in her stiff uncomfortable writer's chair, holding on to her place for dear life, her spine rigid and cold as ice, her eyes glued to the wall in front of her, the fingers of her right hand frozen tight around the pen she'd been using. Gradually, as if deliberately goading her, the unseen presence moved slowly from the space behind her, brushing past her left shoulder like a cold draft from a suddenly opened doorway. But she stayed where she was, scarcely breathing, still staring at the same spot on the bare wall, her frail summery blouse now drenched with cold sweat.

"But I was determined not to leave," she told me, unconsciously stiffening her back as if she were once again sitting in the same room. "There are times when you've got to resist that kind of evil intrusion, and this was one of them."

So she waited there for nearly an hour, the late afternoon shadows darkening the sparsely furnished room, the deathly silence finally broken by her own deep sigh of relief when the presence suddenly left the room.

"But how did you know it was evil?" I later asked.

"Well, it certainly wasn't friendly; I can tell you that."

"So you feel there are friendly and unfriendly visitations?"

"Oh, there's no doubt about that," she said, her voice firm and matter-of-fact. "You can always tell the difference, Hank."

Her unseen visitor reminded me of the *lloronas* who had haunted my childhood in the eastside Chicano *barrio* of Denver, Colorado. All my ghetto friends — in fact, every Mexican I've ever known — had at least one experience with a *llorona*.* No one ever saw one face-to-face, but we knew that a *llorona* was always lurking in the dark alleys and empty lots of our neighborhood, howling like a demented witch on the darkest nights. Once in a while my godfather would tell me he had seen one racing down Larimer Street or through the park, and my Uncle Tomás swore that he had seen a *llorona* running across a snow-covered field without leaving a single footprint.

"I know all about *lloronas*," said Miss Porter when I told her how I'd cower under my blanket, stuttering Hail Marys until I'd finally fall asleep. "I heard about them from the Mexican *rancheros* who worked for my father down in Texas, and they told me a lot of other stories that sounded awful real to me."

One of the older *rancheros* (named Miguel) told her about a strange incident at a community dance he had attended as a child. The whole town — men, women and children — had gathered in a dancehall, sitting at various tables along the walls, eating tacos, drinking *cervezas* (beers) or pulque, dancing an occasional *jarabe* or simply listening to a trio of local musicians. Then just before midnight a tall elegant stranger wearing a black velvet cape entered the hall and quietly sat down at a corner table. Assuming

---

*Spanish word meaning "one who cries."

he was a rich *hacendado* from a neighboring village, some of the dancers nodded politely as they glided past him; but he seemed coolly indifferent. Suddenly there was a wild scream from a young boy who had crawled under the visitor's table to hide from his sister.

"*Tiene cola!*" he yelled, scrambling away. "He's got a tail!"

Leaning forward into a half-crouch while the boy was still screaming, the dark stranger instantly became a huge ball of fire, swishing across the floor and through the open doorway as everyone froze with terror.

Instantly recalling that my father had told me the very same *cuento*, I said, "My God, Katherine Anne! There must have been ten million Mexicans involved in that one little incident. I've heard the same story from three or four different sources during the past thirty years. My father told me it happened in Chihuahua, someone else said it was Jalisco, another one said it was Durango, and your old friend Miguel saw it happen in Queretaro — and all of them swearing and eventually convincing themselves that they actually saw the man turn into a ball of fire."

"That's what made those *cuentos* so wonderful," she said, her eyes sharing a bemused, wistful smile. "They were so convincingly told — and always by someone who claimed he was actually there — so that you couldn't help believing them."

"It's because we wanted to believe them," I said.

She nodded and leaned back on the sofa, her eyes momentarily closed. "Yes, I guess we did," she said. "I felt that way the second time I heard that ball-of-fire story down in Mexico City. One of the maids told me that her parents had seen that same stranger, but the dancehall was in Morelos instead of Queretaro. And, you know, I never let on that I'd heard that *cuento* a long long time ago."

We discussed several other Mexican folktales, some of them amazingly inventive and always macabre, pouring ourselves another drink as the evening shadows gradually darkened the room.

"Let it get dark," she said. "It's always more fun to talk about witches and demons when the lights are out."

"*De acuerdo,*" I said, lapsing into Spanish. "Now tell me, Katherine Anne, have you ever met a *curandera?*"*

"Of course I have," she said, jiggling the ice in her glass. "I had a *curandera* working for me — the best maid I ever had. Her name was Petra."

"How did you know she was a *curandera?*"

"Well, we all knew that. She used to cure everyone in the neighborhood. They'd come around with headaches, bellyaches, stuffed noses — just about any ill you can imagine — and Petra would mix them some herbs, and off they'd go."

"But did she cure them?" I asked.

"I guess so, Hank. They always came back whenever they got sick again. And she cured *me* a couple of times."

"She did?"

"She sure did, honey. I had a sty on my left eye, had it for nearly a week, a nasty swelling that wouldn't go away. Then one afternoon Petra said, 'Let me cure that, señora.' So she tore a thick leaf from a palm tree in the patio, soaked it with some boiled herbs, pressed it over my eye for about a half-hour, mumbling something that wasn't Spanish. Then she took the leaf and burned it in the fireplace."

"And that cured you?" I said, apparently expressing a hint of skepticism.

"Well, all I can say is this: that sty was gone the next morning. Disappeared overnight. Just like that," she said, snapping her fingers.

But Petra was more than an herb doctor, she was also the best midwife in the *colonia* of Mixcoac, the old section of Mexico City where Miss Porter lived. She often delivered two or three babies a week, and very few of them were stillborn.

She was also gifted with what can only be described as extrasensory perception, according to Miss Porter. "Petra would tell me that someone was coming to visit, and an hour later Hart Crane or some other friend would come by. Or she would predict

---

* Female herb doctors, who are often regarded as witches in Mexico and other Latin countries.

a death in someone's family, an accidental death that no one could have foreseen in purely logical terms. And she occasionally would tell me that a storm was coming during the dry season, and the very next day we might get a thundershower."

"That must have been kind of spooky," I said, remembering similar stories about an old lady in my neighborhood in Denver.

"She certainly was," she said, leaning forward as if to recapture a clearer image of Petra. "And she looked like what she was. Her back was slightly hunched, her arms long and skinny, her dry coppery face prematurely wrinkled so that she looked much older than she was, her slender nose hooked like a beak, and her dark black eyes always moist and piercingly alive."

"You seem to be describing a witch," I said.

"But she wasn't a witch, Hank. She was a very kind woman, one of the most lovable people you'd ever want to meet. So it's difficult to describe her, really. She seemed to change a lot."

Her voice had faded to a mere whisper as she talked about Petra, making the room seem darker than it was. Then suddenly I heard a deep intake of breath from Miss Porter as her back stiffened to an upright position.

"She's here!" she said, her eyes widening as she stared across the room.

"Do you mean Petra?" I asked, a sudden chill down my back.

"It's Flannery," she said, her face softening into a vague smile. "It's Flannery O'Connor — she's come to visit. She must have known we were thinking about her."

Knowing that Miss O'Connor had died two or three years before, I simply sat there in dead silence, not knowing how I should react to that sudden change.

Her eyes were focused on the far corner of the room, on a red velvet chair and the antique mahogany table next to it. There was a fragile blue vase on the table, its long slender neck holding a barely visible white rose that seemed suspended in midair. Breathing deeply as though each breath was a sigh, Miss Porter kept staring at the unseen presence for at least ten minutes, her hands loosely folded on her lap, an expression of calm inner happiness in her face.

Finally, she turned to me and said, "Now that was a friendly visitation."

Whenever she talked about witchcraft and other occult phenomena, there was a hint of terror, a certain otherworldliness, in her eyes and in her voice, but none of this was reflected in what she wrote for the Cotton Mather book. Compared to her other work, the three chapters she finally published much later ("Affectation of Praehiminincies," "A Goat for Azazel," and "A Bright Particular Faith") seem flat and remote, like hurried but well-crafted summaries of the thousands of notes she had made in preparation for what she hoped would be the definitive book on the subject. There was no propelling force in what she was writing, and this may account for her failure to finish this much-promised work, which was subsequently announced for publication on two or three different occasions but never produced. As she herself often said, "I think it is the most curious lack of judgment to publish before you are ready."

Yet there were flashes of her wry inimitable irony on almost every page — short pithy comments that emphasized her sense of detachment:

"On Tuesday he prayed for her again, but his mind wandered off to other affairs, and having established the precious necessary mood of intimacy with God he took advantage of it to pray for the political situation in England. . . .

"A note of arrogance crept into his prayers: he demanded the life of Abigail as proof of his own ambassadorship between heaven and earth. . . ."

8

The Hart Crane Tragedy

AFTER five beautiful months in Bermuda, she went back to Mexico in mid-October of 1929, "gradually adjusting from moon time to sun time." The adjustment was necessitated by the fact that she no longer lived alone. Earlier in the year she had established a "fairly chummy" liaison with a minor official in the United States Embassy, one Gene Pressley, who, upon her return, immediately invited her to stay at his home in suburban Mixcoac.

"It was a nice house and he was a nice man, so we were soon living together."

Most of her friends agreed he was *nice*, but they also wondered why she had chosen to live with someone who was so obviously dull, conservative, mundane and pedestrian. Their conjectures ran the gamut from the snide to the presumptuous: "She's broke and has no other place to go. . . . She has become a reactionary in her middle age [close to forty]. . . . He's much more sexual than he seems. . . . She has no desire for sex. . . . She is tired of Bohemian life. . . . He's a secret intellectual masquerading as a diplomat. . . . She is writing a novel about international politics and wants to get a close-up view of the diplomatic world. . . . She is pregnant and he will soon marry her. . . . They are already secretly married. . . . She is dead tired of floating around and simply wants to settle down. . . ."

She herself was never too clear about why she had moved in with Pressley, but it wouldn't be unreasonable to surmise that a need for economic security was a significant factor in her decision. The house was spacious and attractive; there were two servants to do all the cooking and housecleaning; there was a pleasant garden, walled in from a cobblestoned street in a quiet, peaceful suburb; and there was no rent to pay. Moreover, Pressley was a modest unobtrusive man who would not impinge upon her privacy — or so she hoped. Nor was he likely to arouse the tempestuous emotional response that characterized her relationship with John Peale Bishop. He was, in short, a comfortable man to live with, the kind that George Bernard Shaw had in mind when his protagonist in *Don Juan in Hell* airily observes that "the English think they are in love when they are merely comfortable."

Whether or not she got the privacy she longed for (and needed), she apparently was unable to do any serious writing and spent most of her time puttering around the garden and learning to cook new Mexican dishes. Then, quite suddenly, in early December, she went back to New York and rented a flat in Brooklyn, hoping to avoid any distractions from her Greenwich Village crowd. Once again she was ready to bring forth a story that had been germinating in her mind for several years. Thus, between seven o'clock and midnight of a very cold December* evening (1929), she wrote *Flowering Judas* in a five-hour burst of creativity that has few, if any, parallels in American literature. With only a few minor corrections here and there, the first draft was the only draft, and shortly after midnight she dropped the manuscript into the mailbox, having addressed the envelope to Lincoln Kirstein, editor of the literary quarterly *Hound and Horn.* It was published in the spring of 1930.

As indicated in the previous chapter, the characters and episodes in *Flowering Judas* were based on real persons and events which assumed different shapes and guises as they were gradually sifted through her memory, all of which ultimately coalesced into a central theme of self-delusion. Perhaps because of its provocative title, it became a favorite story for symbol seekers. And the

---

* This is the date she gave in the prefatory note in Whit Burnett's anthology *This Is My Best,* but in a subsequent interview published in *Harper's* magazine (September 1965) she said it was January 1930.

most prominent seeker-and-finder was Ray B. West, whose co-
gent and persuasive analysis flowed from an initial assumption
that Miss Porter's central imagery derived from T. S. Eliot's
poem "Gerontion":

> ... In the juvescence of the year
> Came Christ the tiger

> In depraved May, dogwood and chestnut, flowering judas,
> To be eaten, to be divided, to be drunk
> Among whispers ...

And from that premise, West pointed out that the judas tree
symbolized betrayal, and that Laura's eating of the buds was a
sacrament of betrayal. Likewise, the ruthless, self-pitying revolutionary and professional lover of men, Braggioni, was ironically
portrayed as a "world saviour"; Eugenio was a sort of Christ figure; and, like Judas, Laura was directly responsible for Eugenio's
death, since she provided the drugs he used to commit suicide.

Like Eliot's old man, who had lost his sight, smell, hearing,
taste and touch, Laura was seen by West as a wasteland figure
with no capacity for love, religion or revolution. His wasteland-
Christian symbolism clearly focused on Laura's desultory, am-
bivalent involvement in what she considered a sham revolution.
Lacking the courage to disentangle herself, she simply drifted
along in the movement in hopeless despair, feeding on the lives of
others until she finally betrayed herself and Eugenio. Then, as
Hendrick points out, "she realized for the first time the extent of
her betrayal of herself and of her religious, ethical, and humanitarian principles. Some of her Christian precepts were as obviously flawed — her romantic concept of self as Virgin, the hiding of her body, her fear of close human contact, her aristocratic
pretenses — but she was unaware of these faults."

When I read some of these comments to Miss Porter during
one of our lengthy interviews, she responded with a hint of
amusement in her eyes. "Well, I guess some people never tire of
looking for symbols in my stories, especially that one. But I
wasn't thinking of any particular symbols when I wrote it, be-

*Miss Porter's
second husband, Gene Pressley,
who was a minor official in the
United States Embassy in Mexico*

*"Trying to
make myself work,"
in the fall of 1930,
Mexico City*

*Formal portrait by
the distinguished Mexican photographer
Manuel Bravo, 1931*

*On a weekend visit to a
hacienda outside Cuernavaca*

cause it was literally pouring out of me. I think symbolism happens of its own self, flowing out of something so deeply buried in your consciousness and past experience that you're not even aware of any symbols; and I think that's true of most writers. I'm certainly not aware of them until I see them later on. They just come of themselves. So you don't say, 'I'm going to have the flowering judas tree stand for betrayal,' though, of course, it does when you look back on it."

But aside from any symbolic interpretations, *Flowering Judas* was immediately acclaimed by the cognoscenti who read *Hound and Horn*, and it was republished a few months later (1930) as the title story of her first collection of short stories. (Although it was less than fifty pages in length, Miss Porter always insisted that it was a "short novel" and absolutely refused to have it classified as a "novella.") In any event, the slender volume also contained "María Concepción," "Magic," "Rope," "He," and "The Jilting of Granny Weatherall," and there was a limited edition of six hundred copies. Assuming that the book sold for two dollars and that she got the standard ten percent royalty, she would have made no more than one hundred twenty dollars for her first book. Nevertheless, she had finally emerged from the shadowy fringes of the New York literary community, where even the most talented writers (particularly those engaged in "serious" work) often slip into oblivion. She had also earned a firm reputation as an acute and sympathetic observer of the Mexican revolution, a reputation that would later be enhanced by a "short novel" based on an experience she had shortly after returning to Mexico in 1930.

Sergei Eisenstein, the great Russian director, was filming a movie subsequently titled *Que Viva México*; and one of her old friends, either Gamío or Enciso, had arranged for her to visit the hacienda where it was being produced. Located eighty miles southeast of Mexico City, the huge ranch was known as Tetlapaijac and was owned by a rich *hacendado* named Don Julio Saldwar. The main building on the estate was like a rambling fortress, with faded coral-pink walls and two high turrets that overlooked an enormous spread of maguey, the gray-green cactus from which the juice for pulque is extracted. Originally established by the followers of Hernán Cortés, the hacienda had remained in the control of the Saldwar family after the revolution because they had agreed to convert it into an agricultural cooperative for the local peasantry. But as Miss Porter would later observe, there was an army at hand to prevent said conversion.

With a modest budget of twenty-five thousand dollars — personally raised by Upton Sinclair and his wife — Eisenstein had planned a movie in six segments, the first of which was being filmed at the hacienda. But, as so frequently happens with artistic directors, he immediately began exceeding his day-to-day budget by shooting extra footage of key scenes from several angles. Apprised of this worrisome development, Sinclair dispatched his brother-in-law, Hunter Kimbrough, to oversee the production, inevitably arousing the resentment of Eisenstein and his colleagues. He was not only a tightwad but a prude as well, and as Miss Porter watched him fluster and flounder around the set, she carefully noted his most salient defects for future reference. Later explaining Kimbrough's actions, Sinclair emphasized that he was a young but old-fashioned Southerner with high ideals, adding, "I doubt if he had ever heard of such a thing as a homo and he was bewildered to find himself in such company. He discovered that Eisenstein wanted money, money, money, and never had the slightest idea of keeping any promise he made. When Kimbrough, obeying my orders, tried to limit the money and the subjects (to be) shot, there were furious rows."

Hovering behind Eisenstein and his aides, easily within earshot of their shouted conversations, Miss Porter watched scene after scene being shot with extravagant flair as Kimbrough kept shaking his head in penurious agony. The opening sequence was a paean to the maguey, with several Indians extracting the pulque juice from the giant cactus. Then after a scene depicting the ancient process of brewing pulque, the Sebastian-María story began. A simple peon, Sebastian took his new bride, María, to the hacienda owner as an act of homage; but the guards refused to let him in; and as they waited for the *hacendado* to give María a few coins, a carriage arrived with his aloof spoiled daughter, and María was forgotten in the ensuing commotion. Forgotten by everyone except a drunken guest, who savagely raped her. Belatedly informed of this, Sebastian tried to invade the fiesta to free his bride, but was easily repulsed. Now distraught and desperate, he organized a band of peasants, and they, too, were overcome and put to flight by the guards. And during the brief skirmish, the *hacendado*'s daughter was killed, after she herself had killed a peon. Finally captured, Sebastian was summarily put to death, and María found his body among the magueys as the episode came to a close.

Mentally recording each aspect of Eisenstein's artificial and simplistic plot, the quiet unobtrusive Señorita Porter was already conjuring a story about the filming of an altered version of the same plot. Later, much later, when her customary germinating-filtering process had come to a boil, she would sit down and make another short novel that would be called "Hacienda" (she herself often used the word "make" instead of "write," explaining that the *writing* had already taken place inside her head, and all that remained was the simple physical process of *making* it, putting it down on paper).

"Hacienda," then, was the product of her visit to Tetlapaijac. Kimbrough became Kennerly; Eisenstein became Uspensky; and Katherine Anne Porter became the nameless coolly detached "I" who narrated the story, which began with a brilliantly ironic portrayal of Kennerly, the business manager of the film, haughtily reacting to the docile peons whom he considered filthy, inferior, disease-ridden flotsam. With outrageous Anglo-Saxon superiority, he accurately pointed out the graft and corruption in the Mexican government, but was outraged only when his own ox was gored.

Most of "Hacienda" deals with the interaction of various characters on the day Justino shoots his sister. One of the leading actors, an Indian boy, reports that the shooting was accidental and that Justino had run away, only to be captured by Vicente. Someone has said that Justino's brother had also killed a child, and the song writer Montana insists that incest motivated the killing:

> Ah, poor little Rosalita
> Took herself a new lover,
> Thus betraying the heart's core
> Of her impassioned brother.

But whatever the cause of the slaying, the money-conscious Kennerly is merely concerned about a possible lawsuit by the girl's parents. Amused by the irony of Justino playing the role of a boy who accidentally kills a girl (portrayed by his sister), Kennerly openly laments that the dead girl was not photographed because it would have made the movie scene much more realistic. And he is once again perversely amused when Justino has to repeat the killing sequence because the prior "take" had been ruined by poor lighting.

All this — and various subplots of love and betrayal among other members of the cast and the crew — takes place in the overpowering putrid smell that comes from the *pulquería* and hangs heavily over everything, symbolizing the spiritual rot and decay at all levels of society. Meanwhile, poor wretched Indians all over Mexico would be drinking that pulque, swallowing "forgetfulness and ease by the riverful," enriching the haciendas and the government. ". . . Don Gerano and his fellow *hacendados* would fret and curse, the Agrarians would raid, and ambitious politicians in the capital would be stealing right and left enough to buy such haciendas for themselves. It was all arranged."

Once again there was that note of hopelessness, a sense of doom in the phrase *"It was all arranged,"* like the dull hollow sound of church bells tolling for a funeral. *It was all arranged — it was all arranged.*

When this skillfully executed tale of moral and psychological despair and isolation appeared in 1934, the reviews were mixed. In the *Herald-Tribune Books* review for December 16, 1934, Elizabeth Hart frankly disapproved of "Hacienda," complaining that it was incomplete, that it appeared to be a collection of notes for a novel. In a much later critique (1953) for the *Bulletin of the New York Public Library*, Howard Baker observed that "Miss Porter succeeds beautifully in capturing the elusive properties of people and things," but then dampened his praise by calling it inconclusive and lacking in a bold central theme. Still later (1957), Harry John Mooney, Jr., expressed considerable reservations, particularly with respect to the nameless narrator who he felt lacked an integral function and was therefore too detached.

But in the immediate aftermath of her visit to Eisenstein's movie location, Miss Porter had no urgent plan for writing the story that became "Hacienda." Her more pressing concern was the impending arrival of Hart Crane, whose visit would eventually end in tragedy.

One morning, as she was clipping a few roses from a sprawling bush outside her kitchen window, Miss Porter suddenly started telling me about her ultimately tragic friendship with Crane.

She had previously made several oblique references to Crane but always became strangely reticent whenever I asked any follow-up questions about him. "We'll talk about that some other time," she would say, with a slight catch in her voice.

Consequently, I was rather surprised when she commenced talking about him that morning — right out of the blue, with no preface whatever.

"What suddenly brings him to mind?" I asked, instantly regretting my trial-lawyer reflexes.

"There you go again," she said, an amused and forgiving smile lighting her face. "Always cross-examining me — even before I get started."

"Sorry," I said. "I can't shake the habit. But you have a way of springing things on me."

"I guess that did seem a little abrupt," she conceded, glancing at the roses in her hand. "It's this garden that reminded me of Hart Crane."

"How so?"

"Well, down in Mexico I had a perfectly beautiful garden, and

Hart would occasionally help me pull a few weeds here and there.
He was a very kind and thoughtful man — when he was sober.
But he could be an absolute monster when he was drunk."

She had met him in Greenwich Village, probably at Malcolm
Cowley's place, shortly after her futile picketing to help Sacco
and Vanzetti. Like everyone else, she had heard of Crane's still-
unfinished poem about the Brooklyn Bridge and naturally em-
pathized with his slow pace. She herself had often struggled
months and months (perhaps years) on a single short story, so
she wasn't a bit surprised to learn much later that Crane had
taken five years to write *The Bridge.*

"Certain poems and stories take time," she subsequently told
me. "They have long periods of gestation, and you can't force
them against their nature."

There was a studied emphasis in her statement, a well-re-
hearsed defensiveness, as if she had been saying the very same
words to scores of friends and critics who had undoubtedly
pushed her to write more than she had.

As for Mr. Crane, his long-awaited delivery of *The Bridge* was
received with considerable acclaim, and soon after its publication
he was awarded a Guggenheim Fellowship to work on another
book-length poem. Having decided to spend a year in Mexico
City, where Miss Porter was already living on her Guggenheim
stipend, he quite predictably let her know that he was coming.
And she, just as predictably, invited him to stay at her home in
Mixcoac.

"That," she now told me, "was a fatal mistake on my part. I
should have known better. There was simply no way to deal with
that kind of man."

She had been living with Gene Pressley (whom she would
later marry in Paris), but they had enough extra room in their
two-story house for several guests. She was not, however, prepared for the "spontaneous guests" that Crane started smuggling
into his room when he thought everyone was asleep, most of
them young Mexican boys about ten or eleven years old. She had
heard of his homosexual leanings from Caroline Gordon and

Allen Tate, but the little-boy deviance was more than she was willing to accept.

"He hadn't been with us for more than a couple of days when it all started. He would come in blindly drunk, grunting and staggering up to his room with some poor little child trailing behind him. Then there would be all kinds of thrashing about, and I would freeze in my bed wondering what sort of awful perversions he was forcing on those boys, he knowing darned well they were so starved and ragged they would do anything for a few miserable centavos."

But when he would appear in the patio shortly before noon of the following day, clean-shaven and apparently sober, she found it difficult to denounce him. All the anger and resentment she had been nurturing that morning would suddenly dissolve into mere pity. "Like most drunkards, he seemed boyishly vulnerable and as unprotected as an abandoned puppy." He was also an engaging conversationalist, who would keep her amused and fascinated all afternoon and well beyond the cocktail hour, particularly emphasizing certain anecdotes in which he played the fool.

But he was dead serious when he told Katherine Anne about his projected poem concerning the conquest of Mexico, an epic drama featuring Montezuma and Cortés. Though he had originally planned to write the poem in Martigues or Aix-en-Provence, he finally decided that it would be more logical to go to Mexico, where a firsthand acquaintance with native Mexicans — especially the Indians in the remote pueblos — would give him some inner clue to the Aztec character. Like D. H. Lawrence, he also hoped to discover "the primitive Mexico," the ambience that existed there before the white man came.

"When I've captured that essence," he told her, "I'll get to the very roots, the spiritual core, of the greatest theme I've ever heard of."

"You've got yourself a tall order," she told him, remembering her conversations with José Vasconcelos and Manuel Gamío. "I've known some very intelligent Mexicans who have frankly confessed their inability to understand the Indian's psyche."

"But what about Lawrence and his *Plumed Serpent?*" asked Crane. "He seemed to understand them."

"I'm not so sure about that, Hart. There are certain people here who regard that book as pure hogwash. Simplistic nonsense from a romantic Englishman who couldn't even understand kitchen Spanish — much less Nahuatl."

"What's this Nuahatl?" asked Crane, pronouncing the word as if he had a lump of soap in his mouth.

"That's the Aztec language that was spoken by all those natives Mr. Lawrence was writing about," she said. "And there are very few Mexicans — even scholars — who claim to understand it."

But Crane was not easily discouraged. "There are other ways to know people," he said. "I'll get to know them one way or another, Katherine Anne."

Yet the very next morning he expressed grave doubts about his Montezuma-Cortés project. He was, indeed, dubious about writing anything. In sober morning-after sessions of brutal self-analysis, he would tell her about the terrifying angst that seemed to plague him more often now that he was in Mexico.

"He would talk slowly in an ordinary voice (never dramatic), telling me that he was destroying himself as a poet, though he didn't know why.... He said once that the life he lived was blunting his sensibilities, that he was no longer capable of feeling anything except under the most violent and brutal shocks."

He talked of suicide almost every day. Whenever he read of a suicide in the newspapers, he approved and praised the act. He spoke of Ralph Barton's suicide as "noble." He described the suicide of Harry Crosby as "imaginative; the act of a poet." Once while he was still stopping at Miss Porter's house he ran out of his room — it was night, and the moon seems to have been shining, again — rushed up to the roof, which was only two stories high, and shouted that he was going to throw himself off. And she called out to him, "Oh don't. It's not high enough and you'll only hurt yourself." He began to laugh immediately, a curiously fresh sober humor in the laughter, and came down by way of an apricot tree with branches spreading over the roof. He sat and talked a

little while, went in and began to play the piano loudly and inco-
herently — it was very old and out of tune — and after about an
hour of this he left the house, and did not return.

She saw him hail a taxi at the corner and later learned that he
had wandered from one bar to another in a downtown area resembling the Bowery, drinking tequila, beer and rotgut whiskey,
until his cash ran out at a rundown cantina whose owner refused
to extend him credit for the unpaid bill. Protesting angrily in the
few words of gutter Spanish he had managed to learn, Crane was
hauled off to jail and spent the night with several other drunks.
The next day, after a frantic relay of messages from the jail to the
American Embassy to the Guggenheim Foundation, his fine of
twelve pesos (about eight dollars) was paid by the foundation's
local director, Dr. Eyler Simpson; and later that night, after visiting a "friendly bartender" at the Hotel Mancera, he went back
to Miss Porter's house. But during the next two or three days he
prowled around the house and garden like a caged hyena, grum-
bling and snarling about a terrible itch that wouldn't let him sleep
or even sit still. Not even a heavier-than-usual consumption of alcohol could dull the urge to scratch the skin off his private parts,
and she could hear him groaning and stumbling around half the
night. Finally, obviously sensing he was keeping everyone else
awake, he suddenly took off, leaving a note on the dining room
table:

DEAR KATHERINE ANNE:
    HAVE GONE TO THE MANCERA UNTIL THE FIRST. EXCUSE MY WAKE-
FULNESS PLEASE.

    P.S. NO. HAVEN'T BEEN BUSY WITH "LOVERS." JUST YEOWLS AND
FLEAS. LYSOL ISN'T NECESSARY IN THE BATHTUB. HAVEN'T GOT "ANY-
THING" YET. IF YOU KNEW ANYTHING WHATEVER ABOUT IT, YOU'D
KNOW THAT AT LEAST (AND THE LAST THING SYPHILLIS DOES) IT
DOESN'T *ITCH*. OTHER MATTERS DO, SOMETIMES.

He later confessed to a nightmarish seventy-two hour binge at
the hotel, most of it in his cluttered smelly room, yet he somehow
managed to scribble another note to Katherine Anne: "This is as

near as I dare come to you today. Shame and chagrin overwhelm me. I hope you can sometime forgive."

She not only forgave him, she actually helped him negotiate the rental of a house around the corner from hers (15 Calle Michoacán) and also introduced him to one of her dearest friends, Moisés Sáenz, who volunteered to take Crane on a get-away-from-it-all excursion to Taxco.

While waiting for Sáenz at his unfurnished new house, where he had slept on a straw *petate* on his first night of occupancy, Crane wrote another apology which was hand-delivered by one of his newly acquired servants.

Darling Katherine Anne:

I'm too jittery to write a straight sentence but am coming out of my recent messiness with at least as much consistency as total abstinence can offer.

Your two notes were so kind and gave me so much more cheer than I deserve that I'm overcome all over again. God bless you!!! I've got myself in a fix with a hell of [a] bill at the Mancera — but I'll get out of it somehow. My father is sending me some money — meanwhile Hazel Cazes is going to advance some.

This house is a love — and I'm glad to know that it won't be ruined for me now by any absence on your part — and Gene's. The recent cyclone is my last — at least for a year. Love and a thousand thanks.

Hart

When I get D.T.'s again I'll just take it out on police . . . They'll have at least a cell for me — or a straitjacket.

His reference to Gene Pressley was obviously a conciliatory gesture. Miss Porter knew that Crane had disliked her "sourish gentleman" from the very outset. He had, in fact, told her that Gene couldn't stand any of her old friends in Mexico, and that they were equally averse to him. (Looking back on her initial relationship and subsequent marriage to Pressley, she freely admitted to me that he was probably too prim and proper for the writers and artists who were her "natural allies," and that Crane's antipathy was probably justified.)

But now that he had a rented house of his own, Crane could

avoid any personal contact with Pressley. He could (and would in fact) visit Miss Porter while her man was attending his duties at the embassy. Just as soon as he returned from Taxco, apparently determined to "mend his ways by laying off the hard stuff," they spent long hours together discussing a prose poem he had started to write about the bacteriologist he'd met aboard the *Orizaba*. It was titled "Havana Rose," and the very first lines ("Let us strip the desk for action — now we have a house in Mexico . . .") evidenced a new resolve that pleased her, that aroused hopes for even better, more exacting work.

Listening to Miss Porter's reminiscence of that pleasant interlude, a hint of tears glazing her soft blue eyes as her voice faded to a husky whisper, I clearly sensed the profound and special affection they had for each other, an intensely felt love much deeper than mere sexual attachment.

But his expectations (and hers as well) soon foundered when he suddenly started drinking and night-prowling again, often disappearing for two or three days and then coming home with some stranger — usually a young boy — bearded, dirty, rumpled and thunderously drunk, announcing his arrival to all the neighbors with violent harangues against whatever cab driver had suffered the misfortune of picking him up. He somehow suspected that all cabbies were in league against him, that the few pesos they charged him were nothing less than extortion, a continuing ransom that he must pay because he was a defenseless gringo tourist. And his inability to understand them simply aggravated his paranoia.

Quite often his harangues would spill over to a general condemnation of all Mexicans — excluding, of course, the silent mystic *indios* he hoped to meet some day in some faraway village. Then he would get specific again, this time focusing his drunken anger on "certain middle-class intellectual mestizos" whom he classified as frauds and snobs.

Having been closely acquainted with several intellectuals who were deeply involved in *indigenismo*, Miss Porter couldn't let him get away with such arrogant and blanket accusations. "That may be true about some of them," she said. "But then how would you know, Hart? How could you possibly know about their intellectual or spiritual defects without having met them or read anything they've written? What if they were to judge you with the same lack of evidence?"

On such occasions, which were mercifully few since she well understood his continuing insecurity, he would simply twist his lips into a hurt smile and wander back to his house with both hands stuck in the front pockets of the baggy white sailor pants he usually wore. "I hated myself when he walked away like that," she told me. "There he'd go, suddenly straightening his shoulders and trying to sing a song from a Marlene Dietrich film he had once seen, something he always tried to sing whenever he felt uncomfortable or rejected, though he never got it quite right, the lyrics somehow lumping over each other."

Yet there were times when his insecurity would goad him into flights of whimsy that made him totally irresistible.

Miss Porter particularly remembered a pleasant Sunday afternoon, when she and Pressley were entertaining a few Embassy people in the patio of their suburban home. "Most of them were elderly and properly stuffy — not the kind of people you'd want to mix with someone like Hart, especially if he'd been drinking — so we decided not to invite him. In fact, I rather hoped he might be away; otherwise, he would certainly know we were having guests."

No such luck. Promptly at four o'clock, like a matador entering the bullring, Hart suddenly appeared on top of the thick adobe wall overlooking her garden, casually walking toward the patio with all the confidence of a tightrope artist — or a man too drunk to sense any danger. Looking straight ahead without saying a word, blithely ignoring their awed expressions and nervous mumbling, he finally came to a halt at a point directly above the bridge table which served as a bar, proudly standing ten feet above them, his loose sailor pants ruffled slightly by a summer breeze.

Then, with just a brief clearing of his throat that reminded Miss Porter of a "showy Baptist preacher down home," he started to recite *The Bridge* in a beautiful rumbly voice that seemed like the most eloquent music she had ever heard, line upon line of that exquisitely structured poem coming forth as if he were creating each phrase right there and then, "an absolutely stunning performance."

Suddenly it was over, and in the hushed silence that preceded the inevitable applause, Crane smiled and said, "Now that I've sung for my supper, Katherine Anne, may I have a little taco?"

He of course ate several tacos of *carnitas* and *guacamole* and washed them down with rum highballs, dazzling her guests with the charm he could always muster when the occasion demanded, probably causing some of them to assume that Miss Porter had deliberately planned his theatrical coup. "And I saw no point in disillusioning them; I could hardly admit that we had deliberately not invited him."

But as he absorbed more liquor and began to brood about why he had been excluded, he quite audibly told one couple, "Katherine Anne didn't want me — but I came anyway," a remark she chose to ignore for fear of unleashing even more bitter recriminations. "He simply wasn't satisfied with his more subtle triumph, he had to go on and on, 'til there was nothing but a shambles of his torn and bleeding ego." And finally the guests started leaving, mumbling embarrassed goodbyes, as they side-glanced toward the far end of the patio where Crane was now cataloguing a whole series of snubs — some imaginary, others undoubtedly true and sadly warranted.

Hours later, when only she and Crane were left in the darkened patio staring at each other, both of them emotionally drained, she quietly suggested that he go home. Unable to manage more than a guttural blur of expiring vowels, probably meant as an apology, he shuffled through the gate and staggered down the cobblestoned street, reaching sidewise for support against a wall that wasn't where he thought it was and nearly falling as he turned the corner.

He stayed away for two days, then suddenly showed up on Wednesday morning with a sprig of purplish blossoms from a nearby jacaranda tree, a shy can-you-possibly-forgive-me smile on his face, asking if he might borrow a pinch of arsenic for his coffee.

"You can have some of *my* coffee," Miss Porter said, easily adapting to his self-conscious whimsy. "But you'll have to take it straight. I've just exhausted our supply of arsenic."

So once again they somehow managed to establish a certain tentative rapport, joking lightly about witches and poisons as they idly plucked a few weeds from several rows of carrots she'd planted near the rear wall. And when they had settled down for two or three cups of black unsweetened coffee, he started telling her how homesick he had been, how he longed for his "favorite corner of Connecticut" and the Columbia Heights view of the Brooklyn Bridge. He also talked about his home in Chagrin Falls, home-cooked meals and Saturday night movies, about his father, who insisted on calling him Harold instead of Hart, and she offering a few comments about her childhood at a ranch near Indian Creek, Texas, each one laughingly insisting that the other's home town had a fictitious name.

But for all their joking, she sensed that Crane's homesickness was simply a symptom of his inability to feel at home in Mexico. He felt hostility all around him, an inchoate but quite palpable hostility that he considered part of a worldwide antagonism toward all Americans and their "Yankee dollars."

Attributing his sense of alienation to something more personal than a generalized anti-Americanism, Miss Porter felt that some of the difficulty was due to his trying to live in diametrically opposed socioeconomic strata. He wanted to know and (if possible) become part of the common people, the illiterate peons who would give him a clue to "the real Mexico," but he couldn't break his attachments to the coupon-clipping retired expatriate Americans who leeched on any visitor who had even a semblance of celebrity, who gave parties every evening for the same roster of guests plus someone like Crane, eventually becoming so bored with themselves that drugs, homosexuality and mate-swapping were all they could think of to relieve the tedium. Quite obviously, it was easier for Crane to adapt to this latter group, willingly playing their court jester until they tired of him or found someone more amusing.

"He knew what their game was," she observed with remembered bitterness. "But he went along with it. Wasting all that valuable time, draining himself of the energy he should have saved for his writing. And, of course, the guilt gnawed at him."

Still, he did manage to write several long passages of a poem that would never be published, but which Katherine Anne read by accident. It happened on a Saturday morning when he was away. He had, in fact, disappeared for several days, and she had decided to stop by his house to ascertain his whereabouts.

"*No ha aparecido,*" his servant told her. (He hasn't been around.)

Thinking he might have left a note somewhere, she stepped into his living room and immediately noticed that he had pegged several sheets of paper on nine or ten nails that someone had hammered into the wall next to the fireplace. Drawing closer to get a better look, she realized that each sheet contained a long handwritten passage from a poem-in-progress.

"I simply couldn't resist reading it," she told me somewhat guiltily. "But it really wasn't snoopiness, Hank. It was truly an aesthetic curiosity on my part. And it was an absolutely beautiful poem, one of the finest he had ever written. It was a deeply introspective work, heartbreakingly honest and just a bit terrifying — but it was never published."

She looked for it year after year, thinking it might turn up among the poems that would be published posthumously, but she never saw it again. "Nor did I at that time discuss it with Hart, finally concluding that it was *he* who should bring it up."

Unfortunately, she would never know if he intended to show it to her and to ask her reactions to its content or structure. A few weeks later, there came an abrupt and final rupture in their relationship. Miss Porter subsequently provided Crane's biographer with her version of that sorry incident:

The evening before this episode at the gate, I had stopped before his own iron gate and called out to him that his garden already looked like something not made with hands. He came out and we talked for a few minutes. . . . It was just after dark and he had been reading Blake by the light of a single candle. He was drinking somewhat, too, alone in the house. He repeated a few of the vast lines, and added almost in the same voice: "You can't see them from here, but I have hundreds of little plants that I got at the market this morning." Holding to the grill he suddenly began to cry and said, "You don't know what my life has been. This is the only place I ever felt was my own. This is the only place I ever loved."

The next evening, or rather some time after midnight, he arrived at our gate in a taxicab, and began the habitual dreary brawl with the driver, shouting that he had been cheated, robbed; calling for us to come and pay his fare, as he had been robbed in a cafe. At times he accused the driver of robbing him. This time he stood there jingling heavy silver coins in his pocket, and as he shouted, he took out half a dozen, looked at them, and returned them to his pocket. I gave the driver the usual fare and sent him away. (Hart always insisted that he could never remember anything of these events, but he never once failed to come or send the next day to return the money I had paid the drivers.) Hart then demanded to come in, but I was tired to death, at the end of my patience, and I told him plainly he must go home. It was then that he broke into the monotonous obsessed dull obscenity which was the only language he knew after reaching a certain point of drunkenness, but this time he cursed things and elements as well as human beings. His voice at these times was intolerable; a steady harsh inhuman bellow which stunned the ears and shocked the nerves and caused the heart to contract. In this voice and with words so foul there is no question of repeating them, he cursed separately and by name the moon, and its light: the heliotrope, the heaven-tree, the sweet-by-night, the star jessamine, and their perfumes. He cursed the air we breathed together, the pool of water with its two small ducks huddled at the edge, and the vines on the wall and the house. But those were not the things he hated. He did not even hate us, for we were nothing to him. He hated and feared himself.

Crane gave his account of the gate episode in a letter to his friend Lorna Dietz, which was subsequently published in John Unterecker's *Voyager:*

To begin with the same subject which you did in your last — and to continue with what has been almost an obsession with me for the last month — I want to say a few words about Katherine Anne Porter. Not that I can possibly give even the outline of the whole queer situation, but since she has done so much announcing, just a hint at the circumstances.

Those circumstances, Crane went on to say, were much concerned with the influence of Gene Pressley, who he felt was responsible for Miss Porter's coolness toward him. "Maybe you've known like circumstances," Hart wrote.

. . . Anyway, they're very misleading, eventually in any case. Katherine Anne was quite lovely to me on more than one occasion, and since I have always liked her a lot, it was hard to relinquish her company. . . . Everything had been going very smoothly for some time, however; Katherine Anne frequently dropping into my place for afternoon chats, beer, etc. when the apparently decisive moment occurred.

I had asked them both to have dinner with me on a certain day at my house. It was well understood, etc. I made extensive preparations — and was left to keep things warm the entire afternoon, nipping at a bottle of tequila meanwhile, and going through the usual fretful crescendo of sentiments that such conduct incurs. Toward evening, having fed most of the natives in the vicinity and being rather upset, I went to town, where more drinks were downed. But in an argument with the taxi driver at my gate later in the evening I challenged him to arbitration at the local police station. Result: a night in jail; for feeling is so high against Americans in Mexico since the recent Oklahoma affair, that any pretext is sufficient to embarrass one.

K.A.'s place is just around the corner from the house I took, so on the way to the station I passed her gate. She and Mr. Pressly . . . happened to be within speaking distance. I remember having announced my predicament and having said, in anger at her response to the dinner engagement, "Katherine Anne, I have my opinion of you." . . . I haven't seen Katherine Anne since, nor has she offered the slightest explanation of her absence. She told a mutual friend that I said something particularly outrageous to her that evening at the gate; but what it may have been beyond what I have just mentioned I don't know. I wrote her a very humble apology a few days later, but there was no response.

It's all very sad and disagreeable. But one imputation I won't stand for. That is the obvious and usual one: that my presence in the neighborhood was responsible for a break or discontinuance of Katherine Anne's creative work. K-A had been in Mexico a full year before I ever arrived without having written one paragraph of the book she had in mind to write when she went there. If her friends don't already know her habit of procrastinating such matters at least I do. If she wants to encumber herself with turkeys, geese, chickens and a regular stock farm for the fun of it then well and good; but I know that she spent many more hours in nursing and talking to them every day than she ever spent in my company. Neither did the slight amount of extra tippling incident to my arrival impair her health. . . . I think there is a great tendency among her friends to sentimentalize and exaggerate her delicate health. She isn't happy, that's true, and is constantly in a nervous flutter, talks more to herself than others lately, and is a puzzle to all her old friends — but those manifestations originated long before my arrival. I'm tired of being made into a bogey or ogre rampant in Mexico and tearing the flesh of delicate ladies. I'm also tired of a certain rather southern type of female vanity. And that's about all I ever want to say about Katherine Anne again personally.

When I read the Crane-to-Dietz letter to Miss Porter, she turned and stared out the window, tears brimming in her eyes, her lips tightening as if to hold back a sob. Then, with a deep sigh and a sorrowful nod, she said in near whisper, "Oh, that poor, poor man. How awful it must have been to feel that friendless, to think that everyone was deliberately avoiding him. And yet how could he think otherwise?"

Although they remained neighbors for several months, they never saw each other again except at a distance; but she was continually informed of his activities and whereabouts by mutual friends, particularly Mary Doherty, who worked for the local office of the Guggenheim Foundation.

In midsummer Crane's father died, and he went back home for the funeral, returning to Mexico early in September. He had stopped in New York en route to Vera Cruz but apparently avoided most of his old friends, artists and writers "of the Patterson area," later explaining that avoidance in a letter to Malcolm Cowley: "As Bill has probably told you, the Katherine Anne upset accounted for my more than diffidence about seeing most of our mutual friends when I passed through N.Y. Sometime I may say more about it, but I'm sick of the subject just now. . . ."

Although he had no personal contact with Miss Porter after he returned to Mixcoac, she knew that he was having "a rather fulsome" social life. Among his house guests were a young homosexual archaeologist from Wisconsin; David Siqueiros, the great Mexican muralist, who moved in with a whole entourage of political cohorts; and his customary following of what he called "sexually ambidextrous Indians," whom he later described in a letter to Wilbur Underwood:

but he is more stirred by the moon, if you get what I mean, than any type I've ever known. The fluttering gait and the powder puff are unheard of here, but that doesn't matter in the least. Ambidexterity is all in the fullest masculine tradition. I assure you from many trials and observations. The pure Indian type is decidedly the most beautiful animal imaginable, including the Polynesian — to which he often bears a close resemblance. . . ."

But his most constant companion was Peggy Cowley, who had spent her first few days in Mexico as Miss Porter's houseguest.

"It was Peggy who finally rescued Hart from his lifelong addiction to male sex partners," she told me with a tight-smile sarcasm. "He apparently announced his loss of virginity to anyone who would listen, and she was happy to admit — just as openly — to that quite exceptional feat of sexual emancipation."

Mrs. Cowley herself later wrote about their relationship with rare candor: "He was in love and wanted me with him every moment. . . . His energy seemed inexhaustible. He was keyed to the highest pitch. It was his first experience in loving a woman — somewhat frightening to him. . . . He had found something beyond sensuality, he felt purified of a sense of guilt which he had always had as a homosexual."

But Crane's deliverance from homosexuality was apparently not a total one. He would frequently stray off to his old haunts, searching for and ultimately finding a male companion, preferably a young Indian. And Miss Porter occasionally saw him stumbling along the street, bleary-eyed and disheveled, or arguing with a cab driver outside his gate.

She moved to Europe that winter, traveling to Germany on the S.S. *Bremerhaven* (locus of *Ship of Fools*), but she received news of Hart's activities from Mary Doherty and other mutual friends.

On April 27 of the following year (1932) Hart Crane jumped overboard from the *Orizaba* when the ship was about 275 miles north of Havana. (He and Peggy Cowley were bound for New York.) He had been seen on deck clad in pajamas covered by a trench coat. Walking rapidly toward the stern, he tossed aside the coat, climbed on the rail, and jumped into the water. He was never seen again.

Miss Porter was living alone in a boarding house in Berlin when she heard about the tragedy. "Poor man," she later said to an interviewer. "What a terrible time we had with him. He was doomed, I think. His parasites let him commit suicide. He made such a good show and they had no lives of their own, so they lived vicariously by his, you know. And that of course is the unpardonable sin."

9

An Encounter with Hermann Göring

MISS PORTER'S last few months in Mexico were sad, frustrating and unproductive. She had sat hour after hour in her sunny patio, an empty notebook on her lap, listlessly staring at the plants and flowers along the north wall, vaguely aware of children chattering outside in the cobblestoned street, all sorts of half-formed ideas floating around in her mind like vagrant seeds in an errant wind. But none of them seemed to catch hold and germinate; they just kept floating around like the children's echoing voices outside, and her notebook remained empty.

After a while, Pressley, always quiet and apparently imperturbable, would come home from the Embassy and they would have a drink or two (sometimes more) with little or no conversation, finally sitting down to an equally silent dinner, only occasionally commenting on the delicious food Eufemia had prepared. His studied deference — which she came to regard as an oppressive kindness — inevitably made her feel guilty and resentful.

And the next day would be more of the same, one blank day after another, the numbing pattern broken only by the periodic mandatory entertainment of other Embassy people, when she would somehow call upon hidden reserves of "compulsive Southern hospitality," so that she could play the role of proper hostess for whatever time was necessary. But her grudging "niceness" was so apparent that Pressley eventually cut off all social obligation.

But this forced privacy was of no avail: she still couldn't make herself write — at least not fiction. Ironically, for the first time in her life she was free of economic stress, yet the creative urge was as dormant as ever. The Hart Crane debacle was certainly a factor, but she had to admit she'd been "immobilized" before he came to Mexico. Refusing to panic, however, she would occasionally perform what she chose to call "my finger exercises," presumably light inconsequential writing that would reaffirm her technical skills. One such piece was an essay titled "leaving the Petate," a charming, penetratingly accurate picture of Mexican housemaids, perhaps the best ever written on the subject by anyone — American or Mexican. It was an affectionate but unsparing analysis which offered further proof that no American (or any other foreigner) has written about Mexico or Mexicans with greater insight and sympathy.

First describing the *petate* as a woven straw mat that is used for sleeping by Mexican Indians, she went on to say that "there is a proverb full of vulgar contempt which used to be much quoted in Mexico: 'Whoever was born on a *petate* will always smell of the straw.' " And then she pointed out that the *petate* was no longer a symbol of social and racial degradation, that many 1920 revolutionists had insisted on smelling of straw, even though born on middle-class beds, because "it was the mark of a true revolutionary to acknowledge Indian blood" and to profess allegiance to all that was Indian. But, refusing to accept this romanticism, Miss Porter accurately observed that most of the Indians were anxious to leave their *petates* for the "delights of kinder living."

But there were different degrees of "leaving the *petate*," a continuous tug-of-war between strong cultural forces, which Miss Porter effectively summarized when conjecturing about Eufemia's future: "Her children will be added to the next generation of good little conservative right-minded dull people, like Enrique, or, with Eufemia's fighting spirit, they may become *mestizo* revolutionaries, and keep up the work of saving the Indian."

Apparently, "Leaving the Petate" remained unpublished until 1952 (twenty-one years after it was written), when Miss Porter included it in a collection of occasional writings called *The Days*

Before. There were, of course, many other manuscripts that never saw print, some of them having been discarded by her in periodic spurts of "housecleaning." She mentioned this in her journal during the aforementioned period of prolonged ennui in 1931. "My poem as I look at it this morning is not so good as I hoped. It began well and may end well, but there is a long way to go. Sometimes I have regretted destroying all that poetry I worked on for so many years, but now I believe I was right."

She might have been referring to a poem she was writing for Pressley, which she would later complete in Europe. Meanwhile, despite the sporadic lapses in their relationship, they had started to collaborate on the translation of a picaresque Mexican novel, *El periquillo sarniento* by J. J. Fernández de Lizardi. Pressley quickly wrote a literal translation of the text; but, in her continuing lassitude, Miss Porter couldn't bring herself to the less demanding task of polishing his draft. "It will have to wait," she kept telling him. "I am not up to it now."

Not surprisingly, she finally decided that a change of scenery was what she needed. Whether by coincidence or design, Pressley had been reassigned to the United States Embassy in Paris, but she opted for Germany instead, tentatively planning to join him later on. Pressley wanted her to go to France with him, fearing he would never see her again, but he knew it would be futile to argue against her sudden decision. "Well, I hope to see you in Paris," he said. "Don't stay away too long." Consequently, at the age of forty-one, still as restless as ever, she took a train for Vera Cruz, where she would board a ship to Bremerhaven.

Like most port towns, Vera Cruz was a squalid smelly place where unwary outward-bound travelers were easy prey for some of the local citizenry who were experts at extorting all types of *mordida* (petty bribes) for supposed violations of customs regulations. From the moment she checked into a downtown hotel a couple of days before sailing time, she was besieged by a horde of *coyotes* (fixers), who promised to get her through customs for just a few measly pesos, but she assured them — her command of Spanish obviously surprised them — that she anticipated no problems.

On the following morning she toured a few shops in the plaza, making last minute purchases of toilet articles for the long boat ride, and finally took a table on the terrace of the Hotel Palacio which gave her a wide-lens view of the entire square. Slowly sipping an acrid *limonada* made with an artificial extract, she could easily overhear several local businessmen commenting on the latest "birds of passage" waiting for the next boat. They were particularly insulting in their appraisal of the women passengers, with the *norteamericanas* getting special notice: "these painted middle-aged scarecrows ... that fat pale pig ... that skinny young freak with short hair and flat shoes ... the loud-mouthed blonde with the poodle. ..." She could have told these self-styled critics that some of the targeted women were French and German, but that would not have made their comments any less odious and they would have known she was listening to them even though her eyes were fixed straight ahead.

Later that afternoon, she made her first trip to the customs and immigration offices, walking through the crowded *mercado* (marketplace), where she was almost suffocated by the heavy smell of putrifying meat hanging on hooks and swarmed over with buzzing flies, half-rotted vegetables and fruits in adjacent stalls adding their special odor to the general stench. It was almost a relief to get to the relatively odorless Oficina de Inmigración y Aduana (Immigration and Customs). But there she came across a stench of a different sort, the ubiquitous stench of petty corruption. Her tightly packed steamer trunk would have to be opened and her belongings checked for possible contraband, a long tedious task that might take hours — but perhaps (and the message was so unmistakable as to border on farce) a way could be found to expedite matters ... and yet so many people had to be satisfied, señorita, each wanting his share of *mordida*.

She knew from long experience she would have to pay something, but she couldn't help wishing the process were not so blatantly obvious, that some standard of subtlety could be imposed. Yet she would probably have to pay less than those poor frightened travelers who spoke little or no Spanish. She had seen some of them in the waiting room, bleary-eyed and sweatily rumpled

from the long train ride, their hands nervously clutching pass-
ports, visas and other documents as they tried to understand the
rapid mumbling so characteristic of *veracruzanos*.

She offered to serve as interpreter for an elderly couple, who
gratefully accepted, but she smilingly declined their invitation to
dinner at the Hotel Palacio. She simply didn't want to get involved with any of her fellow passengers, hoping to spend most of
her time writing or reading. Consequently, when she boarded the
old German ship a day or so later, she carefully avoided extended
contacts with any other passengers. It was an extremely crowded
ship, particularly in the second-class section, where a vast swarm
of Cuban, Spanish and other European immigrants jammed every
available space. The upper deck, where she had a small cabin, was
occupied by mostly middle-class people of various nationalities,
religions and political beliefs, most of whom would eventually get
involved in all sorts of incidents. There were high drama and low
farce, a tangle of complex relationships that got more and more
confused as the ship slowly churned across the Atlantic, but Miss
Porter resolutely stayed aloof from all of them. "I don't think I
spoke a half-dozen words to anybody. I just sat there and
watched — not deliberately, though. I kept a diary in the form of
a letter to a friend, and after I got home the friend sent it back."
The trip took twenty-eight days, and by the time it docked at
Bremerhaven she had more than enough material for a good-sized
novel — but that novel would be a long time coming, almost
thirty-one years after the voyage that inspired it.

Shortly after her arrival at Bremerhaven, which offered little of
interest, she boarded a train to Berlin, where she took a room in a
small inexpensive hotel and immediately began searching for
more permanent lodging. Within a few days she found a room in
a small pension that belonged to a woman who soon let her know
that she had once been rich and had employed many servants.
Miss Porter's room was standard German, with heavy dark
drapes and carpets, massive furniture and useless knicknacks that
would have been called *cursi* in Mexico.

Her fellow lodgers were a mixed cast of generally dull men,
most of them German and dogmatic. Identifying one of them as

"R" in her journal, she said he was a malicious man who spoke harshly about everyone. And he gratuitously informed her that she could never know the higher realms of religious involvement, "because religious experience belongs exclusively to the masculine principle." Only slightly less dogmatic was the young poet she subsequently met, who sought to discourage her from reading Rilke's *Duino Elegies*, claiming that "he belongs to the old romantic softheaded Germany that has been our ruin." He asked her instead to consider the hard strong new Germany that was producing poets as tough as prizefighters, thereby offering his own poems as fit examples. But she felt his rhythms were gratingly harsh, "the ideas all the most grossly brutal; and yet it was vague weak stuff in the end."

Around December, a cold bleak month, she had several conversations with a couple of Germans (also identified by initials, "L" and "von G," in her journal) about Nietzsche, whom she had always resented. "When I think of Nietzsche and Wagner, at once by simple association I find charlatans of all kinds and degrees. . . . In Nietzsche's case, a real clinical madness: his diseased brain gave his style the brilliancy of a rotting fish." Indeed, she seemed to regard many Germans as oppressive and arrogant, and Berlin more depressing than she had ever imagined. The people struck her as gross and piglike as they muscled their way among the heavy stolid dark buildings. So she found herself spending more and more time in her airless, poorly lit room, trying not too successfully to write. But all she could do was to add a few finishing touches to a poem she had written for Pressley, titled "After a Long Journey," the first two stanzas of which alluded to a happier time of year:

This was never our season. We the spring-born, the May Children,
Put on winter like a hair shirt, we dwell on earth, we wait
For the turn of the year, the leap of the sun
Into the track of spring. Let us turn clasping mittened hands
Idly into the Puppen Allee of the Tiergarten.

This is not a timely season for our love —
Kisses freeze in our mouths, our arms enfold by habit

Talking columns of stone; yet we do not talk of love,
Our love, or say again, once more, once and forever
As if it were for the first time and the last time, a long farewell
  "I love you."

Aside from this poem, she wrote little else. But she was absorbing the total ambience of a Germany that was about to embark upon one of the most evil political developments in modern history, and she was to meet two of the foremost architects of that venture. When Miss Porter told me about this fateful meeting she did so in such an offhand way that I think it bears repeating.

As we were about to eat dinner one evening, Miss Porter mentioned the Nicaraguan poet Salomón de la Selva, instantly reminding me of our first conversation in Mexico.

"You told me about him last winter," I said, pouring the wine she had asked me to uncork. "I remember your saying that he was an evil man."

"Oh, absolutely," she said, her blue-gray eyes reflecting amber glints from the slender white candles on the dark table. "He was totally without scruple. Salomón was the man I wrote about in 'Virgin Violeta,' although I didn't use his real name. But you'll remember that he seduced — deliberately seduced — the teenage daughter of a close friend. So he was worse than immoral, Hank — he was absolutely amoral."

"You also told me — and let me quote your exact words as I remember them — that 'he was one of three such men that I've known, all of them totally evil and without scruple, but somehow they had an undeniable charm.' Or words to that effect."

"That's right," she said, carefully sprinkling wine vinegar on the oiled lettuce in a large wooden bowl. "They were all cut from the same cloth. The kind of men who have no scruple about anything, epecially in their relations with women. They couldn't care a lick who they hurt. But still they've got that damnable charm, that magnetism that draws people to them — even when those people know they're dealing with no-good rascals."

"So one of those three evil men you knew was Salomón de la Selva," I said, handing her the tall pepper grinder. "Now who

*were the other two? You started to tell me in Mexico City, but
someone interrupted our conversation just as you were about to
mention their names."*

*She paused and stared at the barely flickering candlelight, the
mixing fork and spoon poised over the half-marinated salad.
"Well, one of them was Prince Alexis Mdivani" — she stirred the
salad two beats, a slight frown wrinkling her brow — "and the
other one was Hermann Göring."*

*"Caray!" I exclaimed, lapsing into Spanish. "You actually
knew Göring?"*

*Her lips formed an ambiguous smile, as if she were inwardly
debating whether to tell me of her acquaintance with Göring.
"I've told only a few people about this," she said finally. "It's the
sort of thing that's easily misunderstood, because some people are
apt to make instant judgments before they've heard the whole
story."*

Her meeting with Hermann Göring had occurred in the winter
of 1932. Miss Porter was then living in Bambergerstrasse, in a
shabby middle-class section of Berlin, where she had finally
found a rather dismal room in a pension which belonged to a
down-at-the-heels Viennese widow. *The Leaning Tower* was
conceived in that depressing drape-heavy room; and as most everyone has surmised, Miss Porter was the young American artist
named Charles, whose deep and growing distaste for most Germans was but a reflection of her own attitude. "My instincts had
long before settled me against those people, and my notions about
them were not in the least altered by close-up observations of the
passengers on that ocean voyage from Vera Cruz to Bremerhaven, many of whom I've sketched in *Ship of Fools*. There were
exceptions, of course — an occasional good man like Dr. Shu-
mann — but so many of them had that heavy brutish quality
which my Mexican friends used to call *sangre pesada*: heavy
blood."

They resembled, as she later wrote in *The Leaning Tower*, the
most unkind caricatures of themselves, "but they were the very
kind of people that Holbein and Dürer and Urs Graf had drawn,
too: not vaguely, but positively like, their late-medieval faces full

of hallucinated malice and a kind of sluggish but intense cruelty that worked its way up from their depths slowly through the layers of helpless gluttonous fat."

It was her misfortune to see them again in the full fury of their twisted malice at a number of political rallies held by Adolf Hitler's fast-growing National Socialist German Workers party, later to be called the Nazi party. His brown-shirted *Sturmabteilung* seemed to be everywhere, and it was a chilling experience to hear their mad response to the awful venom and hatred that poured from the mouths of Hitler and Josef Goebbels.

Their ranting against the Jews was especially horrifying, and she remembered discussing their vile threats with some Jewish friends she had met during her first few days in Berlin. She used to see them frequently, on weekends mostly, when they would gather for informal musicales and long hours of intellectual talk. All of them played at least one musical instrument ("far better than I played the spinet"), and they would play even the most exacting pieces by Brahms, Mozart, Chopin or anyone else. The scope and depth of their conversation was equally impressive. They were, she felt, about the most civilized and perceptive group she had ever known. But for all their intelligence and aliveness, they were somehow blinded to the obvious dangers that faced them in the god-awful *Götterdämmerung* that Hitler was preparing for them.

"Please, Katherine Anne," they would tell her. "Please don't let all this nonsense depress you. It's only the passing madness of a few rabblerousers. The real Germany won't have it."

They simply refused to believe that Nazis were a serious threat, that their anti-Semitism was anything more than mere demagoguery. And, looking back upon her own experiences in Mexico with certain international rascals who called themselves "humanitarian revolutionaries" and who swore to change the face of Latin America (when in fact they were mere piddlers and do-nothings), she was sometimes tempted to hope that Hitler's gang would prove equally ineffectual. But on meeting Hermann Göring and Josef Goebbels, she quickly realized that the Nazis were hell-bent on the most malevolent venture in all history.

They met at a small dinner party at the home of the Berlin correspondent for the *Chicago Tribune*. "Her name was Sigrid Something-or-other (I simply can't recall her surname), whom I had probably met at one of the American Embassy affairs."

Since she was at that time a Guggenheim fellow, Miss Porter assumed that the cultural attaché felt obligated to invite her to one of his parties for visiting writers and artists, and Sigrid was probably there for the same reason. In any event, she subsequently invited Miss Porter to one of her meet-the-Nazis dinners. "I had been told she was pushing Hitler's gang and trying to introduce them to international correspondents, diplomats and writers. I was amused to learn that she generally invited only one other woman, obviously not wanting to divide the male attention into too many fractions."

Dorothy Thompson had been to one of those dinners, and it was she who told Miss Porter about Sigrid's customary man-woman ratio. Sigrid's mother, who did the cooking, was probably not reckoned in her calculations. The men, needless to say, were usually plentiful and interesting. On this particular evening the principal guests were to be Adolf Hitler, Josef Goebbels and Hermann Göring. "Having seen them at a distance, ranting in the glare of torchlights at various rallies around Berlin, I was morbidly anxious to see them at close range. Consequently, I was somewhat dismayed to note they had not yet appeared when I arrived at Sigrid's home, shortly after seven." There were, however, three or four Englishmen sitting around the fireplace, sipping their cocktails in that cool elegant way that always seemed so British to Miss Porter. In fact, everything about them — their clean-shaven faces, carefully groomed hair, well-tailored clothes and highly polished shoes — seemed to be the very essence of what was later to be called the 'Oxbridge look.' But what really caught her attention most was the high gloss on their beautiful shoes, all those wonderful fine leathers polished and repolished until they glistened like bright mirrors. "You simply can't beat the British when it comes to spit-and-polish; it's born in them, no doubt about it." Well, these particular Englishmen had another distinction aside from their fine shoes: they were all members of the House of Lords. "I believe one of them (and here I must confess that my memory may be tricking me) was Lord Halifax. That name always pops up in a most persistent way when I think back upon that evening, and yet I can't quite visualize the physical characteristics of any of those gentlemen — except their shoes."

Though she was unable to describe the Englishmen in exact detail, she apparently remembered their conversation quite clearly. They were conjecturing, along with their well-informed hostess, about the possibility of Hitler opposing Hindenburg for the presidency in the spring elections. Apparently Chancellor Heinrich Brüning had tried to persuade the Nazis to agree to an extension of Hindenburg's term as president, but Goebbels was advising Hitler to challenge the aging Hindenburg at the earliest opportunity. Sigrid was quite obviously in favor of an early confrontation, but her guests remained solemnly noncommittal. Having neither an official nor diplomatic position to worry about, Miss Porter frankly expressed her horror at the prospect of Hitler actually coming to power. "It was a frightening notion which became all the more frightening when I realized that truly important people were taking him seriously."

Taken aback by her views but nevertheless determined to be a gentle hostess, Sigrid assured Miss Porter that she would think differently once she had met and personally talked with Der Führer.

"Maybe she won't have that opportunity," her mother interjected. "I don't think those men are coming. Let's sit down to dinner."

Visibly annoyed with the old woman, Sigrid softly but firmly suggested they wait another fifteen minutes; but "Mama," a heavy-set woman who was the kind of old-fashioned *Hausfrau* that refuses to let a good meal spoil by overcooking, brushed her daughter aside and led the guests into the dining room. Having first designated three chairs for the tardy guests, she seated the rest of them in fairly random fashion. One of the empty chairs was to Miss Porter's right ("Herr Goebbels will sit there"), and beyond it sat the man she remembered as Lord Halifax. "We nodded tentatively and even attempted some chitchat about the heavy ornate silverware, but the three-foot chasm between us proved insurmountable." Halifax eventually turned his attention to Sigrid's mother, and Miss Porter soon found herself chatting about German *Lieder* singers with a very proper and attentive Lord seated on her left and with a colleague of his sitting directly across the narrow table. Obviously, neither they nor she cared a hoot about *Lieder* singers at that particular moment — what they really wanted to talk about was Hitler — "and yet we all seemed to be engaged in a sudden conspiracy to avoid that topic, like people in a cancer ward not wanting to talk about death."

Still hoping to delay dinner, Sigrid served another round of champagne cocktails, and Miss Porter couldn't help thinking what an awful shame it was to ruin such good champagne by dunking an orange peel into it and diluting it with whatever people use to make such drinks. Be that as it may, that extra round of cocktails seemed to lead them back to the topic which really concerned all of them: the Nazis. After her third sip Miss Porter rather bluntly asked the man at her left if the English were seriously thinking of accepting the Hitler crowd.

"He's nothing more than a common criminal," she said without waiting for a response. "That man — unless he's checked right now — will cause serious damage to this country and to all of Europe. You simply can't do business with him."

He listened with a faint smile that might well have been a restrained grimace. Then, with a slight glance at Lord Halifax, he told her that England had no intention of forming an alliance with Hitler, assuming of course that he might eventually replace Hindenburg. "We know what he's about, and we aren't much taken with what we see," he told her. "But I'll be frank to admit I sometimes wish we had a man like him in England to deal with our miners."

There was an edge of bitterness in Miss Porter's usually soft voice as she recalled his answer. "That, of course, is the attitude of many conservatives when they're about to cuddle up to an incipient dictator: 'We don't like all of him, mind you, but we could sure use a firm hand to take care of so-and-so.' It always starts that way: first of all, it's a *firm hand* that's needed, then a *strong arm*, followed by a *strong man*, and finally you get a full-fledged tyrant."

She didn't remember whether she in fact expressed such misgivings that evening ("though I must have surely felt them") but she did recall a certain coolness in His Lordship's manner when Mama finally began serving a delicious potato-leek soup. The main course was sauerbraten, the best she had ever tasted and a welcome change from the drab food she customarily ate at the pension.

They were about to have after-dinner coffee when the doorbell rang. Sigrid was at the door almost instantly, the worried look in her eyes now vanished. There were mumbled greetings near the door, which was out of Miss Porter's range of vision, and then she reappeared with two guests at her side — Josef Goebbels and Hermann Göring. Hitler, she explained, had gone home with a sore throat, having severely strained his voice at an outdoor political rally. Everyone expressed the appropriate regrets as Mama quickly seated them and brought on their soup. With a curt nod to those nearest him, Goebbels slid into the chair on Miss Porter's right and immediately picked up his soupspoon, holding it in the air even before the bowl was placed in front of him. He looked like a hungry emaciated rat, his eyes set in deep hollows, his thin cheeks pulled in as if he were perpetually sucking a sour lemon. Göring, on the other hand, seemed over-fed and complacent, but he had a tight trap mouth and flat features that accentuated the blue-gray coldness of his eyes.

"How distinctly I remember them," Miss Porter told me, tapping her fingers on the stem of her wineglass. "They sat there in a lean-forward crouch, right elbows resting heavily on the table, their heads leaning against a cradled hand, while they shoveled the food into their gluttonous mouths with the most solemn concentration. Göring sat across from me, and I particularly noticed the sweaty roll of fat that bulged over his tight shirt collar. He had that piggish look I've described in *The Leaning Tower*, the passage where Charles is watching a group of middle-aged men and women who were gathered in silence before two adjoining windows, gazing at displays of toy pigs and sugar pigs. Göring was certainly a prototype of that swinish quality, especially while he was gobbling down the wonderful food Sigrid's mother had prepared."

They had been accompanied by two uniformed escorts, tall strapping young men with clear blue eyes, fine blond hair and the cleanly chiseled features that Hitler erroneously considered typically Aryan. "Well, if 'typical' means what I think it means (though the Lord knows I've never liked that kind of loose word), then those paragons of masculine beauty were certainly the least typical Germans I had ever seen."

Except for Sigrid, the rest of the guests were not aware of their presence until they moved back to the living room. They had been standing guard at the front door, probably as starved as their two superiors, but apparently no one felt the slightest concern for them. Both Goebbels and Göring had cleaned every morsel from their plate, never once pausing in their dead-earnest eating to participate in the somewhat strained conversation that crisscrossed over their heads. However, once they had finished their sauerbraten and swallowed half their coffee, both of them got quite chatty and even friendly. They apologized again for being late and begged everyone to forgive Der Führer for not joining them.

"He sometimes works too hard," Goebbels told them. "His passion for the Fatherland leads him to excessive efforts. Lately everyone wants to hear him speak — thousands come to our rallies — and finally his throat can't stand the strain anymore. He has to rest."

Göring nodded his head in complete agreement. "*Ja, ja* — he has a great passion for the Fatherland."

They were still talking about Hitler's passionate concern for a greater Germany when the guests drifted back to the living room for an after-dinner schnapps. The four Englishmen soon surrounded Goebbels at the far side of the room, and Katherine Anne found herself suddenly alone with Herr Göring on the couch near the fireplace. Now at last, she said to herself with a slight constriction in her stomach, now at last she had a chance to express her horror of fascism to a high-ranking official of the Nazi party. Here was the Number Two man sitting next to her, his ears within easy range of her voice. Then, just as she was about to unleash a few long-pent-up furies, Sigrid moved in from behind them and perched herself on the other end of the couch. Miss Porter's first impression was that she had somehow sensed an impending verbal storm and was determined to ward it off with a barrage of chitchatty nonsense.

But no — she wasn't the least bit interested in peaceful talk. Breaking in with all the aplomb of an assured hostess, she renewed an argument she had apparently initiated with Göring during dinner. (Her high sweet voice, incidentally, was beginning to develop a certain shrillness.) Though Miss Porter had only heard snatches of their brief conversation, she realized Sigrid was challenging his rather old-fashioned notions about women, especially those females who worked for a living. She didn't know whether Göring had said anything earlier to indicate his low opinion of career women, but his views on that subject were fairly well known. Certainly Sigrid was aware of them.

"And now that Herr Göring was sandwiched between us and isolated from his male allies, she probably felt we could both charm him into a more lenient attitude." But Sigrid wasn't relying on charm alone — she had loaded herself with all kinds of statistical ammunition concerning female progress in every vocation. Like any well-prepared advocate, she could instantly spout the names of fifty or a hundred outstanding women scientists, educators, doctors, lawyers and what-have-you. Miss Porter's name was tossed into the latter category. "We're practically human," she kept saying with an embarrassing excess of sarcasm. "Why are you men so afraid to admit that we're as human as you are?"

Herr Göring, who had apparently decided to fall back upon that ancient but often murderous tactic of amused silence, parried each of her increasingly nasty thrusts with a sly smile that infuriated her all the more. Then she began to demean her originally sound arguments with insinuating antimale remarks that caused Katherine Anne to lose sympathy for her.

"Why, I remember asking myself, why do some career women

find it necessary to castrate all men in order to prove their equality?"

And she was wondering how long Göring would sit and listen to her, when quite suddenly he turned and gave Sigrid a withering stare. "Oh, don't talk to me anymore about that kind of woman," he snapped. "The only kind of woman who's important is a *geheiratete Frau*, a married woman."

In other words, to hell with you, career woman! Sigrid, not quite believing what she had heard, stared back at him with her mouth slightly agape — then she blazed off in an awful fury. Whether by design or pure chance, Göring had apparently stabbed her most vulnerable spot. Although she was approaching forty, Sigrid had never been married and her admittedly handsome face was just beginning to develop the drawn and desperate look which one frequently associates with women who have stayed single too long. Since Miss Porter had been married twice by then, his remark meant nothing to her.

With a deep frown clouding his eyes, Göring twisted and squeezed the small knob of his walking stick, whitening the knuckles of his blunt hairy fingers. "That's the Jewish influence for you," he muttered to Miss Porter. "The damned Jews are too permissive with their women. She could be a decent *Hausfrau* if those Jews in America hadn't poisoned her mind with all this nonsense about liberated women."*

"You blame them for everything," said Miss Porter, forcing herself to be calm. "I'm beginning to think your hatred for Jews is a kind of national sickness."

"There is a sickness," he answered. "But not the kind you think. Our sickness comes from the Jew blood that has infected Germany. And we're going to cleanse our old German bloodstream of this dirty poison that has seeped into it. We're going to purify the race by getting rid of them all." Then in the most exacting and sickening detail, he started telling her about some of

---

* Though her parents were German, Sigrid had been reared and educated in Illinois, returning to Germany after her father's death.

the methods the Nazis were devising to "solve the Jewish problem."

Almost instantly her ears turned him off, his words becoming a
mere jumble of meaningless vowels. But she couldn't blot out,
nor even slightly blur, his face — that flat expressionless mask
utterly devoid of any humanizing passion. Had he sneered or
shown any other sign of outright malice, she would have felt less
horror. Yet she was determined to avoid the trap of feminine
hysteria, for nothing was to be gained by mere outrage, certainly
not with this man. So she leaned back and waited for an opening,
meanwhile studying the mechanical movement of his mouth as it
spewed forth the all-too-familiar venom about Jews, American
degeneracy, inferior races, communist conspiracies and whatnot.
After a while it would sound like a broken record, and she
vaguely hoped the German people would finally be numbed into
inertia by this heavy monotonous hatred. ("What a naïve hope
that was.") Eventually Göring paused for a long interval, as if to
flip over his record or rewind the machine, and she rather quixoti-
cally decided to challenge his arguments with cool reason.

"You'll not succeed," she said. "You will fail miserably in the
end. Not only are your goals totally immoral and against every
standard of human decency — but you are also ignoring history.
Remember what happened to Spain when it expelled the Jews,
and look at what happened to England in the twelfth and thirteenth centuries when it decided to mistreat them. If you'll read
your history carefully, Herr Göring, you'll soon realize that —
aside from the moral implications — it isn't good luck to abuse
the Jews. Theirs is a long tradition of survival."

He was leaning forward and staring at the fireplace while she
was talking, both hands idly fingering his walking stick as if it
were a flute. But his face, except for an ever-so-slight tightening
of the lips, remained impassive as ever. Not knowing whether he
was really listening or merely lost in his own musings, she resumed her monologue.

"But what bothers me most is your strange notion that the
Jews have poisoned this country. I simply can't accept your reasoning. As a matter of fact, they help build up every country they

ever live in. Having no country of their own, they've devoted all their creative energies to building up other countries, and Germany is no exception."

She was about to cite a few examples of scientific and cultural contributions by German Jews when Göring suddenly interrupted her with a light touch on the wrist. "That's the trouble with you Americans," he said. "You're all so sentimental: that may be your fatal weakness. You will never understand the Jews the way we do in this country. But we are determined to rule the world and we can't do it without first ridding ourselves of these people. Only the pure Aryans can do the job that's needed."

She finally realized it was futile to discuss the matter any further, that it wouldn't do any good to argue with this man. She had always felt that anti-Semitism is so deeply ingrained in some people that nothing will uproot it.

Sitting there next to that cozy fireplace on a cold February night in 1932, listening to Göring and occasionally glancing at those polite Englishmen huddled around Goebbels, she simply could never have imagined even one percent of the horror that was to follow. Somehow Göring's boast — "We are going to change the course of history for the next thousand years" — struck her as thoroughly ludicrous. Having spent several years in Mexico, she had heard fifth-rate politicians brag the same way and was never impressed. And as she listened to Göring's plans for "the great Fatherland," she felt the same disdain for him as she felt for the man she named Braggioni in "Flowering Judas." There was a certain demented quality to his thinking, and she remembered fleetingly that he had once been (perhaps still was) addicted to drugs. Later she learned that he had apparently been cured of his addiction at the Langbro Asylum, somewhere in Sweden, where he had once worked for an aircraft company. His wife, Carin von Kantzow, had been one of the famous beauties of Sweden. But sometime after their marriage she became an epileptic invalid and was confined to a Swedish sanitarium, where she eventually died in 1931.

When he told Miss Porter about his wife that evening his cold expressionless eyes suddenly softened with deep-felt emotion, his voice becoming a shade huskier. He had obviously been quite fond of her, and she was sure he meant every word when he said he had not had a single happy day since her death six months before. "It seemed so strange, in the light of our previous conversation, to hear him talk with such tender affection. But there was no soft mushiness in what he said, no false sentimentality. It was a manly kind of sorrow, unashamed but controlled, and I must frankly confess it touched me."

She particularly remembered that he had a firm resonant voice — no wavering, no hesitation — giving her the impression that he always knew what he wanted — and how to get it.

Later, as he was reminiscing about their early-marriage years in Munich (where he attended the university on a haphazard basis), he abruptly switched the topic of conversation. "And how about you?" he asked. "Are you married?"

Now that was a rather difficult question to answer because, although she considered herself married to Eugene Pressley, they had not formalized the union. So she simply said, "Yes — but my husband is in Paris."

Then with a most candid look in his eyes, he bluntly asked her if she was happy in her marriage. Well, that kind of question always unsettled her in those days (Can we ever say an absolute *yes* or *no* when we're talking about marriage or any other relationship between a man and woman?), and yet she usually found herself nodding in the affirmative or mumbling something like "Yes, of course." That's probably what she said that night, though she really couldn't remember.

However, she distinctly recalled that during this rather awkward turn in their tête-à-tête she felt a sudden chill through her entire body. Here I go again, she said to herself, another siege of pneumonia! She'd had it so often in so many different places, sometimes without a moment's warning, that even the slightest chill could alarm her. Her face must have shown considerable distress because he immediately leaned forward and placed his hand on her shoulder. "Is something wrong?" he asked.

"I'm not sure," she said. "But I really must go. It's getting rather late."

Without a moment's hesitation, he offered to drive her home. Indeed, it was more of a command than an offer, and all her feminine protestations were shushed aside with such cool assurance that they sounded foolish even to her. "He wasn't one of those weak and flabby men, who are so easily manipulated by women and easy to say 'no' to," she told me, pausing a moment. "There was, instead, a strange forceful confidence in his manner, that subtle evil charm that is somehow strengthened by a lack of human commitment, because it's never sidetracked by the ambivalence of moral compunction. Some people call it sex appeal, but I think that's a shallow way of putting it."

While he was getting their coats, Miss Porter walked across the room to thank Sigrid and her mother (Goebbels and the Englishmen were so deeply engrossed in their conversation she had decided not to disturb them), and they both accompanied her to the door, expressing the usual regrets. Oddly enough, she felt completely well again — no trace of a chill. Herr Göring warmly thanked them for a pleasant evening as he helped her with her heavy coat and asked them to relay his good wishes to "those four good gentlemen from England who seem to be caught in Herr Goebbel's web."

Turning to her with a bemused, rather impish smile, he said, "That man is magic with words." Since Goebbels had not spoken more than ten words to her during the entire evening, she was in no position to dispute his judgment. "My apparent function insofar as Sigrid was concerned was to distract Herr Göring with small talk while the other guests were engaged in more serious conversation with Goebbels. But I'm sure our conversation, rambling as it was, proved to be more interesting than theirs, because Göring was probably playing it straight with me."

He was in the kind of candid relaxed mood which comes on when a man is tired and having a few drinks after a good meal. As a woman, she was no threat to him, and he apparently felt no need to be on guard. His eyes were drowsy but a shade pixieish (could it be that he was on drugs again?) and his speech was soft and slow, creating an easy flow of language, the kind of talk she would never expect from a sober fox-wary politician.

At one point he said, "I understand you're a very famous writer."

"Well, no," she said. "I couldn't possibly say that. I've just written a little book with three stories. Nothing more."

"Will you write anything about us?"

To which she flatly replied, "No — not a single word."

"*Gott sei Dank!*" he said. (Thank God!)

When they got outside, a long sleek chauffeur-driven limousine pulled up to the front curb. It was one of those fancy cars which Edmund Wilson once described as the kind a gangster's widow rides in to the funeral. One of the aforementioned bodyguards had preceded them and was now opening the rear door of the limousine, then snapping to attention beside it. Göring motioned Miss Porter into the commodious rear seat and asked her to scoot over to the far side. Then he slid into the middle and ordered the guard to sit on his right side. What a strange seating arrangement, she thought to herself; he was apparently determined to keep her well away from his handsome military aide.

They were just getting settled when Göring ever-so-casually put his left arm around her shoulder and said, "Why don't we stop by my favorite beer garden for a little drink?"

She stiffened a bit and remained deadly quiet. Never moved an eyelash. "In fact, I just went dead as a mackerel and stayed that way for quite a spell." After several awkward minutes (perhaps only a few seconds, though it seemed longer) he abruptly took his arm away and pretended to blow his nose, turning slightly away from her. It was a rather schoolboyish ploy but probably served his purpose. Then, having regained his composure, he repeated his invitation. "Just a short while," he said. "You don't really have to go home right away, do you?"

"Oh, yes, I must — I really must." Her voice less positive than her words.

"But couldn't I persuade you to visit this place I know — for just one drink and maybe a little dance?"

There was an appealing persistence in his voice, aided and abetted by still another voice inside her which was saying, *Why, hell yes — why not? — it might be interesting.* "Now I don't claim I'm *naturally* discreet, but discretion was so thrashed into me when I was a child that it sometimes seemed completely inborn. It was all based on the notion that young girls have to stay away from men (especially strangers) in every sense of the word. Thus, when you were dancing you had to keep your elbow crooked at a right angle and firmly positioned so as to force a wide space between you and your partner, the way Mrs. Treadwell had been instructed to do in *Ship of Fools*. But we only did it mentally, you know: that genteel elbow was purely symbolic. Well, that night I simply disregarded all my Southern upbringing — uncrooked my elbow, as it were — and accepted Herr Göring's invitation."

Ten minutes later they pulled into a parking lot next to a beer garden called Otto's Hofbräuhaus. Even before they reached the side entrance she could hear the dull steady *oompa-oompa* of a bass horn. But as the door swung open the strident guttural voices of the high-spirited crowd seemed to drown out the horn and three other instruments played by four solemn bullnecked musicians tightly squeezed together on a small bandstand near the bar. About two hundred customers were jammed into booths along the walls or more comfortably seated at checkered-clothed tables clustered around the dime-sized dance floor. Göring's aide immediately and most efficiently got them a table opposite the bandstand, then quietly stationed himself several feet away, rigid and attentive as ever. He would have looked completely and properly military had he not been standing next to an arched trellis skimpily decorated with faded crepe-paper vines. Those rickety trellises seemed to be the sine qua non of restaurant decor all over Germany, and that loud bumptious music was equally pervasive. Miss Porter supposed it was meant to be cheerful music, but it was rendered with such fierce determination that the hoped-for cheerfulness came out as mere frenzy, a curiously solemn frenzy. In fact, most of the people dancing to Otto's four-piece band moved around the floor with the same intense fervor, their heavy feet clomping on the floor as if they were hammering invisible nails. How different they were from her carefree feather-light Mexican friends, who could always manage to have a good time without working at it: pleasure was such a hard chore for these Germans!

Sipping from a heavy stein of beer which she had to lift with both hands, she watched a particularly clumsy man whirling his buxom partner past their table and vaguely wondered if Herr Göring would dance as clumsily. Well, she didn't have to wait long to find out. On the very next number he led her to the floor and completely surprised her. In spite of his hefty bearlike physique, he moved around with graceful ease, only occasionally bouncing when the bass horn's *oompa* got too emphatic. And he was probably the only man there who didn't pump his left arm.

When they returned to their table, two couples in a nearby booth turned and pantomimed an applause for Göring. At first she thought they were teasingly congratulating him on his dancing skill, then quickly realized they were fellow Nazis merely acknowledging his presence. Several times thereafter they would smile in his direction and lift their foamy steins to toast the Fatherland. They seemed so jolly and sociable, so full of drunken good cheer, that she found it difficult to imagine they were actually bent on persecuting their Jewish neighbors, thousands of men, women and children who had done them no harm. And there was Göring, big and friendly as a corner grocer, telling her about the beautiful house he had built as a sort of monument for his dead wife. Less than a decade later she would learn that some of these cheerful sentimental Germans were indeed capable of spending a pleasant evening at home — perhaps playing nice family games with their children — then, after a good night's sleep, getting up in the morning and hustling off to stoke the furnaces at Dachau.

Perhaps a dim premonition of that horror sent another cold chill through her, so she abruptly told Göring she would have to leave. The long ride to Bambergerstrasse was rather quiet. In her confused and weary state, she was in no mood for even perfunctory conversation, and he probably sensed it. However, as they drew near her pension he said, "I'll see you tomorrow for dinner." Not a suggestion, mind you, but a flat statement.

"That won't be possible," she said. "I'm leaving Berlin fairly soon and won't have time to see you again." Paying no heed to what she had said, he informed her that he would come by at five P.M. "Since I had no intention of ever seeing him again, I just let him prattle on to his heart's content. One would think my cool demeanor would have put him off, but not at all." As she turned to thank him (they were now at her front door, which she had partially opened), he bent over intending to kiss her. And when she twisted her head away his lips brushed her left ear. He was still standing in an awkward position, arms half-extended, when she slipped inside the door and turned the latch.

She spent the following afternoon at a farewell party given for her by Naomi and Peter Schecter, the most active members of the informal musical group she mentioned earlier. They were all so kind, so full of good advice and genuine concern about her writing career, she hesitated to tell them how worried she was about *them*. Finally — no longer able to hold her tongue — she frankly urged them to leave Germany, to get out before Hitler should come to power and thereafter launch his campaign against the Jews. They all sat there patiently listening to her like children receiving advice from an old-fashioned aunt, politely attentive but not in the least impressed.

"Dear Katherine Anne, you're sweet to worry about us — but please don't let Herr Hitler distress you too much. He won't get out of hand."

It wasn't mere bravado that prompted such remarks — they actually believed they were safe. They seemed completely secure when she left their home that evening. Behind her, as the door softly closed, she heard them resume a rather lively quartet by Mozart.

Shortly before midnight she got home and found a note from the landlady pinned to her pillow: "Herr Göring was here at five o'clock and waited until six. He was quite annoyed."

When I asked Miss Porter if she still had the note, she told me she had carried it around in one of her notebooks for many years but had apparently lost it while living in Hollywood.

10

A Second Book and a Second Husband

I N the spring of 1932, after living less than eight months in the gloomy environs of Berlin, she suddenly decided to move again and took a slow meandering train ride to Basel, Switzerland, a lovely city on the eastern bank of the Rhine.

Her constant "moving about" had become an established pattern which would persist for the rest of her life, the eternal pilgrimage of a restless soul. In a span of fifty years (from 1910 to 1960) she would eventually move from one domicile to another at least fifty times, occasionally two or three times in a single year. Increasingly disturbed by her restlessness, her family and friends would urge her to settle down, to find a permanent home somewhere. "I will," she would tell them, "just as soon as I find the right place and the right people."

Many psychologists would attribute her restlessness to a neurotic inability to make a firm commitment to either people or places, and they would undoubtedly reach back to her childhood to find the cause or causes for this lifelong neurosis. In his monumental study, *Childhood and Society*, Erik Erikson stresses the need for a child to develop a "basic trust" in people, particularly in his or her mother.

"The infant's first social achievement," he declares, "is his willingness to let the mother out of sight without undue anxiety or rage, because she has become an inner certainty as well as an outer predictability. Such consistency, continuity, and sameness of experience provide a rudimentary sense of ego identity which depends, I think, on a recognition that there is an inner population of remembered and anticipated sensations and images which are firmly correlated with the outer population of familiar and predictable things and people."

In Miss Porter's case, that protective mother never existed. She died before her infant daughter could know her or develop any sense of her being, died as a result of complications from the infant's birth — which in itself provoked a guilt that would plague Miss Porter the rest of her life. And when young Katherine Anne tried to create an image of her mother — asking her brothers and sister what she looked like, what she wore, and how she talked — her father would refuse to let anyone talk about her.

Fortunately, her grandmother moved into the household and provided some degree of stability and affection, even though she was often too strict and demanding. (She was also cared for intermittently by a black "nanny," so that there was no single and constant person tending her.) One cannot be sure if the grandmother was indeed able to create a "basic trust" in her youngest granddaughter — but if she did, that trust was probably shattered when the grandmother herself died while Katherine Anne was still a child. Thus twice "abandoned," by her mother and grandmother, before she was seven years of age, she probably developed an early mistrust of close personal attachments for fear of being abandoned again.

Consequently, she was never able to achieve what Erikson calls "a readiness for intimacy," the capacity to commit oneself to concrete affiliations and partnerships and to develop the strength to abide by such commitments, even though they may call for significant sacrifices and compromises.

"The counterpart of intimacy is distantiation," according to Erikson, "the readiness to isolate those forces and people whose essence seems dangerous to one's own, and whose territory seems to encroach on the extent of one's intimate relations." Thus, by constantly moving about, Miss Porter made it difficult (if not impossible) for anyone to invade her psychic terrain.

Painfully aware of this inability to find permanent roots, she

With her father in San Marcos, Texas, June, 1937,
just after his eightieth birthday

promised herself to "stay put" when she got to Basel. She would find a house — not just a room — where she could feel free from the kind of intrusion she had to suffer from her fellow lodgers in "that awful *pension*." Fortunately, she was able to find (at a reasonably low rental) an elongated, steep-roofed cottage which had been built in 1390.

But even with this much-hoped-for solitude, she found it difficult to produce anything worth publishing. Her enormous notebooks were gradually filled with a neatly scribbled accretion of random current observations and fleeting memories from childhood, from long confinements in various hospitals, from happier days in Mexico — acute but isolated memories from every place she had lived in during her lonely never-ending pilgrimage. Now and then, as she strolled along the river in idle contemplation, some long-forgotten incident would suddenly jell in her mind and would expand into a possible motif for a story, but most of the time such ideas would remain mere notations in her thick notebook.

"If I didn't know the ending of a story, I wouldn't begin," she once told an interviewer. "I always write my last lines, my last paragraph, my last page first, and then I go back and work towards it."

Apparently those crucial last lines kept evading her, and the resulting frustration inevitably gave rise to feelings of guilt. Not only was she failing herself as an artist, she was also failing as a grantee of the Guggenheim Foundation. They had given her a stipend to write fiction, and she had not written a single short story. So one evening she sat down and wrote a letter "full of contrition" to Henry Allen Moe, the foundation's executive director, confessing she had not turned out the book she hoped to write that year.

Well aware of so-called "writer's block" in even the most gifted people, he immediately wrote her a most comforting letter, saying that no one expected her to write on a fixed schedule, that she had been given a general grant to help sustain her life's work.

Thus, partly relieved of guilt, she temporarily set aside her own work and buried herself in the previously abandoned translation of Lizardi's *El periquillo sarniento,* a picaresque novel first published in 1830 and thereafter republished many times for millions of readers in Mexico, Spain and South America. Starting with Pressley's first draft, she eventually produced a final version of "four big fat typewritten volumes," including a map of Mexico City *circa* 1770, several illustrations from the 1884 edition, and a tintype portrait of Lizardi. But, as things turned out, it was mostly a labor of love — and not much appreciated. During the next ten years, no fewer than fourteen publishers would reject it. When finally published as *The Itching Parrot* by Doubleday & Company in 1942 (one must assume they were heavily influenced by the fact that it was translated by the now quite prominent Katherine Anne Porter), it aroused very little interest despite her long explanatory preface. As she later explained in an over defensive answer to a harsh critique,* the novel had been drastically cut by the editors, and she had reluctantly agreed because she knew there was absolutely no prospect of getting the full text published.

Although it was an excellent translation, certainly more artistic than the original, her friends and colleagues quite reasonably wondered why she had expended so much time and energy on secondary work. One plausible explanation was that she felt obligated to Pressley, whom she had persuaded to do the initial draft. On the other hand, she unconsciously might have been creating an excuse to avoid her own work. Her on-and-off study of the life of Erasmus and the Reformation possibly served the same function.

Nevertheless, she did manage to jot down an occasional note that could conceivably germinate into something more substantial. One such notation appeared in her journal that summer:

> Remember: The serious, bitterly humiliated little boy, about three years old, on the dusty country train in Central Texas, with a tin chamber pot wedged on his head; over his ears. . . .

---

* "Miss Porter Adds a Comment," *The Nation,* March 6, 1943.

With that eye-catching introduction, she further recalled the shamed and forlorn expression on the boy's not-wholly-hidden face as the other passengers gawked at him and asked his worried mother how it happened. Anxious to explain, she had told everyone that the boy had been bored and restless. He wouldn't play in the yard and wouldn't keep quiet inside the house, so she had finally given him his potty to play with, assuming it to be harmless. And the next thing she knew it was wedged down over his skull "tight as wax." She had tried everything to dislodge it — soap, sweet oil and even a can opener — and had finally decided it would be safer to let a doctor handle it. Remembering the child's distress, Miss Porter noted that "he gazed past her and the surrounding strangers with the solemn awful humiliation of one whose predicament is beyond pity, and so should never have been exposed to curious eyes."

A subsequent entry in her journal (November 1932) announced that she had "worked this afternoon on some notes for Noon Wine," but said nothing more about the story. It was actually a brief comment on the problems of a timid shabby painter who had been slowly painting the same scene from a certain spot on the Rheinbrücke bridge, changing the colors on his picture as the seasons progressed from spring to summer to autumn. Then one morning, a fat bald beggar with a barrel organ had deliberately stood in the painter's way, blocking his view and even jogging the artist's arm each time he cranked the organ. "I decided, then, the beggar should never have another pfennig from me," Miss Porter wrote, "even if he loses a hundred pounds from starvation."

Like so many entries in her voluminous notebooks, neither of these provocative incidents was ever used in her stories. In fact, there was nothing in her subsequent writing that would indicate that she had ever lived in Switzerland. She herself later said that Basel had merely provided a sort of vantage point from which she could look back at her "usable past," and where she could find enough isolation to permit her a few clear perspectives regarding herself, for there were certain personal problems she had left hanging in limbo: Should she resume her informal liaison with Pressley? Or should she marry him and settle down to the presumably secure and probably dull, circumscribed life of an embassy wife? Or should she terminate the relationship and go back to the States, where she would have to find a job teaching at some college or doing the kind of hackwork magazine editors would pay for? At the age of forty-two, she was increasingly aware of the need for a firm economic base. But aside from such security, Pressley would provide emotional stability, being there when she needed support, yet giving her the privacy she would sorely need.

It was this consideration (among others) that eventually led her to Paris, where she married Pressley in March 1933. Ford Madox Ford, an old friend and one of her favorite writers, served as best man at a simple ceremony attended by very few friends. "Since we had already lived together, there was no need for the traditional white-lace wedding gown and all the other folderol." Yet there was a tinge of regret, an undeniable wistfulness, when she momentarily recalled her grandmother's elegant satin brocade wedding gown and the crystal chandelier holding fifty white candles that gleamed over a huge table laden with the richest foods one could possibly imagine.

But her marriage to Pressley had other compensations. First of all, they would be living in Paris, still the center of literary and artistic ferment. And at the very core of that ferment was Sylvia Beach, who managed the famous bookshop known as Shakespeare and Company, located at 12 rue de l'Odéon. Like most English and American expatriate writers and painters, Miss Porter became an habitué of Miss Beach's store and occasionally visited her flat immediately above the shop. There she would meet rare conglomerations of people whom she was "surprised to find on the same planet together, much less under the same roof." Some would be lounging on the bare floor, leaning against one of the packed bookcases that lined every wall. Others would crowd into Miss Beach's kitchen for long intense discussions of this or that new book, unaware of the silk stockings and underwear drying near the window or perhaps charmed by such insouciance. Meanwhile Miss Beach and some favored guest would be sitting and gossiping on her narrow bed, which was usually covered by a tiger skin. "If it was not a tiger," Miss Porter later surmised, "then some large savage cat with good markings; real fur."

Small-boned, thin, quick-moving and quick-minded, with chestnut brown hair and greenish brown eyes, Miss Beach was the daughter of a staid Baltimore preacher, and she had decided early in life to get out of that dull gloomy town and the farther the better. She was, in Miss Porter's estimate, "a wild free spirit if ever I saw one, fearless, untamed to the last, which is not the same as being reckless or prodigal, or wicked, or suicidal." She was also irrepressibly persistent when she set her mind on some particular project; and the major all-consuming project of her life was the publication of James Joyce's *Ulysses*. She had literally prodded him to get the book written, then arranged for the printing and partial distribution, meanwhile supporting the half-blind author and his family under the most trying circumstances.

Still, she had time and energy for her perpetual self-assigned task of bringing together writers and painters of diverse talents and personal idiosyncrasies. She had a genius for friendship and depths of sympathy that could reassure anyone who came within her ambit. Even the distrustful and pathologically wary Ernest Hemingway let down his guard when he met Miss Beach, so that an hour after meeting her, he had taken off his sock and shoe to show her the still-painful war wounds he had suffered in Italy. Later on, he would help her distribute *Ulysses* by bootlegging numerous copies into the United States, and he would always touch bases with her whenever he came back to Paris.

Indeed, it was in Miss Beach's shop that Miss Porter saw Hemingway for the first and last time. She had dropped into the bookstore on a cold, rainy evening, looking for something to read. And just before leaving she paused to chat with Sylvia near a big round table piled high with books when suddenly the door burst open and Hemingway came into the room, wearing his familiar old trenchcoat and wet floppy hat. He was every inch the "dark-haired, sunburned muscle boy of American literature," and watchful as a panther.

Greeting him with schoolgirlish excitement, Miss Beach ran toward the door and they hugged each other with great affection. Then, still holding his left hand, she reached out for Miss Porter's hands as she introduced them, very deliberately pronouncing their full names: "Katherine Anne Porter, this is Ernest Hemingway. . . . Ernest, this is Katherine Anne, and I want the two best modern American writers to know each other!"

Realizing he probably had never heard her name, much less read her meager collection of stories (printed in a limited edition of only six hundred copies), Miss Porter cringed at the pretentious though well-intentioned introduction. To make matters worse, the phone rang in the back room at that very instant, and Sylvia ran off to answer it, cheerfully commanding them to get acquainted, "and I'll be right back."

But Hemingway and Miss Porter just stood there, staring at each other with unblinking eyes for about ten seconds, neither saying a single word. Then, turning suddenly in an awkward swinging motion, he dashed out of the shop into the cold wet night. (Some thirty-one years later, she recalled the incident in an article for the *Ladies Home Journal,* ruefully observing that "it must have been galling to this famous young man to have his name pronounced in the same breath as a writer with someone he had never heard of, and a woman at that. I nearly felt sorry for him.")

There were, of course, more pleasant occasions at Miss Beach's Shakespeare and Company bookstore. She particularly enjoyed the evening on which T. S. Eliot read some of his early poems ("Gerontion," two parts of "The Wasteland," and parts of his recently finished "Ash Wednesday"), but she was surprised to see how different he looked from the frequently published photograph that showed him as a young Harvard undergraduate, with hair slicked down and a fairly benign expression on his face. As he read in a brittle nasal voice, his face was "as severe as Dante's, the eyes fiercely defensive, the mouth bitter, the nose grander and much higher bridged than his photographs then showed." Seemingly unaware of the small group around him, his thin bony fingers clasping the book he was reading, he reminded her of a bird of prey.*

Sitting near him was James Joyce, slouched in his chair and totally motionless throughout the prolonged reading. From her vantage point less than ten feet away, Miss Porter could see that his eyes (always concealed by dark glasses) were closed most of the time, yet he seemed extremely attentive, his fine handsome head bowed slightly so that his beard nuzzled his chest. Every now and then, she would notice a sudden tightness around his mouth as if he were suffering sharp pain, and Miss Beach later explained that his teeth were severely diseased and were, in fact, the principal cause of his half-blindness. Small wonder that he was so difficult to deal with. Yet he was surrounded by a covey of "faithful friends," some of whom became jealous of each other in their petty struggle to be first among the chosen few. Witnessing this internecine scuffle from a safe distance, Miss Porter felt "he had reached the point of near defenselessness against the peculiar race of people who live in reflected glory." On the other hand, she finally concluded that Joyce had been callous in his use and abuse of Sylvia Beach and that she had ample reason for her belated resentment.

While Miss Beach easily aroused her sympathy and friendship, Miss Porter had a completely contrary reaction to another American woman who lived in Paris — namely, Gertrude Stein, whose famous salon drew many of the same people who frequented Sylvia's shop. But Miss Stein seemed more selective and less gregarious. Her atelier in rue de Fleurus had been (and still was) the mecca for some of the most creative painters and writers — Hemingway, Picasso, Fitzgerald, Gris, cummings, Miró, Dos Passos, *et al.* It was "the place to go" if one could somehow wangle an invitation, and visiting American writers seemed especially anxious to meet her. So it came as no surprise to Miss Por-

---

* Having apparently forgotten that evening in Paris, Miss Porter subsequently wrote a letter to a distant relative, in which she said that she first saw Eliot in New York just after the opening of his play, *The Cocktail Party,* describing him as "a charming, sweet-mannered man."

ter when her friends Allen and Caroline Tate asked her to accompany them on what she called "the mandatory pilgrimage to the shrine."

"I should never have thought of going if the Tates had not asked me," she subsequently declared, "for I had long since lost my early notions that there was any vitality in her work."

Miss Stein had evidently not heard of Katherine Anne Porter and was thus unaware of Miss Porter's bitingly amusing parody of her *Useful Knowledge;* and if she were aware of it, she certainly managed to conceal it. She was, in fact, quite courteous and friendly as she quietly acknowledged the Tates' compliments on her extraordinary collection of paintings, later described by Miss Porter as "ranging the walls from floor to ceiling, giving the impression that they were hung three deep, elbowing each other, canceling each other's best effects in the jealous way of pictures."

Yet there was no sense of disorder in the room itself. The heavy divans and armchairs, covered with dark horsehair, and several small tables with vases, books, photos and other objects — all seemed to contribute to a general air of solid bourgeois respectability. And her obviously pampered dogs, Basket and Pepe (as well as her lover, Alice B. Toklas), seemed to strengthen that impression. As for Miss Stein herself — with her no-colored heavy woolen clothes and drab woolen stockings — she reminded Miss Porter of an "old Jewish patriarch who had backslid and shaved off his beard."

Nevertheless, in spite of Miss Stein's courteous manner, Miss Porter insisted (some twenty years later) that she experienced a "deep feeling of boredom and futility and sense of suffocation," which she took as a message from her deeper instincts that she was "in the wrong place with the wrong people." Whether or not she included the Tates in that judgment was never made clear. In any event, she left that famous atelier at the first opportune moment and never went back.

Her extremely negative reactions might have been prompted by a nagging dissatisfaction with herself. She was still plagued by the persistent ennui which had virtually immobilized her for two or three years. Instead of settling down to "the serious writing" she had hoped to do, she spent days on end puttering around the house, taking long ruminative walks on the Champs Elysées, browsing in open-air bookstalls along the River Seine, or sitting alone in some small café on the Rive Gauche sipping black coffee and rereading hand-scribbled menus until she had practically memorized every item on the page. Indeed, she herself could have cooked most of the dishes listed, for she was taking lessons in haute cuisine (one more distraction?) and would eventually earn a *cordon bleu.*

But preparing excellent *escalopes de veau panées* was not what she was meant to do. There were stories to write — all kinds of stories about all kinds of people — many of which had been slowly filtering through her mind in an ever-so-gradual process that too often seemed completely dead-still and beyond revival. How she envied the quick and decisive and monumentally productive writers like Ford Madox Ford, who could boast of one book for every year of his life, while she had produced but a single slim volume of collected short stories at the age of forty-three. She had sometimes alluded to economic insecurity in rationalizing her meager output, but Ford had suffered even more privation, had often worried about where his next meal would come from — yet he would sit down every day and write his self-imposed daily quota of usually good fiction, filling page after page with his "crabbed fine hand," somehow ignoring or forgetting the gnawing pains of hunger and the lack of heat in his nearly empty room. He had once told Miss Porter that he was "an old man mad about writing," and she had called his madness "an illuminated sanity."

Then, as if Ford's good example were the necessary catalyst, she finally broke through her own impasse in the latter months of 1933. Several stories, which had been stirring in the depths of her creative conscience, started surfacing all at once. On the upper level were two stories from her days in Mexico, and at deeper levels were several others from early childhood. Working backwards in time, she first produced "Hacienda" and "That Tree," both with Mexican locales. As indicated in a prior chapter, "Hacienda" is a fictionalized account of her visit to an old estate where

Sergei Eisenstein was filming *Que Viva México*, and the name-less first-person narrator was Miss Porter herself.

"That Tree" is a dramatic monologue with two unnamed char-acters, an expatriate American journalist and his companion, pre-sumably a woman. Uninterrupted except for a brief quarrel with a fellow newspaperman, the journalist's monologue is a garrulous account of his failure to lead the bohemian life he had dreamed of, the failure of his marriage to a woman apparently frightened of sex and life itself, and the concomitant failure of the Mexican so-cial revolution he had been writing about. Though he is often self-revealing in his snarling cynicism, he presents a fascinating pastiche of truths and half-truths about American expatriates in Mexico, American liberal magazines, Mexican bohemians, mid-dle-class mores in the Midwest, journalistic codes of conduct, and more personal comments on his Indian mistress and some of his pseudoartistic friends.

His heaviest irony is directed at his wife Miriam, a prim and proper woman from the Midwest, who had hated Mexicans and everything else in Mexico, refusing to hire an Indian maid and forever holding her nose as she walked through the *mercado*. Then, as so frequently happens in such antispouse tirades, he criticizes her for doing something that any sane person would have done, something that had occurred during the installation of a new government. Four generals had "infested the steam baths, where they took off their soiled campaign harness and sweated away the fumes of tequila and fornication" and later got drunk again on champagne with several French whores who had been imported for the inaugural festivities. Then, as they started quar-reling among themselves and reached for their pistols, all the Mexican girls on the dance floor swung their escorts around to serve as shields — but his wife Miriam had ducked under the table. Thus, according to the journalist's Hemingwayish code of conduct, she had humiliated him.

They had gotten divorced shortly thereafter, he tells his com-panion, but he had remarried her after two intervening marriages. Talking on and on as the café starts closing and the orchestra leaves, he finally turns to "the shadow opposite" — a symbolic

wasteland image from Miss Porter's previous Mexican stories —
and says: "I suppose you think I don't know" — then he paused
for effect — "I don't know what's happening, this time," he said.
"Don't deceive yourself. This time I know."

Once again, Miss Porter had mercilessly dissected certain aspects of expatriate life in Mexico, cutting through the diseased
ganglia and dead tissue of that alienated society with the cool expert precision of a fine surgeon. At least one critic, Professor
Harry J. Mooney, later complained that she had been too detached, that she had failed to generate any sympathy for her protagonist — but, of course, she had never meant to.

Certainly, there was no lack of compassion — indeed, there
was the most poignant and delicate sympathy — in the stories she
had started writing about a child whom everyone recognized as
the author herself, the series that launched what would later be
called "the Miranda cycle." Though Shakespeare had used the
name Miranda in the Latin sense, in which it means "strange and
wonderful," Miss Porter preferred its Spanish meaning — "the
seeing one" — for in all these stories, Miranda would have the
ability to see through the shams of her quintessentially Southern
society and particularly the adults in her own family. In the later
stories, the narrative point of view would offer a wide range of
perspectives; but in the earlier ones the emotions and perceptions
were those of a child and were therefore expressed in a vocabu-
lary suited to that purpose.

The first of these, in a chronological sense, was "The Fig
Tree," where the child Miranda was introduced to some of the
facts (and mysteries) of birth and death. In the opening sequence
she was seen struggling with Aunt Nannie, who was combing her
hair and firmly tying her bonnet, which her father had insisted
she wear because he didn't want her face spoiled with freckles —
the two adults restricting her innocent joys to "protect" her, and
incidentally pushing her toward a loss of innocence. They were
preparing for an outing at the family farm named Cedar Grove,
which her father called "Halifax" because it was hot there. Ignorant of its slang meaning, Miranda repeated the word and was
scolded by Grandmother Rhea, who told her to call things by

their right name; but Miranda had noticed that Harry never called the grandmother by her right name, Mammy or Mama, which then reminded her that "Mama was dead. Dead meant gone away forever. Dying was something that happened all the time, to people and everything else." And she remembered a long string of carriages slowly crossing a rocky ridge toward the river as a bell tolled and tolled, "and that person was never seen again by anybody."

It was a simple natural acceptance of death, and its naturalness reflected her acceptance of the cycle of birth and death in both animals and human beings. Moreover, she had learned the rituals of death from the death of her mother and of certain neighbors and relatives. Consequently, when she found the dead chick in the fig grove, Miranda immediately followed the burial rituals she had seen before, carefully choosing the right-sized shoebox and making the little chicken as attractive as possible. She had to hurry, of course, because if someone found out why she needed the box and thus required her to get permission for the burial, she would lose the instant joy of doing it. But just after she had made a mound over the grave, she heard a strange noise, "weep, weep, weep." Thinking she had buried the chick alive, though she knew when all kinds of animals were really dead, she had wanted to dig out the box, but couldn't because the family was ready to leave. And when she started to cry and couldn't bring herself to explain why she was crying, her father simply assumed she was having a tantrum over some doll she had left behind. (He had never noticed that Miranda loved only live things, that dolls had no interest for her — except that it was fun to put doll clothes on kittens, who tore them off.) She was finally calmed when someone mentioned forty kittens at Cedar Grove, life once again triumphing over death.

Arriving at the farm, they were greeted by Great Aunt Liza, an amateur scientist and a wonderfully comic figure, who wore snuff-colored clothes, had snuff-colored eyes and dipped snuff just like a man. Though fascinated by Aunt Liza's telescope and microscope, Miranda felt differently about the snuff-flavored gumdrop the old lady gave her, slyly washing off the smell before eating it. Meanwhile, Aunt Liza and her grandmother were bickering about this and that, and she listened carefully "for everything in the world was strange to her and something she had to know about." And among the things she learned was that her grandmother's social code was not overconsistent, for she had always said that snuff-dipping was a low-class habit, yet she easily ignored her own sister's addiction to snuff.

Later that night, when Aunt Liza allowed them to gaze at the stars through the telescope, Miranda asked if the millions of other worlds were like the earth. And when she answered, "Nobody knows, child," Miranda began singing "Nobody knows" inside her head, overjoyed that there were mysteries not even adults could solve. She also learned from Aunt Liza that the "weep, weep" sound she had heard at the chicken's grave was the same sound frogs made as they shed their skins and then ate them. " 'Thank you, Ma'am,' Miranda remembered finally to say through her fog of bliss . . . ," happily trusting the answer.

Thus, Miss Porter had commenced the awakening and life initiation of the child Miranda, drawing heavily upon her own personal experience and recalling her childhood emotions and perceptions with a fidelity so clear and poignant that it all seemed to have happened just yesterday. Written in early 1934, "The Fig Tree" was to have been included in a collection titled *The Leaning Tower and Other Stories*, but the manuscript went astray, was finally found twenty-six years later, and was published in *Harper's* magazine in June 1960. ("I lost several stories that way," she later explained. "I would stash them away in a box or suitcase for more revisions; then I would store the box somewhere, generally with friends, and would eventually lose track of where I'd left it.")

The initiation process was continued in "The Circus," where Miranda and her family and relatives were first shown inside an enormous circus tent, which one critic characterized as "a microcosm of the world." Glancing down through the plank seats, Miranda saw several sniggering boys staring up at her and innocently asked Dicey what they were doing. Instantly drawing her knees together, Dicey scoldingly warned her to "stop throwin' yo' legs around that way."

Unable to understand the sexual connotations in Dicey's reprimand, Miranda turned her attention back to the arena and was immediately horrified by the smells, the riotous colors and the blaring music, crying in panic and shutting her eyes. Then, opening her eyes again when the crowd started laughing, she was even more horrified by the white-faced clown with a huge red mouth, teetering on a thin wire, feigning several falls as the crowd roared and shrieked. Too sensitive to bear any more, Miranda started crying and screaming again — louder this time — and was finally sent home with Dicey, who naturally resented it.

Later, when her father casually said that no harm had been done, Grandmother Rhea was not so sure. "The fruits of their present are in the future," she said, "so far off, neither of us may live to know whether harm has been done or not. That is the trouble." (Here again Miss Porter was reiterating Katherine Mansfield's dictum that all our character is formed by the age of ten, after which nothing much matters.)

In any event, the shock had been sufficient to cause Miranda a terrible nightmare that very same night, especially when she remembered the grinning ugly dwarf standing by the exit as she was carried away by Dicey. Screaming again, she begged Dicey not to leave and not to be angry with her. And the old black nanny, dutifully controlling her resentment and exasperation, tried to soothe her: "Now you jes shut yo eyes and go to sleep. I ain't going to leave you. Dicey ain't mad at nobody . . . nobody in the whole worl. . . ."

Though quite brief, "The Circus" once more revealed Miss Porter's keen understanding of childhood trauma, and it also laid bare a lifelong conviction that her father (perhaps most fathers) had little or no understanding of children. She had also focused on the demeaning role of black servants and the helpless rage that seethed just below the surface of their forced goodwill, although that may not have been her intention. (It's interesting to note that the story was published in the Southern Review in 1935.)

"The Grave" was the third of the Miranda stories written in the latter part of 1934. Once again, Miss Porter was exploring the meaning of life and death through the eyes and sensibilities of children. The story began with a brief résumé of the Rheas' family history, with the grandmother moving her dead husband's body from Kentucky to Louisiana and then to the family burial plot on their Texas farm; and in the next paragraph, the body was being moved again to the public cemetery. (Some biographers have assumed this actually happened to Miss Porter's grandfather, but the family tomb in Kyle indicates that he died in 1879, apparently after the Porters moved to Texas.) In any event, Miranda and Paul had started playing in the newly empty grave and suddenly found a ring and a dove-shaped screw head from the coffin. After trading what they had found (Miranda getting the ring and Paul pocketing the dove), they continued on the hunting expedition they had previously planned. But then they started quarreling about their hunting rights, Paul claiming the right to shoot first if they should spot a rabbit or dove, and Miranda ironically asking if she could fire first if it were a snake.

Soon losing interest in the hunting, Miranda started playing with the gold ring on her thumb, suddenly wanting to go home to bathe, to dust herself with violet talcum powder, and to wear her nicest dress, symbolically shedding her tomboy role. She also fantasized about certain luxuries and family grandeur. But as she started to tell Paul she was going home, he shot a rabbit; and inside the dead body they found several unborn rabbits, each one covered in a flimsy veil. Carefully studying each fetus, Miranda had instantly intuited the process of birth and would have discussed it with everyone — but Paul, fearing their father would think he had exposed her to things she should not know, exacted a promise of secrecy from her.

Having kept that secret for twenty years, Miranda suddenly remembered the family grave as she walked through a market in Mexico, where the smells of decay and a ragged old vendor carrying a tray of sugared animals — including some tiny rabbits — inevitably evoked a Proustian recollection of that long-ago afternoon. Initially horrified by the stark remembrance of the unborn rabbits curled inside scarlet membranes, she further recalled her grandmother's possessiveness in moving her husband's corpse, and her father's squeamish refusal to discuss such things as birth and death so that she'd been forced to keep secret what she had learned that day. But through the montage of past images that reflected a world of corruption, decay, disaster and chaos, there was a momentary vision of Paul still standing in a bright afternoon sun, gently smiling as he fingered the cracked silver dove, perhaps a symbol of his own flawed innocence.

Here, again, Miss Porter was endowing Miranda with much of her own personal background and psyche, this time projecting her into a strange land twenty years later. And like Miss Porter, who had also rejected family legend and tradition, Miranda had started wandering from here to there in a restless pilgrimage — forever an alien in the corrupt worlds she was finding everywhere.

"The Grave," which was published in the *Virginia Quarterly Review* in 1935, clearly indicated that Miss Porter was planning to make Miranda and her family the key figures in a larger work that would span several decades. In fact, she was quite specific about her intentions in a speech she made before the American Women's Club in Paris just about the time (1934) when she was writing the initial Miranda stories: "*Legend and Memory* is the title of the first section of a long novel I am now working on, and I called it that because it is from these two sources I am attempting to recreate a history of my family. . . ."

Meanwhile, *Hound and Horn* had published "A Bright Particular Faith A.D. 1700," one of the eleven chapters of her still unfinished book on Cotton Mather. Although lacking the compelling force of her fiction, the Mather material nevertheless had occasional glints of Miss Porter's slyly irreverent attitudes. In the closing paragraph, for example, Mather is at the bedside of his daughter Nancy, who has had a malignant fever and convulsions. Having resigned himself to her dying, he has fasted and prayed for an easy and speedy death for her. But "in the evening she suddenly revived and remarked with some spirit: 'I heard my father give me away today, but I shall not die this time, for all that!' "

Though pleased by the publication of the Mather chapter and by the editors' quick acceptance of her two Miranda stories, Miss Porter was still plagued by a persistent malaise that kept recurring even during her most productive periods. The incipient failure of her marriage was certainly one cause of her distress. Pressley had tried to give her enough *Lebensraum*, had most thoughtfully respected her privacy, yet she still felt imprisoned and frustrated and jitteringly restless. Resenting his concern, which she couldn't possibly reciprocate, she would suddenly rush away from the house with no particular place to go, wandering from one street to another, idly staring through store windows and seeing nothing but her own reflection, stopping for tea at a small café and letting it grow cold as she stared at blank walls, browsing for hours in bookstores and never buying a book.

Sad and contrite and inutterably weary, she would finally go home and apologize once more to Pressley, and they would have a drink or two "to settle their nerves." The next time there would be two or three drinks. Then more drinks and more apologies. And one evening she came home and found Pressley already into his fourth or fifth highball, sullen and peevish, full of recriminations about her "goddamned independence" and bitingly sarcastic about her writing.

He drank more often after that, usually alone. "And I guess I was drinking more than was good for me," she subsequently said. "So I had to get away from there."

Taking what she called "a short vacation from marriage," she packed a few belongings and manuscripts and went to Vienna, where she continued working on the opening sequences of her novel. It was during this period that the second edition of *Flowering Judas and Other Stories* was published, she having added four new stories: "Theft," "That Tree," "The Cracked Looking Glass," and "Hacienda." She also got fresh new copies of *Southern Review* and the *Virginia Quarterly Review*, which featured her two Miranda stories. She was glad now that she had not submitted them to *transition*, which had previously published her "Magic" and "The Jilting of Granny Weatherall," for she had finally concluded that it was a "sinister" magazine, which was supposedly the vanguard of international experimental thought, while "its real voice was hoarse, anxious, corrupted mysticism speaking in a thick German accent." This she attributed to the editor, Eugene Jolas, an Alsatian who was "bilingual in irreconcilable tongues, French and German . . . with no mother tongue, nor even a country." Consequently, according to her, Jolas had frantically demanded that language be reduced to something he could master, exploding the verb, defending "hallucinative forces" and the "occult hypnosis of language," and finally proposing a "chthonian grammar." She further accused him of hating reason and defending "the voice of the blood," as well as advocating the disintegration of syntax.

Needless to say, *transition* would never again have the opportunity of publishing anything by Katherine Anne Porter.

Returning to Paris in 1936, she immediately informed Pressley that their marriage was over, and he accepted her decision with no great show of emotion. "We had both made mistakes, and perhaps getting married was the biggest mistake of all. But there was no sense moping about it — I had my work to do."

So she went back to her novel — or to the short stories that would be part of the novel — occasionally breaking away from her fiction to jot a few more notes in her journal. She had become increasingly fascinated by some of the bizarre stories in the Paris newspapers, several of which she permanently recorded. One of the more amusing news stories was about a rich South American who wanted to get married, but had destroyed his manhood by too much high living. He had solved his problem by purchasing one testicle from a poor but virile young Italian for ten thousand lire. "The operation was a success," Miss Porter noted. "But busybodies of the Italian's family, thinking to make more of the bargain, decided the operation was a crime in spite of his consent for payment, and brought the case into court." But a Paris judge had dismissed the suit, judiciously observing that the South American had married and become a father, while the young Italian had become solvent and could still father a child, all parties thus prospering from the transaction.

Judging from this particular entry in her journal, Miss Porter periodically scanned some of the sensational sex and crime stories in the tabloid press, which might have been another idle time-consuming diversion from her work. Yet it was often more than mere idle reading. Being as fluent in French as she was in Spanish, she was always probing for the news behind the news, for the seldom-reported motivations and neurotic compulsions that drove people to commit atrocious crimes or to engage in odd sexual practices. And her observations were generally cool and detached, free of sob-sister sentiment but occasionally sharpened with biting irony.

She could be equally penetrating and objective in probing herself, seeking to understand the process of her own psyche as an artist. Here, for example, was another notation in her journal for 1936: "This constant exercise of memory seems to be the chief occupation of my mind, and all my experience seems to be simply memory, with continuity, marginal notes, constant revision and comparison of one thing with another. Now and again thousands of memories converge, harmonize, arrange themselves around a central idea in a coherent form, and I write a story. . . . I must know a story 'by heart' and I must write from memory."

She also noted that some of her fellow writers, people whose judgment she admired, would often tell her that her writing lacked detail and exact observation of the physical world, that her people seldom had any distinguishable features, that they lived in empty houses. "At one time, I was so impressed by this criticism, I used to sit on a camp stool before a landscape and note down literally every object, every color, form, stick and stone before my eyes." But when she later described that landscape she couldn't remember any such details, and she felt "it was no good pretending I did." She also mentioned that she had ridden, saddled and harnessed hundreds of horses in her lifetime, but still didn't know the names of the different parts of the harness. Nor did she care.

She probably made these observations during a Writers' Conference at Olivet College (Michigan) that same summer (1936).

She had never before spoken to a group of student writers and had initially considered rejecting the invitation to participate in the workshop, but she had finally decided, "It would be fun to see some of my old friends." On her way back from Olivet, firmly convinced such conferences were a waste of time, she spent a few days in New York. She hoped to see John Peale Bishop, whom she had seen at a party in Paris, but she was then still married to Pressley. And now that she was single and free (though not yet formally divorced), Bishop was away from the city — so once again they seemed to be missing each other when circumstances seemed otherwise propitious.

On her return to Paris she found several complimentary copies of the *Southern Review*, featuring "The Old Order," which had also been selected for *Best American Short Stories*. Moving back and forth in time, the story spanned the whole life of Grandmother Rhea, ending with her death as the "new order" was about to begin. Drawing upon some of her own grandmother's recollections, Miss Porter had depicted two old ladies, Sophia Jane and Nannie, constantly talking about the past and reluctantly agreeing that the world was changing swiftly, "but by the mysterious logic of hope they insisted that each change was probably the last or that certain changes, going full circle, would bring back the old ways.

Part of the "old ways" — which the white grandmother particularly yearned for — involved slavery, and she recalls her father buying Nannie and her parents at a slave auction in 1832. (Miss Porter's grandmother Catherine was born in 1827 and would have been five at that time.)

Sophia Jane had married her cousin Stephen, a weak ineffectual man who had dissipated her fortune, then died at a fairly early age, leaving her with several children. Transplanting her family to Louisiana (moving his body from one grave to another), she had tried unsuccessfully to manage a sugar refinery, finally selling at a loss and moving her household to central Texas. There her children had grown up and married, and one of her sons had married Miranda's mother, who had been too sickly and delicate to manage her own house and children. So the old woman had moved in with her son and daughter-in-law, taking charge with a domineering hand. Then one afternoon, completely ignoring the express wishes of her daughter-in-law, she had decided to reorganize the garden, which would require moving a fifty-foot adobe wall — but she had fallen dead as she commenced the project.

And with her death, the family had started coming apart at a frightening pace, for she had been the cohesive force — the mythic force — that had kept it together. The same could be said for Miss Porter's grandmother.

11

The Seven-Day Cycle

PARIS seemed rather empty when Miss Porter returned from the United States. Perhaps the brief stay in New York had made her homesick, or — more probably — her impending divorce had cast a pall over everything. She could no longer feel at home in Paris — if, indeed, she could feel at home anywhere. Clearly, it was time to leave.

Within a few weeks she packed all her belongings, first having discarded some of what she considered "excess" manuscripts and books she had accumulated. Then, after a few tearful farewells, she took a train to Le Havre and boarded an old ship destined for New York. Not wanting to share a cabin with anyone in third class, she permitted herself the luxury of a second-class cabin, characteristically choosing the least expensive one she could find. Very much alone and preferring it that way, she would spend hour after hour, day after day, leaning on the rail of the afterdeck, staring back at an invisible Europe. Now and then she would notice one of the crew members watching her from a distance, and after a while she wondered if he were fearful that this always-alone female might be contemplating suicide, so she would occasionally smile and wave at him in her most reassuring manner. Had the crewman been able to read her mind he would have had no cause to worry, for on those long contemplative days she was in the throes of furious creativity. Three short novels had begun to jell inside her all at once, sequence after sequence coming into a clear crystalline focus. Quite soon each of them would be ready to set down on paper.

She arrived in New York late in October 1936, and within a few days she went to see her old friend and favorite editor, Carl Van Doren.

"I'm ready to make three stories," she told him. "But I've got to find some place where I can be alone, where absolutely no one can disturb me."

"I've got just the place for you," he said almost instantly. "It's an old inn down at Doylestown, Pennsylvania — not too far from here, but way off the beaten track."

Thanking him for the suggestion, she hurried back to her hotel room to write a few "I'm back in the States" letters to friends and relatives and to make certain necessary arrangements for her trip to Doylestown.

She arrived at the rustic rural inn on the afternoon of November 7, 1936, rented a small room, ordered a pot of coffee and a dozen oranges, and began to write "Noon Wine" that same evening. In a state of trancelike absorption, in which nothing else existed except the story itself, she wrote it in seven days, finishing the last paragraph in the early morning hours of November 14. "I wrote it as it stands except for a few pen corrections," she later said, though she had written some of the middle section — the scene between Mr. Hatch and Mr. Thompson, which leads up to the murder — while she was in Basel four years earlier.

That same afternoon, with only a few hours of sleep, she began writing *Old Mortality*, once again immersed in a deep trance that blanked out everything except the steadily unraveling sequences of a story that had been gestating in her mind for twenty or thirty years. And like *Noon Wine*, it was also written in just seven days. Commenting on her working habits several years later, Miss Porter told an interviewer, "I know where I'm going. I know what my goal is. And how I get there is God's grace."

Apparently, God's grace was still very much with her when she sat down to write *Pale Horse, Pale Rider*. With only a brief interlude, during which she went down to Louisiana "to get acquainted with my editors" at the *Southern Review*, she isolated herself in a modest hotel room in New Orleans and immediately started writing as if compelled by an irresistible force. "I paused

Miss Porter with her third husband, Albert Erskine

only to catch a few hours of wakeful sleep and to let the chamber-maid do her chores." She ate a few sandwiches and drank a considerable amount of black coffee and orange juice, "but my real sustenance was the work itself." Once again she seemed attuned to a mysterious cosmic rhythm, working mostly by "moon time," so that she was able to produce *Pale Horse, Pale Rider* in seven days. "That was my magic cycle, I guess — at least in those blessed days. Each of those stories was written in just seven days. But I hadn't planned it that way; it just seemed to happen."

Each of the three manuscripts was about twenty-five thousand words in length, and there were very few revisions on the first and only drafts she wrote. Some people called them long short stories; others preferred the terms "novella" or "novelette"; but she adamantly insisted they were *short novels* and openly resented anyone calling them novellas. Certainly, no one could deny that they had the impact of novels five or ten times longer, and thousands of students who later read them in college literature courses would subsequently remember them as if they *were* full-sized novels.

Noon Wine was published in a small but distinguished literary magazine called *Story* in June 1937, and was instantly acclaimed by most of its unfortunately limited number of subscribers. The setting for this tightly constructed story is a small farm in central Texas from 1896 to 1905, approximately the same period when Miss Porter lived in that region. In the opening sequence a stranger appears at the farm of Royal Earle Thompson and asks for work as a hired hand. It's a fortuitous moment, for Thompson is engaged in a chore he resents and therefore immediately hires the man, who subsequently identifies himself as Olaf Helton but says nothing about his background. A quiet hard worker, who passes his spare time playing the same boring tune on a harmonica, Helton helps the farm prosper during the next few years.

Then nine years later, another stranger comes to the farm. He is a professional bounty hunter named Homer T. Hatch, and he's looking for Helton, who had escaped from an asylum, to which he had been committed after killing his brother in a dispute over a harmonica. Instantly disliking Hatch, who exhibits an annoying superiority about everything (including the kind of tobacco he chews), Thompson demurs at the prospect of losing his hard-working, low-paid employee. In his ambivalence, he mistakenly thinks that Hatch intends to injure Helton, and he suddenly kills Hatch with an ax he has been holding all along. He is acquitted of murder in a local court — but thereafter keeps making the rounds from one neighbor to another, doggedly trying to explain his innocence, dragging along his reluctant wife as a "witness." Then one night his wife has a nightmare and screams, "Oh, oh, don't! Don't! Don't," and her sons rush in to rescue her, one of them coldly warning Thompson, "You touch her again, and I'll blow your heart out."

Thus finally realizing that everyone, including his own family, believes he is a murderer, the old man writes an agonized note protesting his innocence and then shoots himself through the mouth with a heavy shotgun.

Although there was nothing directly autobiographical in *Noon Wine,* several sequences and the general ambience of the story were admittedly culled from experiences in her early childhood. She quite clearly remembered a certain afternoon, while she was still a small child, sitting alone on the wide lawn next to the house, when the explosion of a shotgun echoed and rolled across the sky, shaking the air around her. Almost instantly there was a piercing long-drawn scream, a sound she had never heard before. ". . . but I knew what it was — it was the sound of death in the voice of a man. How did I know it was a shotgun? How should I not have known? How did I know it was death? We are born knowing death."

Sometime later — she couldn't remember when — she saw a funeral procession creeping along a nearby ridge, the hearse a simple old spring wagon, and someone from the Porter household sadly remarked, "Poor Pink Hodges — old man A—— got him just like he said he would." All sorts of questions ran through her mind: Was it Hodges who screamed? And who was A—— ? What had been done to him? She had started to ask these and many more questions, but some adult invariably hushed her, telling her she was too young to understand such things. Yet the unanswered questions never ceased to plague her.

Still later, when she was about nine, she noticed a strange horse and buggy in the drive. Impelled by her customary curiosity, she crept toward the half-open door of the living room and saw a man and woman talking to her grandmother, who was listening with a doubtful smile. The woman was a pale beaten-looking creature in a faded cotton print dress, who kept looking down at her hands twisted tight in her lap, her eyes hidden behind dark glasses.

While staring at her, young Katherine Anne suddenly heard the man almost shouting in a rough, hoarse voice: "I swear it was in self-defense! His life or mine! If you don't believe me, ask my wife here. She saw it. My wife won't lie!" And she would answer in a low, unwilling, muffled voice, "Yes, that's right. I saw it." Looking into the room, nine-year-old Katherine Anne saw this "great loose-faced, blabbing man full of guilt and fear . . . his eyes bloodshot with drink and tears."

Soon thereafter, Katherine Anne saw a poor tired-looking farm worker, a thatch of straw-blond hair hanging between his eyebrows, sitting on a kitchen chair tilted against the wall of an old shack, playing a sad tune on his harmonica, "the very image of loneliness." She later learned he was a Swedish alien who spoke very little English, which made him seem all the more lonely and helpless.

On the other end of the human scale, she and her father had once seen a "tall, black-whiskered man on horseback, sitting so straight his chin was level with his Adam's apple," his flamboyant black hat tilted at a rakish angle. "That's Ralph Thomas, the proudest man in seven counties," said her father with a faint smile. And when she asked what he was so proud about, her father said, "I suppose the horse. It's a very fine horse." Which made her realize that Mr. Thomas was sort of ridiculous — and yet pathetic.

Each of these incidents, distilled and crystallized to their very essence, were eventually transformed into the basic elements of *Noon Wine*, Miss Porter once again drawing upon the vast reservoir of her *usable past*. In so doing, she was able to delve deeper and deeper into one of the central themes of her fiction: the efforts of man to cope with evil, within himself as well as in others. For example, she reveals how Thompson is unable to comprehend, much less combat, the evil Homer Hatch represents; nor is he able or willing to face up to the ambiguous evil in Olaf Helton. Consequently, he can never understand his own motives in killing Hatch and is thus driven to suicide. On the other hand, Mrs. Thompson cannot bring herself to tell, much less believe, the ultimate lie that will exculpate her husband. Helton has apparently overcome his violent compulsions but lives in a private hell which no one can penetrate.

As Robert Penn Warren cogently argued, "The issue here . . . is not to be decided simply; it is, in a sense, left suspended, terms defined, but the argument left only at a provisional resolution. Poor Mr. Thompson — innocent and yet guilty — and in his passion for absolute definition unable to live by the provisional."

Except in the most abstract sense, *Noon Wine* was not a specific reflection of Miss Porter's personal history, but *Old Mortality* was about as autobiographical as anything she ever wrote. The title was taken from Sir Walter Scott's *Old Mortality* (1816), which dealt with a deeply religious man who wandered around rural Scotland, caring for the graves of fellow Covenanters who had been killed in the reign of the Stuarts.* Nicknamed "Old Mortality," he searched for the most obscure and neglected graves, cleaning moss off the tombstones, renewing wornout inscriptions, and repairing damaged emblems. He felt this was his sacred mission, and many people superstitiously believed "his graves" would never decay again. So, too, on a symbolic level, Miranda cleansed the past in *Old Mortality;* but unlike Scott's old renewer of graves, she would eventually reject that past.

Part I of her story (1885–1902) begins with two children, Miranda and Maria, listening to the adults' comments on the photograph of the now-deceased Amy, saying how lovely she

---

* From Miss Porter's "The Source," we learn that the Rhea (i.e., Porter) family had a set of Scott's works, which young Katherine Anne read in her early teens.

was. But Miranda inwardly notes that Amy was caught in a pose of being photographed and that her supposedly elegant clothes look old-fashioned and a bit faded, like some of the "finery" her grandmother had kept through the years. Yet the child Miranda *wants* to believe the family legends about Amy, in spite of the contrary evidence she keeps noticing. Just as she believed that Mary Queen of Scots actually died on stage when she saw the play,* Miranda can believe that Aunt Amy was so lovely men would fight over her, that she could torment her fiancé Gabriel with impunity, and that she would defy her father by wearing a daring gown to a party. She could also believe that Amy's behavior had encouraged a former suitor to flirt with her (perhaps secretly kiss her), and that her enraged brother Harry had shot the interloper and forced Gabriel to challenge the already-wounded man to a duel of honor. And the legend Miranda heard went on and on: Harry fleeing to Mexico to escape prosecution, Gabriel being sent away for a while, Gabriel being disinherited, Amy marrying Gabriel in spite of his troubles, and the chronically ill Amy dying a most romantic death six weeks after the wedding.

But all these scenes of romance, beauty and honor — so often repeated to the children as reality — are seen as sham or exaggeration in Parts II and III. In the opening sequence of Part II, the children are leading a dull sequestered life in a New Orleans convent school, their grandmother having suddenly died. Their safe, sedate existence is in stark contrast to the harrowing anti-Catholic novels they had read, in which babies were killed by nuns "immured" in convents. Having somehow managed not to break any regulations, Miranda and Maria are permitted to leave the convent for a Saturday visit with Uncle Gabriel, who takes them to the horse races. But when they first meet him, Miranda immediately sees that he's not the romantic figure of family legend — that he's gross and fat and red-faced from too much drinking. He is also still enamored with the mythic Amy. Though obviously disillusioned, Miranda is momentarily excited when his horse wins the big race, at one-hundred-to-one odds, but her romantic

---

* Young Katherine Anne Porter had a similar reaction when she saw the play (see page 15).

view of racing is instantly shattered when she sees the horse's nose bleeding. And her disillusion deepens when Uncle Gabriel takes them to a slum hotel in Elysian Fields to meet his second wife, Miss Honey, whose name belies her sharp vinegary manner. But Miranda's and Maria's greatest disappointment comes when they learn that the money they've won at the race has to be saved in a bank.

In Part III the teetering Amy legend virtually collapses. Uncle Gabriel has died and is being buried next to Amy. Miranda, now eighteen, is returning to Texas for the funeral and has a long myth-shattering talk with Cousin Eva in the sleeping car. Poor chinless Eva has failed as a belle and devoted her life to teaching Latin in a female seminary and also fighting for women's suffrage. But in her rancor of past slights by men, she shows her resentment of Amy and other pretty women who attended all the gay parties, which she characterizes as "markets" for marriage and love affairs. "Cousin Eva wrung her hands, 'It was just sex,' she said in despair; 'their minds dwelt on nothing else. They didn't call it that, it was all smothered under pretty names, but that's all it was, sex. . . .'" Moreover, she never regarded Amy as a ravishing beauty, nor did she consider her tuberculosis romantic. In her opinion, Amy had been driven to illness by sexual rivalries.

Seeing through Cousin Eva's envy, Miranda nevertheless realizes that she's speaking more truth than her family ever had. But her temporary rapport with Eva dissipates when they get home. Miranda's father, who still resents her elopement, holds back from her and chooses instead to gossip with Eva.

Feeling isolated but suddenly free from myth, Miranda begins rejecting her family ties and the world they represent. She also decides not to go back to her husband and his family, because marriage and families demand too much. "I hate loving and being loved," she declared. And as a final personal declaration of independence, she says, ". . . Let them tell their stories to each other. Let them go on explaining how things happened. I don't care. At least I can know the truth about what happens to me, she assured herself silently, making a promise to herself, in her hopefulness, her ignorance."

Here, surely, is the unmistakable voice of a young defiant Katherine Anne Porter when she was the same age as Miranda, when she herself was bitterly estranged from her unforgiving father and had decided to break off her impulsive runaway marriage to a young man whose name she would never reveal.

In the exquisitely poignant and poetic *Pale Horse, Pale Rider*, Miranda had become a young woman in her middle twenties and (like Miss Porter) was working as a reporter for the *Rocky Mountain News* in Denver, covering plays and movies. While being interviewed during a television adaptation of her short novel, Miss Porter reemphasized its autobiographical source: "I met a boy, an army lieutenant. . . . Our time was so short and we were much in love. But we were shy. It was a step forward and two steps back with us. Then I was taken ill with the flu. They gave me up. The paper had my obit set in type, and I've seen the correspondence between my father and sister on plans for the funeral. . . . I knew I was dying. I felt a strange state of — what is it the Greeks called it? — euphoria. . . ." But, as we've seen, she somehow mustered the will to live.

"And the boy, Miss Porter?"

"It's in the story," she told the interviewer, fighting back tears. "He died. The last I remember seeing him. . . . It's a true story. . . . It seems to me true that I died then. I died once, and I have never feared death since."

The aforementioned factual situation furnished the core of *Pale Horse, Pale Rider*, but there were numerous other references to Miss Porter's early childhood in the opening dream sequence, particularly emphasizing the close ties with her grandmother and the family mystique she represented, with its excess ancestor worship, its false conventions and repeated deceptions — yet that was the only past she had.

Since Miranda's story parallels Miss Porter's similarly unfortunate experience in Denver, as described in Chapter III, I shall forgo a detailed analysis of the plot. There were, of course, certain added elements that served as poetic enhancements of the original facts. Take for example the tenderly beautiful scene where Miranda and Adam sang an old Negro spiritual, "Pale horse, pale rider, done taken my lover away" — which seemed to restate the dramatic theme of the first dream. But by the time the story ended, Miranda had put aside her conscious fears as she envisioned a world without war, houses without noise, streets without people, and "the dead cold light of tomorrow." As one who had been exposed to death, to her own version of heaven and hell, she could not resist adding an ironic afterthought: "Now there would be time for everything."

Thus, in spite of an apparently romantic ambiance that would have lured most writers into mawkish sentimentality, Miss Porter ultimately forced her fictional alter ego to look at herself and others in a "dead cold light." It was precisely this quality in her three short novels (indeed, in all her short stories) which prompted some readers to accuse her of antihumanism and chronic despair. But the very humane Eudora Welty had a diametrically contrary view of Miss Porter's fiction:

> If outrage is the emotion she has most strongly expressed, she is using outrage as her cool instrument. She uses it with precision to show what monstrosities of feeling come about not from the lack of the existence of love but from love's repudiation, betrayal. From which there is no safety anywhere. Granny Weatherall, eighty, wise, affectionate and good, and now after a full life dying in her bed with the priest beside her, "knew hell when she saw it."
>
> The anger that speaks everywhere in the stories would trouble the heart for the author we love except that her anger is pure, the reason for it evident and clear, and the effect exhilarating. She has made it the tool of her work; what we do is rejoice in it. We are aware of the compassion that guides it, as well. Only compassion could have looked where she looks, could have seen what she sees. *Real compassion is perhaps always in the end unsparing; it must make itself a part of knowing. Self-pity does not exist here; these stories come out trenchant, bold, defying; they are tough as sanity, unrelinquished sanity, is tough.* [Italics mine.]

As for the critics who saw little (if any) hope for most of the characters in Miss Porter's autobiographical fiction, Miss Welty cautioned them to take a second look, to probe beneath the surface of what seemed like hopeless despair:

... It is a despair, however, that is robust and sane, open to negotiation by the light of day. Life seen as a savage ordeal has been investigated by a straightforward courage, unshaken nerve, a rescuing wit, and above all with the searching intelligence that is quite plainly not to be daunted. In the end the stories move us not to despair ourselves but to an emotion quite opposite because they are so seriously and clear-sightedly pointing out what they have been formed to show: that which is true under the skin, that which will remain a fact of the spirit. . . .

With specific reference to *Old Mortality*, Miss Welty reminds us that Miranda was rebelling against the ties of the blood, "resenting their very existence, planning to run away now from these and, as soon as she can, from her own escape into marriage." And when Miranda says, "I hate loving and being loved," Miss Welty chooses to believe that she "is hating what destroys loving and what prevents being loved." She goes on to observe that "seeing what is not there, putting trust in a false picture of life, has been one of the worst nightmares that assail Miss Porter's characters." Thus one sees the romantic and the antiromantic pulling each other to pieces; but, in Miss Welty's view, the romantic is never fully defeated. "Even if there rises a new refrain, even if the most ecstatic words ever spoken turn out to be 'I hate you,' the battle is not over for good. That battle is in itself a romance."

As one might expect, Miss Porter admired the same quality of unrelenting honesty and toughness in Miss Welty's work, and she expressed that admiration some twenty-four years *before* Miss Welty wrote her laudatory comments. Thus, in reviewing Miss Welty's *A Curtain of Green* (1941), she said that dullness, rancor, self-pity, baseness of all kinds could be most interesting material for fiction provided these were not also the main elements in the mind of the author, further declaring that there was nothing in the least vulgar or frustrated in Miss Welty's mind, that her eyes and ears were sharp, shrewd and true as a tuning fork. "She has given to this little story all her wit and observation, *her blistering humor and her just cruelty* [italics mine]; for she has none of that slack tolerance or sentimental tenderness toward symptomatic evils that amounts to criminal collusion between author and character."

Four years earlier (October 1937), just about the time *Noon Wine* was published, Miss Porter had similar praise for the "toughness" in one of her most favorite writers, Katherine Mansfield. Her main virtue, she felt, was "a certain grim, quiet ruthlessness of judgement, *an unsparing and sometimes cruel eye, a natural malicious wit,* an intelligent humor; and beyond all she had a burning, indignant heart that was capable of great compassion." Alluding to the fact that some critics had criticized Miss Mansfield for an almost finicking delicacy, Miss Porter said, "She was delicate as a surgeon's scalpel is delicate."

Not surprisingly, she would later praise the *just cruelty* and *malicious wit* in the work of Flannery O'Connor, especially her searingly honest novel *The Violent Bear It Away.*

When compared to these four women — Porter, Welty, Mansfield and O'Connor — most tough-guy writers like Hemingway and Mailer seem blabbily sentimental and incurably romantic. Which would appear to verify Miss Porter's lifelong conviction that most men are basically weaker than women because they are afraid to look at themselves (and others) square in the eye. "Our presumed feminine weakness is mostly a physical matter." Yet she, too, had an occasional momentary lapse, most notably on that long-ago afternoon in Mexico City when she told a revolutionary colleague, "But can't you see that I'm all applesauce inside?"

When *Story* magazine published *Noon Wine* in June 1937, several major publishers immediately approached Miss Porter and urged her to start writing full-length novels. And the clamor became more intense when she got a special award of twenty-five hundred dollars from the prestigious Book-of-the-Month Club. "Those New York publishers wouldn't let me alone," she later remembered with a sudden burst of emotion. "They kept yanking at me from all sides, and I felt as if my flesh were being torn apart by a million hooks. They simply wouldn't understand that I had to write my own way and in my own good time, that I couldn't and *wouldn't* write to their specifications."

However, most of the pressure from publishers was at long range, for she had suddenly moved to Baton Rouge, Louisiana, and soon thereafter married Albert Erskine, a young professor of

English at the University of Louisiana and managing editor of the *Southern Review*, which published *Old Mortality* and *Pale Horse, Pale Rider* in the spring and summer issues of 1938.* She had met Erskine on an earlier visit, and there had been an instant rapport. Conscious of his youth, which was partly obscured by his mature manner and sophisticated mind, she at first resisted any serious attachment. But aside from having fallen in love with her writing, he quite understandably found her extremely attractive. With her soft unblemished skin and her beautiful violet eyes, which were becoming a smoky blue-gray, she looked several years younger than her real age.

"I honestly didn't want to get involved," she subsequently confided, "but Albert was so persistent, so wonderfully attentive, I simply couldn't resist any longer."

So they were married in 1938 and were soon settled down in a two-room apartment on the second floor of an eighteenth-century Spanish-French house near the campus. She was then forty-eight years old and he was twenty-seven. But in spite of that age difference, they had a warm, loving relationship, firmly based on mutual interests in literature, art, music and Southern lore. They also liked the same kind of people and were especially fond of their good neighbor Robert Penn Warren, affectionately known as "Red" among his close friends.

Both poet and novelist, Warren was just finishing his powerful and complex *Night Rider*, having done so while teaching at the university, and Miss Porter had been amazed by his ability to make use of even thirty minutes of free time. "He would simply go to his typewriter, pick up where he left off, and pound away at a steady pace. That was a tremendously complicated book to write, yet he went right through it as though he was simply making notes in a journal."

Warren's exemplary work habits undoubtedly made her feel increasingly guilty about her own failure to write. After that furious burst of creativity that helped her produce three short novels in three weeks, she had been "lying fallow" for more than a year,

---

* The year before, she had obtained an uncontested divorce from Pressley in a New York court.

either "socializing too much" but enjoying it, or reading scores of books she had been wanting to read for years and years. It was during this period that she had wept uncontrollably while reading a book about the fall of Richmond in the Civil War, and her young husband had consoled her with the utmost subtlety and loving affection.

Eventually, however, she became restless and frustrated, feeling hemmed in — indeed, imprisoned — by her marriage. It wasn't anything she could validly blame on Erskine; it was marriage itself that was becoming difficult to bear, for she needed privacy and psychic space in order to pursue what she properly considered her prime function in life. So once again she began spending hours and hours, then days and days, by herself, restlessly wandering all alone around Baton Rouge and occasionally New Orleans. She also wrote a few "diversionary pieces," which merely accentuated her inability to do more serious work. One of these pieces was about a pilgrimage she had made through an area which featured a number of old Southern mansions that clearly evoked a deep nostalgia for the bygone days her grandmother had so vividly described. One of them was called "Greenwood," which she characterized as a "typical Southern mansion of too many songs, too many stories." Observing that it was quite improbable that anyone would again build a house so large and lavish, she dreamily invisaged "the hostess sitting in her drawing-room with the green-and-gold chairs, the lace curtains fine as bride veils drifting a little; the young girls in jodhpurs going out to ride. . . ." Then, commenting on the absence of noisy radios, Gramophones and telephones, she said, "It seemed to me suddenly that this silence, the silence of a house in order, of people at home, the silence of leisure, is the most desirable of all things we have lost."*

Still avoiding her real work, she wrote another short piece couched in a question-and-answer form which had a few scattered hints of her frame of mind at the age of forty-nine. When asked if Henry James's work was more relevant to the present and

---

* From "Audubon's Happy Land," finally published in *Collected Essays,* 1970.

future of American writing than Walt Whitman's, she unequivocably sided with James, "holding as I do with the conscious, disciplined artist, the serious expert against the expansive, indiscriminately 'cosmic' sort." She went on to say that "the influence of Whitman on certain American writers has been disastrous, for he encourages them in the vices of self-love (often disguised as love of humanity, or the working classes, or God). . . ." As for the influence of critics on her writing, she commented: "It is true that I place great value on certain kinds of perceptive criticism but neither praise nor blame affects my actual work, for I am under a compulsion to write as I do." Regarding the practical problem of earning a living as a writer, her answer was quite candid: "If you mean, is there a place in our present economic system for the practice of literature as a source of steady income and economic security, I should say, no." Furthermore, she seemed to question the artistic freedom of writers who attain security: "In the arts, you simply cannot secure your bread and your freedom of action too. *You cannot be a hostile critic of society and expect society to feed you regularly.*" (Italics mine.) In the final question about a writer's responsibility in time of war, she forthrightly declared herself a pacifist, adding: "If you are required to kill someone today, on the promise of a political leader that someone else shall live in peace tomorrow, believe me, you are not only a double murderer, you are a suicide, too."

Aside from this question-and-answer article and "Audubon's Happy Land," she wrote nothing of consequence while living in Baton Rouge; but there was a brief flurry of excitement in April 1939, when Harcourt, Brace published *Pale Horse, Pale Rider*, which included *Noon Wine* and *Old Mortality*. The book was highly praised in *The New York Times, The Nation, Time* magazine and several other newspapers and journals. The review in *Time*, accompanied by a picture of Miss Porter at her typewriter, was a fairly typical sample of critical reaction:

Not many writers can sustain a literary reputation on the strength of one short story. But for almost ten years that has been the achievement of Katherine Anne Porter. Probably no U.S. writer has been praised so highly while writing so little. The story that made her reputation was

Flowering Judas, a sensitive finely-grained piece of prose, but hardly a lifework in itself.

Critics threw their hats in the air, hailed Miss Porter as one of the most promising American writers when it first appeared in 1930. They tossed them again, finding her just as promising, when it was republished in 1935.

Last week she kept her promise. *Pale Horse, Pale Rider* is a collection of three short novels which belong with the best of contemporary U.S. writing in this difficult form. A distinctive book, elusive as quicksilver, it has the subtlety that has marked all Miss Porter's writing, none of the preciousness that has previously marred it. . . .

It's interesting to note that Miss Porter fudged a little regarding her age while being interviewed in New York: she told the *Time* book critic she was forty-four, and a day or so later "admitted" she was forty-five to *The Nation* reviewer. She was, in fact, forty-nine at the time, but her youthful appearance completely justified the slight through inconsistent alteration.

She also informed *Time* that she was living on tree-shaded American Avenue in Baton Rouge, keeping herself busy in a two-room apartment, cooking, gardening, sewing, collecting old records and music, reading medieval documents and modern poetry. Presumably her slow writing bothered her not at all. "There are too many bad books without me trying to turn out two a year." Nevertheless, she told the interviewer she was working on a novel titled "Promised Lands" (conceivably a different title for the novel-in-progress previously called "Legend and Memory") and hoped to write four more books, one for each section of the United States.

Considering her gift for procrastination, it is difficult to determine whether she was in fact engaged in writing what she had mentioned or was merely expressing an intention. Suffice it to say, she never published a novel or short story bearing either of those titles. In any event, she was becoming increasingly restless and dissatisfied with her marriage, once again wondering if it would ever be possible for her to forgo the privacy one must almost necessarily sacrifice in marriage or in just living with someone.

Consequently, while visiting in Manhattan to accept the Gold Medal annually awarded by the Society for Libraries of New York University in April 1940, she apparently made inquiries about a fellowship to Yaddo, a writers' retreat near Saratoga.

A few weeks later she packed her suitcases again and left Baton Rouge, taking a train to New York on her way to Yaddo. Without her husband.

12

Divorce and Wanderlust

FROM the moment she left Baton Rouge to join the Yaddo writers' colony, Miss Porter knew that her brief marriage was breaking apart. She also knew — or was beginning to realize — that she would never again be married to anyone, that she would never be able to accept anything as permanent and confining as marriage. Her young husband summarized his reaction quite succinctly when he later told a friend, "I got married to someone with a prior commitment." Presumably, that prior commitment was to her writing.

But if one accepts Erik Erikson's analysis, the reasons for her sudden departure were far more complex than her young husband realized. Had he been more objective, he might have surmised that she suffered from a chronic inability to form close personal attachments for fear of being abandoned, a fear dating back to childhood. Thus, Miranda's bitter admission, "I hate loving and being loved," could well be interpreted as a defensive expression of Miss Porter's own unshakable fear of ultimate abandonment.

Whatever the reason for the failure of her third marriage (and the reasons were probably multiple and commingled), she felt unutterably lonely and depressed as her train slowly chugged northward to New York. Yet there was also an undeniable sense of relief, for she was free again, free from all the day-to-day constraints of wedded bliss. She would some day write that marriage had to be accomplished in a physical situation of the direst intimacy, in which either spouse or both spouses might casually dis-

*With Marc Chagall at
"one of those cultural functions
that go nowhere," December, 1943*

*Portrait by Paul Cadmus,
December, 1943*

In a playful Romeo-Juliet pose with her friend George Platt Lynes,
Hollywood, 1947, when Miss Porter was fifty-seven

Paul Cadmus and Miss Porter at South Hill, May 15, 1943

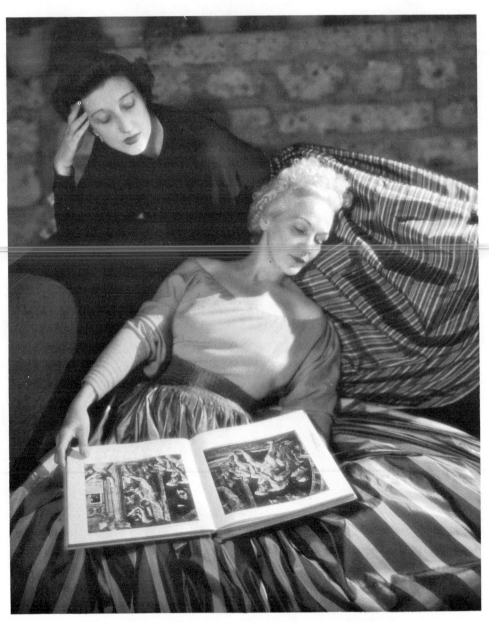

With a Hollywood friend, Jane Gray, in "one of the terribly posey pictures which George liked to take"

Another portrait by George Platt Lynes

regard one another's most ordinary privacy. "I shall not attempt to catalogue the daily accounting for acts, words, states of feeling and even thoughts, the perpetual balance and check between individual wills and points of view, the unbelievable amount of tact, intelligence, flexibility, generosity, and God knows what, it requires for two people to go on growing together and in the same direction instead of cracking up and falling apart."

Knowing that this constant invasion of one's privacy would be compounded by the presence of children, Miss Porter had long since decided to forgo the pleasures of motherhood. Indeed, she could be quite specific in her appraisal of very young children: "They lie flat on their noses at first in what appears to be a drunken slumber, then flat on their backs kicking and screaming, demanding impossibilities in a foreign language. They are human nature in essence, without conscience, without pity, without love, without a trace of consideration for others — just one seething cauldron of primitive appetites and needs. . . ."

That would have been answer enough to any well-meaning friend who might have suggested that a child or two could have helped salvage her marriage to Erskine. If, indeed, she wanted to salvage it.

In any event, she was burdened by neither children nor spouse when she got to Yaddo. Free and alone, she now hoped to produce a number of stories that had been germinating inside her for several months. Yet nothing seemed to come forth. She would sit for hours and hours at her desk (actually a table) or take long solitary walks through the lovely woods nearby, hoping some stray thought would suddenly lead to a burst of creative energy. Still nothing came. And perhaps one of the reasons for this impasse was that she was not really alone at Yaddo; there were other writers living there — and, as could be expected, they seemed to socialize perhaps more than they should. One of them was a nineteen-year-old Southerner named Truman Capote, who latched on to Miss Porter from the very outset.

"Truman has always been a climber," she told me with a tolerant smile. "And I guess he thought I was some kind of celebrity. I don't know why, except that I seemed to be one in his young eyes."

Still, she was flattered by his attention and genuinely enjoyed his company. Consequently, they had several dinners together and even went dancing at a sleazy roadhouse near Saratoga. They usually sat in a corner booth, their faces reflecting the feeble red light of a neon beer sign as they gossiped about this or that writer or magazine editor. He had a frankly malicious wit which was accentuated by his soft high-pitched lisping Southern drawl, and he obviously appreciated the cool trenchant irony of her humor. The thirty-one years' difference in their ages was of little consequence, since there was no threat of sex between them.

"It wasn't that kind of relationship," she later said. "So we were completely relaxed and free of sexual tension."

Aside from their delicious gossip, they discussed several ongoing projects, Capote evincing considerable interest in her still-unfinished book on Cotton Mather, which Harcourt, Brace had hopefully announced on its "catalogue of coming publications" at least three or four times. One of the chapters, "A Goat for Azazel," had just been published in the May–June 1940 issue of *Partisan Review*, but she had to admit — with a hint of bitter frustration — that she hadn't done much more on the Mather project than the eleven chapters she had written ten years earlier while in Bermuda.

"And what about your fiction?" he asked. "Like novels or short stories?"

"Well, I've burned the manuscripts of at least four novels that weren't coming out the way I wanted them to," she told him. "But there are others still churning around inside me."

Pending their hoped-for emergence, she wrote a long preface on the author of *El periquillo sarniento*, the Mexican novel she had translated eight years before. Meanwhile, she made several trips to New York City, often staying with some friend for a week or so. These were generally pleasant interludes, but she was always glad to get back to the Yaddo estate, where she had "taken root" at the cottage known as North Farm. On her return, as the train left Albany, she would always experience an exhilarating sense of homecoming that was rare for her.

"One day, hardly knowing when it happened, I knew I was going to live [in this area] for good and all, and I was going to have a house in the country."

Remembering that travelers in Europe usually believe it's *de rigueur* to taste the wine of the country they are visiting, she considered it mandatory to live in a house that belonged to the area. "Here, the house of the country is plain, somewhat prim, not large, late Colonial; perhaps modified Georgian would be a useful enough description."

Her house-hunting began on the first day of January, 1941, in deep snow frozen solid by zero weather. She had found a reputable real estate agent who knew every farm for miles around, telling him she wanted a house fairly near Saratoga Springs, then her favorite small town in all America. "It must be handsomely located in good, but domestic, landscape," she said, "with several acres, well watered and wooded, and it must not cost above a certain modest sum."

Apparently not understanding her notion of nearness, he drove her at once sixty miles away to a rockbound spot in Vermont, where he showed her an old nineteen-room house that would have been a perfect setting for a gothic novel. Unabashed by her immediate negative reaction, he took her to several other places within the next eighteen days, showing her houses of every possible description, including pink brick mansions on a quarter-acre to wooden bungalows in wild places far removed from any neighbors. They slogged through deep drifts of snow to look at a huge ugly Victorian house large enough for a boarding school, later inspecting a desolate crumbling shack where leaves and snow had drifted through broken windows and were piled in corners of the living room.

After each wild-goose chase she would patiently tell him that she was looking for something simple but well kept and not too far away. She finally had to remind him that mutual friends had told her she could believe every word he said, but unless he was willing to believe every word *she* said, there could be no progress in their search for the kind of house she wanted. Finally getting the message, he called her on January 21 and said he had perhaps found the right place.

Just as they were driving away from Yaddo, a hen pheasant suddenly flew past them, lightly brushing the radiator cap of his car and losing a few breast feathers. Asking him to stop, she hurriedly got out and picked the feathers off the ground and stashed them in her handbag, solemnly explaining that they might bring her good luck.

Declining any comment on her superstition, the none-too-talkative agent drove for several miles around Saratoga Lake, finally turning into an uphill road between a spread of pine and spruce, then turned again toward a small rise on the right. When they got to the crest, he pointed toward the valley just below them. There she saw a rather small and very old Colonial house, modified Georgian, with a slanting red roof and several small porches and sheds attached on all sides like architectural afterthoughts. Surrounded by tall, bare trees, it sat against a small hill covered with thick evergreen.

"But that is my house," she exclaimed. "That's mine!"

Nodding, but cautiously refraining from any comments that might be construed as oversell, he led her around the vacant house, plowing the way through knee-deep snow, both of them peering through the windows into the half-dark interior.

"We'll have to get someone to let us inside, so you can see what condition it's in," he said.

"Let's not bother," she said. "I'll take it."

"But you must see inside first," he quite logically insisted.

"I know what's inside," she said from hidden depths of knowledge firmly based on pheasant feathers. "Let's go to see the owner."

The owner, a woman about fifty years old, had apparently lost hope of selling the house at South Hill, which had been for sale no less than seven years. Consequently, she had to be told several times that Miss Porter actually wanted to buy it; and in the euphoria of having at last found a buyer, she gave a brief history of the house. It was one of the first houses in that area, having been built by settlers related to Benedict Arnold. Some people claimed that he himself had lived there, an ancient rumor which Miss Porter herself would occasionally repeat as established fact, although her subsequent essay on this matter ("A House of My Own") made no such claim.

Thrilled at first by her new acquisition, she soon came down from the clouds. Recalling that E. M. Forster had once remarked that acquiring land made him feel heavy, she, too, quickly felt "a ton weight of moral, social, and financial responsibility, subject to state and county taxes, school tax, and an astonishing variety of insurance."

The dream house eventually became a nightmare of time-consuming, energy-draining problems she had never bargained for. Ironically, she had saved the lucky pheasant feathers to burn (again for luck) on the first fire she made in the fine old fireplace, but thirteen months later she moved out of the house and never went back.

Somehow, in spite of almost continuous distractions related to owning a house, she had managed to finish another short novel while living at South Hill. Titled *The Leaning Tower*, it was published in the 1941 Fall issue of *Southern Review*. The central character of this story, Charles Upton, was given a background similar to Miss Porter's. He had gone to Berlin from a farm in central Texas to pursue a career in painting, ignoring objections from his family — just as Miss Porter had ignored family objections to her writing career. Upton also moved into a shabby *pension* managed by a once-rich widow who talked compulsively about her former staff of servants; and the dark heavily draped room he occupied closely resembled the room Miss Porter lived in. There was also a similarity in their reactions to the German people and to the general ambience of Berlin as Nazism was beginning to take hold in 1932.

Indeed, as the story evolved from one sequence to another (there was very little plot or dramatic tension), one could easily visualize Miranda substituting for the sensitive rather naïve Upton, except that she probably would have been less naïve. In the opening café scene, for example, the young man's recollection of childhood illusions and southern hypocrisy could easily be those of Miranda–Katherine Anne. So would his reactions to the dressed-alike students, the streetwalkers and beggars, and the fat red-faced Germans peering at displays of candied pigs like drooling pig worshippers. The same comparison could be made with respect to Upton's reactions toward his fellow boarders, particularly if one recalled Miss Porter's observations about fellow boarders in her journal.

Considering this obviously autobiographical aspect of *The Leaning Tower*, some critics wondered why Miss Porter had gone out of her way to create a male protagonist when Miranda could have served just as well and probably better, for much of her personal history and psychic background was already familiar. Others wondered why there was no specific mention of Hitler and his budding Nazi party, but one could easily argue that certain passages clearly alluded to the imminent threat of that political disaster. Take, for example, the New Year's Eve celebration at the small cabaret, when Charles was listening to other young men from his *pension* truculently discussing race and war:

And even at the moment, like the first symptoms of some fatal disease, there stirred in him a most awful premonition of disaster, and his thoughts, blurred with drink and strangeness and the sound of half-understood tongues and the climate of remembered wrongs and hatreds, revolved dimly around vague remembered tales of Napoleon and Genghis Khan and Attila the Hun and all the Caesars and Alexander the Great and the dim Pharaohs and lost Babylon. He felt helpless, undefended, looked at the three strange faces near him and decided not to drink any more, for he must not be drunker than they; he trusted none of them.

Evoking the names of brutal conquerors in past history, Charles sensed the ominous emergence of a new tyrant whose name he had not yet heard but who was certain to be spawned by the dreadful hate that simmered in the German people. He was experiencing a "dislocation of the spirit" because he now realized that society was beginning to fall apart, that he himself could not escape it. Yet he felt that "no crying jag or any other kind of jag would ever, in this world, do anything at all for him."

A few critics felt that *The Leaning Tower* was unduly harsh and prejudicial in its characterization of the German people, particularly when Miss Porter's protagonist inwardly pictures their faces as "full of hallucinated malice" and "intense cruelty."

That judgment was admittedly harsh and all-encompassing, but in the fall of 1941, when millions of Jews were being led into the ovens at Buchenwald and Dachau with no discernible protest from the German population, most people were inclined to agree with Miss Porter.

Interestingly enough, it was the United States joining the war against Hitler that led to Miss Porter's decision to abandon her newly acquired home in South Hill. The rationing of gasoline and other war-related products aggravated the difficulties she was having in the repair and maintenance of the old farmhouse. "Owning that lovely place was getting more complicated than marriage," she later complained. "The day-to-day crises were causing an awful drain on time and energy that should have been spent on my writing. So I finally decided to cut loose, even though I had been there less than thirteen months."

Once again packing all her unfinished manuscripts, her wardrobe and other belongings, she moved away from her dream house in the spring (March or April) of 1942.

As if to heighten the irony, she got a divorce from Albert Erskine that very same year, but it was a fairly amicable denouement. In fact, when Miss Porter informed her mother-in-law that she was returning the family silver, Mrs. Erskine immediately rejected the offer: "Now see here, Katherine Anne, it's all very well for you to go off into the world and take up other people's customs, but you ought not to forget your raising. The silver belongs to the wife. Don't you give him a teaspoon."

She, of course, loved her son deeply, but she was not about to abandon Southern tradition, which was based on the Code Napoléon, wherein all the movables (*les meubles*) were legally vested in the wife.

Though relieved by the formal termination of her marriage, Miss Porter nevertheless had a profound feeling of personal failure when the judge issued the decree. During the preceding six weeks she had written the first forty-eight pages of *Ship of Fools*, but the divorce was so traumatic she found it impossible to resume what she had been doing, and she didn't get back to page 49 until several years later.

Meanwhile, she took part in a three-week writers' conference at the University of Colorado and quite understandably resented spending most of her time correcting papers and consulting with students. (During that period, I took a bus to Boulder, hoping to interview her for the University of Denver student newspaper. But when I approached her just after one of her lectures, she politely but very firmly told me that she couldn't spare the time. Two of her students, who had been listening to our brief colloquy, approached me after Miss Porter left the room. "She's a real prima donna," one of them said. "She hasn't got time for anyone." Needless to say, I was inclined to agree with him at that particular moment; but, in retrospect, I can readily understand how harassed and put-upon she must have felt.)

Restless, frustrated, unable to settle down to serious writing, she spent the next two years (1942–1943) wandering back and forth from New York to Boulder to New York to Connecticut and back to New York again. Now and then she would write a short essay or biographical note, none of which added much to her stature as an artist but nevertheless had occasional glimpses of her irony and wit.

"No Plot, My Dear, No Story" was a three-page "fable" about a great big little magazine with four and one half million subscribers, which made it possible for the publishers to charge advertisers $3,794.36 for an inch of space. Offering prospective writers a bit of professional advice, the narrator says, "There are all sorts of schools that can teach you exactly how to handle the 197 variations on any one of the 37 basic plots. . . . They can teach you the O. Henry twist; the trick of 'slanting' your stuff toward this market and that . . . then you are all set, maybe. After that you have only to buy a pack of 'Add-a-Plot' cards (free ad.) and go ahead. . . ."

"Homage to Ford Madox Ford" was a two-page remembrance of an old friend, who had been best man when she married Gene

Pressley. Recalling that Ford had referred to himself as "an old man mad about writing," she had added that "his madness was an illuminated sanity."

On learning of the death of James Joyce, she wrote a three-page notation in her journal, recalling the night she had heard T. S. Eliot reading his early poems, while Joyce sat nearby, his half-blind eyes concealed behind dark glasses. She also added some observations on W. B. Yeats and Ezra Pound.

"The Charmed Life," was a six-page biographical essay about the old American archaeologist who took her to the ruins of Teo-tihuacán (near Mexico City), where she met the beautiful Indian woman who was the protagonist of her memorable "María Concepción." Her notes for this essay had been scribbled twenty-one years earlier (1921).

"Miss Porter Adds a Comment" was a letter she wrote to *The Nation* magazine (March 6, 1943) in response to a negative review of her translation of the Mexican picaresque novel *The Itching Parrot*. The opening line set the tone for this much-too-defensive reaction: "A number of persons, some of them good friends, all of them well disposed to my work, have confessed that they simply (simply!) could not be interested in *The Itching Parrot....*"

"The Winged Skull," also published in *The Nation*, was a review of *This Is Lorence: A Narrative of the Reverend Laurence Sterne*, by Lodwick Hartley. Reaffirming her long-held admiration of Sterne, she had this comment about *Tristram Shandy*: "That book contains more living, breathing people you can see and hear, whose garments have texture between your finger and thumb, whose flesh is knit firmly to their bones, who walk about their affairs with audible steps, than any other one novel in the world, I do believe."

"The Days Before" was an extended biographical essay of Henry James, much longer and more carefully written than any of the aforementioned occasional writings. Aside from several comments on the economic security enjoyed by James, she very astutely analyzed his character and background: "His intuitions were very keen and pure from the beginning, and foreknowledge of his ineducability in any practical sense caused him very rightly to kick and shriek as they hauled him however fondly to his first day of school." Commenting on both William and Henry James, she further noted that "their father taught them a horror of priggishness, and of conscious virtue; guarded them, by precept and example, from that vulgarity he described as 'flagrant morality.' . . ."

Near the beginning of this two-year period and before she had written any of these minor essays, *Accent II** published a third chapter from the eleven she had written thirteen years earlier for her long-heralded but never published book on Cotton Mather. This chapter was titled "Affectation of Praehiminincies" and dealt with the birth and early childhood of Mather.

She published no fiction during this time, but it was later learned that she had written three different versions of "Holiday," none of which satisfied her. She simply stashed them away with several piles of yellowing manuscripts that had followed her from Texas to Mexico to Germany to Switzerland to France to Austria and to several sections of the United States.

In 1944 she wrote a fascinating autobiographical essay called "Portrait: Old South," which was actually a portrait of her grandmother. The opening lines must have sent chills down the spine of any Southerner who read it and probably still do: "I am the grandchild of a lost War, and I have blood-knowledge of what life can be in a defeated country on the bare bones of privation." Much of what she said has been covered in earlier chapters of this book, but one ought to mention her comment on some of the family legends she heard as a child: ". . . they were the merest surface ripples over limitless deeps of bitter memory. My elders all remained nobly unreconstructed to their last moments, and my feet rest firmly on this rock of their strength to this day." Which seemed a far cry from Miranda's repeated rejections of what she considered a false past, but at the age of fifty-four Miss Porter seemed a bit more nostalgic than she had been during the preceding decade.

---

*Spring 1942.

Her sudden spate of regional chauvinism may have been prompted by something that happened earlier in the year. In late January (1944) she was appointed to the Society of Fellows of the Library of Congress by Archibald MacLeish. Her exact title was Fellow of Regional American Literature. In what must have seemed a cruel irony, she was to fill out the unexpired term of John Peale Bishop, who had been forced to resign because of a severe debilitating illness. She had been recommended for the vacancy by the poet and critic Allen Tate. Continuing the work of Bishop and his predecessor, she did extensive research into source writings of pioneers and of transient visitors in the early history of this country, which consisted of letters, journals, folk tales, poetry (or rather verse) and published fiction. Not surprisingly, she paid special attention to stories of the great migration from Virginia and Pennslyvania to Kentucky. "It was an unbelievably rich and vast field," she subsequently reported, "even the small corner I chose for my own, for the whole project would take the working lifetime of one individual." The ultimate goal was to locate all existing documents and rare printings in all the libraries and private collections, and to catalogue them for public reference.

She had temporarily moved to Washington to pursue her research and found the work "deeply interesting and exciting," but after several months she felt a nagging urge to get back to the job that was her first (and presumably only) priority. No doubt, the publication of *The Leaning Tower and Other Stories** served to remind her of the many stories she had been promising to write. The new collection included "The Circus," "The Grave," "The Old Order," "A Day's Work," and four additional stories which had not been published before: "The Source," "The Witness," "The Last Leaf" and "Downward Path to Wisdom."

"The Source" was an introduction to Miranda's grandmother and her family within a framework of Southern society. It provides an engrossing though fragmentary account of the somewhat romanticized world of Sophia Jane Rhea, which was to influence the character of Miranda — just as Katherine Anne Porter and

---

* Published by Harcourt, Brace and Co., 1944.

her society were crucial in the molding of Katherine Anne Porter, both as a person and as an artist.

"The Witness" emphasized the role of Uncle Jimbilly, a former family slave who had stayed on with the Rheas after the Civil War. The accounts of slavery the children heard from Uncle Jimbilly inevitably contradicted what they had heard from their elders (". . . Dey used to take 'em out and tie 'em down and whup 'em wid gret big leather straps inch thick long as yo' arm . . . so's evey time dey hit 'em de hide and de meat done come off dey bones in little round chunks. . . ."), leaving the children to wonder who was telling the truth.

"The Last Leaf" was a fitting close to the opening phase of the family chronicle. The grandmother has died, and her lifelong servant Nannie had surprised the family by moving away from the main house to a small cabin symbolically located across the creek. The children had tried to dissuade the old woman, assuring her that they loved her and would care for her; but Nannie simply didn't care, for she was part of the Old Order, and she was now preparing for her own death: "I've served my time, I've done my do, and dat's all."

Although *The Leaning Tower and Other Stories* was well received, it failed to arouse the kind of enthusiasm which greeted Miss Porter's two previous collections. Nor did the book yield anything resembling a bonanza, since such collections seldom get into the lists of "best-sellers." In fact most publishers stay away from short story collections, printing them only if the author has agreed to write (or has already written) a full-sized novel, a contractual obligation which Miss Porter could not or would not accept.

Consequently, she found herself getting perilously short of cash as 1945 rolled around — this despite her customary Spartan frugality. So at the age of fifty-five she began traveling throughout the country, giving lectures and singing ballads and once more resenting her inability to find more time for serious writing.

"I've spent about ten per cent of my energies on writing, and the other ninety per cent to keeping my head above water," she once remarked, pointedly adding that even Saint Teresa had refused to starve herself or wear a haircloth shirt, insisting she could pray better when she was comfortable. Miss Porter further added that "living in cellars and starving is no better for an artist than it is for anybody else."

On another occasion, she wistfully remarked, "You know how life is. I've never had any protection or margin, nor any buffer between me and the economic grimness of life."

Aware of her chronically unstable financial status, her friends were not at all surprised when she suddenly decided to accept an offer to write screenplays for a Hollywood film producer. Her friend Robert Penn Warren was already in Los Angeles, collaborating on a scenario for one of his recent novels, and he was probably instrumental in getting her hired shortly after the beginning of 1946.

"Although the salary was modest by Hollywood standards, it was much more money than I had ever earned,"* she later told friends. "So I packed my bags again, manuscripts and all, and hurried out to California."

She was accompanied by a charming, extremely handsome photographer named George Platt Lynes, with whom she lived in a pink stucco Spanish-style house in Santa Monica. "But there was no sex involved in our relationship. He had no interest in women in that particular respect. He was simply a good, loyal and very witty friend, whose company I greatly enjoyed."

In explaining her liaison with Lynes, she candidly alluded to what she called "a most comfortable alliance" with three homosexual friends (two of them fairly well-known writers), who were her constant companions and escorts during a ten- or fifteen-year period. "It was so nice to relax with that kind of man, to enjoy his delightfully malicious wit and intelligence, without having to worry about bruising his male ego, his machismo, and having to deal with all that ritualized wrestling around at the end of an otherwise cheerful evening."

Aside from being an easy person to be with, Lynes was an ex-

---

* Probably five hundred dollars per week.

cellent and imaginative photographer, whose favorite nonprofessional model was Miss Porter herself. On one occasion, using a timing device, he photographed Miss Porter and himself in a fascinating pose — she standing on an overhead balcony with the rapt expression of a middle-aged Juliet, while he stood just below her, clad in white swimming trunks, flexing the sleek muscles of his elegant bronze body like a young Adonis.

"It was an awfully silly picture," she subsequently admitted. "But it was great fun when we did it. Southern California lent itself to that kind of silliness; some people might have called it *going Hollywood.*"

Apparently, her old friend Truman Capote had also *gone Hollywood* in a big way, sporting dark sunglasses, flamboyant silk scarves, salmon-colored shirts, navy-blue blazers with shiny brass buttons, and a snappy yachting cap.

"Still on the prowl for celebrities, he couldn't have been in a more promising ambience," Miss Porter observed with a knowing smile. "He was surrounded by famous people he had always wanted to know. And he was determined to meet them."

Although Capote was naturally interested in some of the other writers in Hollywood — Aldous Huxley, Christopher Isherwood, William Faulkner, Robert Penn Warren, William Saroyan, *et al.* — he was even more fascinated by the actors, actresses, directors and producers, many of whom he managed to meet one way or another.

One afternoon, as he was lunching with Miss Porter at a studio cafeteria, Capote leaned toward her with a smile that was both conspiratorial and smug. "Guess who I had lunch with yesterday?" he said. "In the star's dining room, I'll have you know."

"I can't possibly imagine, Truman, but I'm sure you're going to tell me."

"Well," he said, ignoring her remark. "It was Greta Garbo herself, and she was perfectly delightful."

"How wonderful," said Miss Porter, barely suppressing a yawn. "But how did you manage this magnificent coup?"

"Well, I've got my ways, Katherine Anne," he said, his smile broadening into a grin. "I've got my ways."

Although not entirely immune from the lure of Miss Garbo and her less mysterious colleagues, Miss Porter was far more interested in the truly creative artists like Aldous Huxley. Consequently, when Robert Penn Warren asked her to accompany him to a Sunday afternoon party at Huxley's home, she happily accepted. It was a rather intimate gathering and full of stimulating conversation about hallucinogenic drugs and extrasensory perception. One of the more amusing guests was Christoper Isherwood, who subsequently asked Warren for a ride back to Santa Monica.

Miss Porter was riding in the back seat of the car but leaned forward to join the conversation between the two men, one of whom happened to mention a child who was suffering from an incurable disease.

"That reminds me of some children I met at a sanitarium near San Antonio," she interjected."They were all afflicted with tuberculosis. I was teaching them how to read and write, but it was heartbreaking to realize they would soon be dead."

"My oh my," said Isherwood, mimicking her soft Southern drawl. "We've got a sure enough Texas Joan of Arc ridin' with us."

Reacting instantly, she quietly reached forward and grabbed his hair with both hands and yanked it slowly but firmly, jerking his head back and forth two or three times. Momentarily stunned, Isherwood didn't make a sound until she let go. Then all he could say was a befuddled "Jesus."

Recalling the incident some twenty years later, an impish twinkle in her eyes, Miss Porter told me that she had experienced a remarkable sensation as she pulled his hair. "It was a visceral thrill that I could feel in every fiber of my body," she said. "But, of course, that's a womanly pleasure which you men know nothing about."

Then pointing at a picture of Norman Mailer on the front page of the *New York Times* literary review section, she said, "Now there's a bunch of hair I'd like to yank — it's so thick and curly. It's just about perfect for pulling."

Several months later I mentioned her remark to Mailer, and he responded with an amused eye-crinkling grin: "She's about the meanest little old lady in tennis shoes that I've ever met. And I guess you know that hair-pulling is a sure sign of sexual frustration."

The Isherwood episode calls to mind a similar scene from Miss Porter's memorable *Noon Wine*, where Mr. Thompson gives his wife "a good pinch on her thin little rump":

> Mrs. Thompson looked at him opened-eyed and blushed. She could see better by lamplight. "Why, Mr. Thompson, sometimes I think you're the evilest-minded man that ever lived." She took a handful of hair on the crown of his head and gave it a good slow pull. "That's to show you how it feels, pinching so hard when you're supposed to be playing," she said gently.

If, indeed, Mailer was correct in his Freudian comment on this particular syndrome, there was no discussion of hair-pulling when Miss Porter was interviewed about her sexual attitudes and habits by Dr. Alfred Kinsey, who was in the process of completing research for his book on the sex life of American females. Hair-pulling would have seemed much too prosaic to Kinsey; he was obviously interested in more bizarre behavior, and he wasted no time with the usual prefatory questions.

"Have you ever made love to a dog?" he asked without the slightest change in his bland expression.

"Why, no, Dr. Kinsey!" she exclaimed. "Have you?"

"B-b-but, I'm asking th-the questions," he stammered, momentarily losing his poise but quickly recovering. "But, no, I haven't."

He actually blushed, she later said, and quickly moved on to the rest of the questions on his questionnaire. And when he had completed the list, they had a rather extended and cheerful talk about art, music, literature and gourmet cooking. But before he left, Kinsey asked if she had ever read the works of Krafft-Ebing or Stekel.

"Not a word," she said. "Some of my friends have advised me to read them. But I have no interest in the sex life of other people — only my own."

As she declared in a devastatingly effective essay on D. H. Lawrence, "Lovemaking surely must be, for human beings at our present state of development, one of the more private enterprises. Who would want a witness to that entire self-abandonment and helplessness?"

She was referring to what she considered a grotesquely awkward scene in *Lady Chatterley's Lover*, which she had always condemned as highly overrated trash. Nevertheless, she strongly opposed any attempt to censor Lawrence's controversial novel — or any other novel. In fact, during her brief residence in Los Angeles, she joined hundreds of writers and sympathizers who picketed around the courthouse where a local book dealer was being tried for selling Edmund Wilson's *Memoirs of Hecate County*, which the District Attorney characterized as "pornographic filth."

She felt that her defense of Wilson's novel was "a misguided act of guild loyalty and personal admiration I cannot really regret, so far as friendship is concerned. But otherwise the whole episode was deplorably unnecessary." She went on to say that she much preferred his "magnificent" *To the Finland Station* or any of his essays on literary or public affairs.

Several years later she would appear as a defense witness in a similar trial involving the censorship of Henry Miller's *Tropic of Cancer*. After a long journey on a bitterly cold day, she sat in a New York City courtroom for several hours before she was finally called to the witness stand. But every time Miller's lawyer tried to ask her a hypothetical question, the prosecutor would jump to his feet and object to the question. Somehow, after a long series of queries that drew similar objections, she managed to convey her abhorrence for any kind of censorship. Then, just before leaving the courtroom, she quietly told Miller's attorney, "Some day I hope to be given a chance to stand up in defense of a book I really like and not one that is being censored because it used two dirty little words which I happen to find obnoxious anyway." But she resisted a strong impulse to tell Henry Miller to put away his chalk and stop writing on walls.

Aside from her opposition to governmental censorship of

morals, Miss Porter was also vehemently opposed to the political thought-control which was sweeping across the nation at the time she was working as a screen writer. She clearly expressed her liberal sentiments in a journalistic report on a "Town Meeting of the Air" broadcast from the Philharmonic Auditorium in the summer of 1947.* Four local celebrities debated the pros and cons of "Communism in Hollywood," and there was an overflow crowd, carefully guarded by a record number of police, whose presence was ironically noted by Miss Porter: ". . . Or am I just prejudiced against seeing public assemblies, when political debates take place, being treated as if they were composed of potential criminals? It always reminds me unpleasantly of Berlin in 1932."

Miss Porter was disturbed by the sizable minority of spectators who raised their hands when the moderator asked how many people believed that communism was a genuine threat to the film industry, but this did not alter her final judgment: "I still don't know how many communists there are in Hollywood, nor where they are; but I will trust Mr.Dekker and Mr. Lavery and that audience to fight them more effectively than any number of Anti-American Activities Committees, whose activities have seemed to me from the beginning the most un-American thing I know."

Though she was a member of the controversial Screen Writers Guild, Miss Porter had no active role in any of its functions, political or otherwise. "As a matter of fact, I felt it was rather presumptuous of me to belong to the guild, since none of my scripts was ever converted into actual film." In view of her extensive firsthand knowledge of Texas ranch life, she had hoped one of the studio bosses would ask her to write a scenario for a blood-and-guts western; "but they wouldn't listen to me — they wanted me to write all that saccharine drivel about swooning Southern belles in perpetual distress, or some equally stupid nonsense about some poor rich woman imprisoned in a haunted mansion."

Bored with her scripts and angry at herself for writing them, she apparently vented some of her frustration by writing a scathing critique of Gertrude Stein. In 1927 she had praised Miss Stein

---

* She reported the meeting for the *Westwood Daily*.

as "the great influence on the younger literary generation," further stating that she was free of pride and humility: "She is honest in her uncertainties. There are only a few bits of absolute knowledge in the world, people can learn only one or two fundamental facts about each other, the rest is decoration and prejudice. She is very free from decoration and prejudice."

But now, more than twenty years later, Miss Porter had decided to write about her intervening disenchantment with Miss Stein, which probably dated back to the winter of 1933, when she has visited the famous atelier in rue de Fleurus with Caroline and Allen Tate. Her revised opinions in "The Wooden Umbrella" amounted to an almost complete turnabout. Referring to some of Stein's former admirers, who had left her and became successful writers on their own terms, Miss Porter said, "Humanly, shamefacedly, they then jeered at their former admiration, and a few made the tactical error of quarreling with her. She enjoyed their discipleship while it lasted, and dismissed them from existence when it ended."

Here and there, Miss Porter seemed to concede a certain primal wisdom in Miss Stein's work, but such concessions would usually be vitiated by an astringent put-down in the very next sentence or paragraph:

... in that slow swarm of words, out of the long drone and mutter and stammer of her lifetime monologue, often there emerged a phrase of ancient native independent wisdom. . . . Of all those G.I.'s who swarmed about her in her last days, if anyone showed any fight at all, any tendency to question her pronouncements, she smacked him down like a careful grandmother, for his own good. . . . Like all talkers, she thought other people talked too much. . . . Wise or silly or nothing at all, down everything goes on the page with the air of everything being equal, unimportant in itself, important only because it happened to her and she was writing about it. . . . Considering her tepid, sluggish nature, really sluggish like something eating its way through a leaf, Miss Stein could grow quite animated on the subject of her early family life, and some of her stories are as pretty and innocent as lizards running over tombstones on a hot day. . . . The mind so long shapeless and undisciplined could not now express any knowledge out of its long wilful ignorance. But the heart spoke its crude urgent language. . . .

As Miss Porter no doubt anticipated, "The Wooden Umbrella" provoked violent reactions from all sides when it was published in 1947. No reader could have remained neutral. There was still some fallout on the campus of Stanford University when Miss Porter arrived to take up her appointment as writer-in-residence in October of a subsequent year. Most of her colleagues in the English Department disagreed with her harsh appraisal of Miss Stein but managed to keep their objections within the bounds of academic civility. Some of the younger professors and instructors felt no such compunctions and openly hinted that there was personal animosity in Miss Porter's criticism. They got even more hostile when she started declining invitations to various faculty social functions.

She shrugged aside their hostility with an air of amused forbearance, which someone characterized as "grande dame bitchiness," but she was much less forbearing when another Gertrude Stein admirer (Professor Donald Sutherland) renewed the controversy six years later (1953). In a memorandum to Yale University, a copy of which Miss Porter received, Sutherland indirectly surmised that Miss Porter's stinging critique was an act of revenge, and that she had waited until Miss Stein was dead to launch her attack. As a possible explanation of Miss Porter's "malice," he cited a passage from a letter he had received from Miss Stein:

. . . you know there was a funny story, one day a young gentleman called and he sent in a note saying that he was a nephew of Katherine Anne Porter. Then he came in and I said gently and politely, do I know your aunt, I am afraid said he you have never met, and I said politely who is she, and he went quite white and said you know and I said no, and then he decided to take it as a joke, but it was a blow, he had evidently traveled far on his nephewship. . . .

Miss Porter's response was quick and angry. After some preliminary comments about her 1932 visit to Miss Stein's atelier and some acerbic appraisals of her writing and overall influence ("I thought her a blight on everything she touched, and I think so now more than ever"), Miss Porter came to the core of her disclaimer:

... My nephew told me this story about Gertrude Stein. But not before my article was written, and not before I had decided to publish it. ... She had died meanwhile, and I brought it up to date a little — the original piece, as you see, had been begun nearly ten years before; and I was troubled that I had not finished it and published it before her death because I realized that I could also be accused of base motives in withholding it. I had not withheld it. I simply finished it in its own time, an editor of *Harper's,* a friend of mine, who knew it was in existence, thought it very timely, and asked me for it. ... But I did not know this story of my nephew's until *afterward.* ... However, this gave someone his big chance to write to *Harper's* magazine and tell the story and accuse me of taking my base revenge in the form of this article. I did not answer it because I did not know yet. It is a thing too cheap and mean even to talk about, and yet the circumstances certainly do give such minds all they need to work on. It is a matter exactly of my word against theirs — a very loaded kind of dice, for they are not interested in facts. Nice fresh dirty gossip is good enough for them. ...

In a subsequent letter, Professor Sutherland expressed an appalling machismo that would have set any woman's teeth on edge: "But I do think the feminine mind lives and breathes in the personal and the sensory, and when you go on the attack, even with fasting and prayer and purity of heart, you come out with the substance and texture of gossip and cannot really get beyond moral ideas, so that there has never been a woman critic and I think there never will be, except where the specific gifts are at their best, as when Edith Sitwell is on the subject of the texture of Pope or the misdeeds of Wyndham Lewis. *So I think you are wasting your time on criticism. ...*" (Italics mine.)

In her return letter, Miss Porter told Sutherland that his reviews of Miss Stein's work carried a charge of the personal and sensory that "fairly pulsates between the lines." She also said that men were "the most virulent and persistent gossips I know, and at a level which shames me for the human race." Then once again confronting the male chauvinist professor on the issue that nettled her the most, she said, "Let's not play that silly game. . . . You are welcome to disagree with me as much as you choose, criticize my work as severely as you like; but please don't expose yourself by putting it on the grounds that I am a woman."

Had her younger colleagues at Stanford University known back in 1948 about the "nephew episode," they probably would have chosen to believe that she had indeed been motivated by revenge in her virulent attack on Gertrude Stein. But at least a portion of their hostility could be attributed to their prior resentment of Miss Porter's refusal to socialize with anyone.

"They wouldn't allow me any privacy," she later complained. "I had been promised plenty of time to do my own work, but then I had all those student papers to correct and personal conferences with them — and all those faculty teas and cocktail parties I was expected to attend as some sort of star attraction. And if I said 'No,' however graciously, I was sure to be called a prima donna. They simply wouldn't recognize my right to a little privacy."

Once in a while, she would escape to San Francisco for a few days, usually staying at an inexpensive hotel near Chinatown. But she seldom got down to any serious writing, for there were too many fascinating distractions in that lovely city. One of them was a young man she had met either in Greenwich Village or at the writers' workshop at Olivet College. He was a "very mature" thirty and she was fifty-eight, although she could have passed for someone in her early forties. "Nevertheless, we had a brief fling that winter. Nothing too serious, mind you, no great emotional investment on either side. But I'll admit it was rather intense." (Remembering that she had once told me, "When I fall in love, the meeting between us is like an exchange of signals with lightning — and when I've gotten over the shock and sorted out the damage, I can then remember what really happened . . . ," I couldn't help wondering if this particular affair had provoked a similar trauma.)

It is interesting to note that during this period (1947–1948) she wrote a disturbingly penetrating analysis of love and hate titled "The Necessary Enemy," in which she said,

Her hatred is real as her love is real, but her hatred has the advantage at present because it works on a blind instinctual level, it is lawless; and her love is subjected to a code of ideal conditions, impossible by their very nature of fulfillment. . . . Hatred is natural in a sense that love, as she conceives it, a young person brought up in the tradition of Romantic Love, is not natural at all. . . . [Her vow was] the statement of honorable intention to practice as well as she is able the noble acquired faculty of love, that very mysterious overtone to sex which is the best thing in it. Her hatred is part of it, the necessary enemy and ally.

13

The Ezra Pound Controversy

ALTHOUGH embittered by her experience as writer-in-residence at Stanford University, Miss Porter soon thereafter began a grueling lecture tour with brief stops at numerous universities throughout the country. It was an exhausting and often boring chore, which left her no time for serious writing, but she hoped to accumulate enough money to "buy" a year or two of uninterrupted freedom.

Now approaching sixty, she was still unable to make a decent living at her chosen profession. Her kind of fiction had never been published in the popular big-circulation magazines, and the so-called "little" magazines could pay her only nominal fees of fifty or a hundred dollars per story. Teaching and lecturing, both of which she hated, offered a more secure source of income, but the sheer physical strain and drudgery of constantly moving from one campus to another had a debilitating effect on her morale, particularly for a fifty-nine-year-old woman whose health had always been somewhat precarious. One could sense a benumbed weariness in a letter she wrote to her nephew while lecturing at Purdue University in the summer of 1948: "Now it is only four days until I must be on the road again, but only for two days' work and then I shall stop in the Missouri University Sorority House until time for a big show in Kansas. Then another short rest and on to Seattle, Nebraska, Indiana —"

She went on to say that the North and Middle West had always seemed like foreign lands to her, in a way that Mexico and France never had. Compared to what she called the "stylish literary communism" of New York and California, she felt that Midwesterners were "quite innocently, you might say almost unconsciously, Fascist or Nazi —"

Observing that the population around Purdue was largely German and that the university "crawls with them," she was frankly concerned about their continued sympathy for the Germans who had followed Hitler. "I have always admired the way the French hate the *sales Boches* steadily and for good reasons and without foaming at the mouth, without screaming for revenge, but without any intention ever to let them get the upper hand again."

But her periodic comdemnation of any type of totalitarianism — communist or fascist — was only half-heard in most of the Midwest colleges. They applauded her tough remarks about communists but blithely ignored her attacks on fascism. "They seemed to be living in a political vacuum," she later concluded. "They were getting no input from the outside." After a while she herself began to feel isolated, with no newspapers or magazines from New York — and practically no mail from friends and relatives.

Because of her constant travels, her mail could never catch up with her, lagging farther and farther behind with each passing day, which simply exacerbated her sense of loneliness. She would occasionally imagine a small blizzard of tattered letters swooshing into her room and covering her from head to toe. "I realize most of it would have been junk mail, but I'm sure there were some letters I would have enjoyed receiving."

Some of the missing letters were from the Library of Congress — more specifically, from the Society of Fellows in American Literature, which was in the process of selecting a recipient of the Bollingen Award for Poetry. Several poets had been considered in preliminary balloting by mail, but none of these ballots were ever received by Miss Porter. Consequently, the list of candidates had been pared down to four poets when she finally got a chance to participate, and she voted for Ezra Pound. Although she was not overly enthusiastic about *The Pisan Cantos*, which she considered inferior to his previous work, she felt they were better than the poetry written by the other three poets, ". . . and

*Miss Porter in the library of the University of Michigan, where
she lectured in 1954. Shortly after this picture was taken, she
collapsed in class and was rushed to a local hospital.*
Photograph by Eck Stanger

if I had voted against him, or had abstained, it would have been because I abhor his treason and detest his emotional perversities, for they cannot be called ideas, in politics, and not at all on the grounds provided for in my vote."

She would have considered such action a "sidestepping of a serious problem," and she had never been known to sidestep any controversy. Still, she regretted that the award was not withheld until "a luckier year," and would have preferred to vote for John Crowe Ransom, Wallace Stevens, Louise Bogan, Léonie Adams, Robert Penn Warren, Randall Jarrell, Marianne Moore, Allen Tate, Robert Graves, W. H. Auden, Archibald MacLeish, e. e. cummings, T. S. Eliot, Edith Sitwell or the late Paul Valéry, whose "The Cemetery by the Sea" had deeply moved her. But, of course, some of these poets were foreigners and thus ineligible for the Bollingen Prize, and the others had not published a volume of poetry in the prescribed year, 1948.

The Fellows who participated in the final vote were Katherine Garrison Chapin (Mrs. Francis Biddle), Willard Thorp, Paul Green, Theodore Spencer, Conrad Aiken, Karl Shapiro, Robert Lowell and the aforementioned Tate, Bogan, Eliot, Auden, Warren, Adams and Miss Porter.

The award to Ezra Pound was announced on February 20, 1949, and the public outcry was even worse than Miss Porter had anticipated. Angry letters flooded the editorial offices of newspapers and magazines all over the country, far too many to print in the limited available space. There were also hundreds of public discussions in college campuses and local forums, with Pound's reluctant supporters usually in the minority. In one memorable debate between Professors Harry Levin and F. O. Matthiessen, held at Harvard University before an overflow crowd, Matthiessen eloquently defended the award, saying that he abhorred Pound's treasonable broadcasts every bit as much as Levin did, "... but even though I cannot agree with Ernest Hemingway, who would forgive the *man* because of his poetry, I cannot condemn the poetry because I hate the man who wrote it. In other words, *The Pisan Cantos* must be judged on its own merits, free of these outside considerations."

A completely contrary view was expressed by the Pulitzer Prize–winning poet Robert Hillyer in a two-part essay published on June 11 and 18 (1949) in the prestigious *Saturday Review of Literature*. Announcing his intention to analyze the much-disputed award from two points of view, the political and cultural, Hillyer titled his article "Treason's Strange Fruit" and forthwith launched his attack:

Ezra Pound is quite simply under indictment for treason because during the last war he served the enemy in direct poetical and propaganda activities against the United States. The defense has been that he was insane, which may be an interesting commentary on his prize-winning poetry. His poems are the vehicle of contempt for America, Fascism, anti-Semitism, and, in the prize-winning "Pisan Cantos" themselves, ruthless mockery of our Christian war dead. That fact may place the award, and the committee on the Bollingen Prize, in an observable relationship to our war dead and to the nation they died for. Lastly, the award was sponsored by the Library of Congress and its Librarian. The Library is the property of the American people; the Librarian is their paid custodian. Should this matter come up for investigation by Congress, neither the Librarian nor the Bollingen group will have the right to argue that it is an attempt on the part of the government to control literature; on the contrary, this group has apparently invoked the sanction of government for its own ends. . . .

After a lifetime of writing characterized by William Butler Yeats as "nervous obsession and nightmare, stammering confusion," this alienated citizen produced the "Pisan Cantos," certainly the worst of the lot. Yet the Bollingen jury stretched a point to consider Pound a citizen and defied all critical standards by finding in the "Pisan Cantos" the best American poetry of 1948.

Observing that the Bollingen Foundation had been granted ten thousand dollars for ten annual thousand-dollar prizes by Paul Mellon, the multimillionaire son of the former Secretary of the Treasury, Hillyer wryly commented that few, if any, of the jurors knew where the name Bollingen came from. Then he himself provided the answer and thereby stretched his argument to remarkable lengths:

Bollingen is the Swiss lakeside retreat of the psychoanalyst Dr. Carl G. Jung. It is near Zurich. There, in an idyllic cottage, dwell Dr. Jung and his wife, receiving the visits, adulation, and gifts of many, including such millionaires as Paul Mellon. It is said that his first wife was one of Dr. Jung's patients. There is no implication in what follows that Mr. Mellon had any knowledge of Dr. Jung's former connection with Nazism.

The issue of Dr. Jung's pro-Nazism has been hotly argued, though certain facts are a matter of record. For a time Dr. Jung's admiration for Hitler was warm, and his services to the Nazi cause, including propaganda activities during his trips to this country, were considerable. Among his sympathies were included such Nazi flourishes as racism in general, the superman, anti-Semitism, and a weird metaphysics embracing occultism, alchemy and the worship of Wotan. . . .

I had personal contact with Dr. Jung's Nazism. At luncheon during the Harvard Tercentenary of 1936, Dr. Jung, who was seated beside me, deftly introduced the subject of Hitler, developed it with alert warmth, and concluded with the statement that from the high vantage point of Alpine Switzerland, Hitler's new order in Germany seemed to offer the one hope of Europe. . . .

The alien, or expatriate, T. S. Eliot was not in the original group of Fellows in American Letters; he is a disciple of Dr. Jung; and he has been for years an intimate of Pound. Both Pound and Eliot, and especially Eliot, have a stranglehold on American poetry through the so-called "new criticism." . . . Eliot's whole life has been a flight from his native St. Louis, Missouri. He has gone far, and doubtless, if he survives Masefield, he will be the next English Laureate. In America he is so enhedged with nebulous divinity that people are shocked, as by blasphemy, at anything said against him. . . .

Hillyer made no specific reference to Katherine Anne Porter, except to list her name as one of the jurors, but it was she who wrote the most effective rebuttal to his lengthy articles. Having first reiterated her abhorrence of Pound's treason and his "emotional perversities," and further regretting that the committee had not withheld its award to a "luckier" year, she admitted not knowing the origin of the prize, nor the meaning of its name — and she did not inquire as she had not inquired into the sources of a great many other prizes and fellowships, "because I have a general knowledge that, in many instances, a very small part indeed of some very ill-got fortunes have been returned to society in the form of benefits to the needy."

As for Mr. Hillyer's firsthand knowledge of Dr. Jung's Nazi beliefs, she quite logically asked "What was a professed Nazi doing as the guest of Harvard so late as 1936, when his vicious ideologies were already so well known?" And more to the point, she asked if Hillyer himself had rushed from that luncheon to speak to some member of the faculty, to the trustees, to the president of Harvard himself, warning them against Dr. Jung? "Did he write and publish a piece about it? Did he do anything at all about it? Or did he just forget it until now, when suddenly it pops up as a convenient weapon to use against poets not of his school?"

As for Hillyer's reference to T. S. Eliot as an alien and expatriate, who would thus have no right to serve on the Bollingen jury, Miss Porter surmised that "he would not like Mr. Eliot any better if he had stayed in St. Louis."

Like so many emotionally overwrought advocates, Mr. Hillyer had weakened a basically sound premise with scattershot arguments that were far off target, allowing his bias to lead him into captious remarks tinged with envy and narrow self-interest. Had he confined himself to the mean-spirited racism and the confused maunderings of the poetry itself, emphasizing the fact of Pound's presumed insanity when he wrote *The Pisan Cantos*, Hillyer would have been much less susceptible to Miss Porter's skillful rejoinder. Indeed, the weakest aspect of her answer was her failure to refute Mr. Hillyer's well-buttressed accusation that Pound's poems were grossly anti-Semitic.

Soon after her rather acrimonious dispute with Hillyer and *SRL*, Miss Porter found herself in a most charitable and loving mood as she reviewed Edith Sitwell's *The Canticle of the Rose*. Comparing Sitwell's lifelong excellence to that of W. B. Yeats and Henry James, she likened Sitwell's early poems to the courtly music of Lully, Rameau, Purcell and Monteverdi, whose festival music was meant to be played at christenings and weddings or in sweet-smelling gardens under a full moon. But there was a less romantic quality in Miss Sitwell's poetry which struck a deeper chord in Miss Porter's admiration: "So many peevish and obscene little writers of late have been compared to Swift I hesitate to set his name here even where I feel it is not out of place. In *Gold Coast Customs* I find for the first time in my contemporary reading a genius for invective as ferocious as Swift's own, invective in the high-striding authoritative style, the same admirable stateliness of wrath, the savage indignation of a just mind and generous heart outraged to the far edge of endurance."

One could now add Miss Sitwell to Miss Porter's select roster of brilliant women writers who were gifted with a "just cruelty," the others being Eudora Welty, Katherine Mansfield and Flannery O'Connor.

Although the Sitwell review and the response to Hillyer's articles were fairly lengthy and time-consuming, Miss Porter spent most of her creative efforts during 1949 in preliminary drafts of the long-awaited *Ship of Fools*. All the separate pieces seemed to be coming together into a fascinating mosaic, but there were cracks to be filled, colors to be changed — and, as usual, she was demanding the utmost perfection of herself. That, of course, required complete isolation from all outside distractions, an isolation that was breached only for the most special reasons, one of which was a quick trip to the University of North Carolina, where she was awarded an honorary degree as Doctor of Literature.

Finally, in the early months of 1950, she finished writing three long segments of her novel, which were published in the October, November and December (1949) issues of *Harper's* magazine, the title having been changed to "No Safe Harbor." The public response was generally favorable, ecstatic in some quarters, and once again she was under tremendous pressure to complete the novel for book-length publication. "They wouldn't let me do it my way," she subsequently complained. "They just kept hounding me, they simply wouldn't understand that I had to work at my own pace."

Meanwhile, she managed to write three essays, on Ezra Pound, Rainer Maria Rilke and Virginia Woolf, all of which were subsequently published in *The Days Before.* The eight-page critique on Pound, significantly titled "It Is Hard to Stand in the Middle," seemed to gloss over his anti-Semitism and mainly dealt with his influence as a critic and tutor of other writers, also alluding to his obstreperous nature: "Pound was one of the most opinionated and unselfish men who ever lived, and he made friends and enemies everywhere by the simple exercise of the classic American constitutional right of free speech. His speech was free to outrageous license. He was completely reckless about making enemies."

Her essay on Rilke, "Orpheus in Purgatory," was largely devoted to the poet's full love life and his boredom with public adulation. "As much hysterical nonsense has been written about him as about D. H. Lawrence, if that is possible. Like Lawrence, his personal attractiveness drew to him the parasitic kind of adorers who insist on feeding on the artist himself instead of on his work."

Her brief commentary on Virginia Woolf spoke admiringly of Mrs. Woolf's perfectionism, her painstaking ways of working, her many revisions and rewritings, and her refusal to allow any of her work to be published unless it was completely satisfactory. "She was one of the writers who touched the real life of my mind and feeling very deeply; I had from that book (*The Voyage Out*) the same sense of some mysterious revelation of truth I had got in earliest youth from Laurence Sterne, from Jane Austen, from Emily Brontë, and from Henry James."

These short essays were fairly typical of the kind of writing she would do for the next ten years. She would publish no fiction whatever from December 1950 to June 1960, and many of her admirers would occasionally ask, "Whatever happened to Katherine Anne Porter?"

Much of that time was spent on the college lecture circuit, Miss Porter always hoping to accumulate enough money to buy another year of "freedom" for her truly serious work. Not wishing to yield ten or twenty percent fees to an established lecture bureau, she would arrange her own tours, which were predictably haphazard and more time-consuming than they should have been.

Sometimes she would have extended periods as a writer-in-residence at some university, but she usually resented the constant pressure of students seeking personal advice and the even more onerous pressure from faculty colleagues inviting her to social functions.

"Oh, I yearned for a nice, quiet, very private cabin in the mountains or a house on an isolated beach!"

It is doubtful, however, that a mere period of isolation would have been sufficient to break through the writer's block that constantly plagued her. Indeed, considering her monumental reputation, she had produced very little fiction, far less than most writers of comparable reputation. Now past sixty — after forty years of episodic bursts of creativity — she had published three slender volumes of short stories and short novels, which altogether would amount to one average-sized novel.

The factors that lead to a creative impasse are of course numerous and complex. Dr. Edrita Fried, whose *Artistic Productivity and Mental Health* is widely quoted by fellow psychologists, says that writers and artists are uniquely vulnerable to internal and external pressures. "Vulnerability, or a state of being not too heavily protected by various mechanisms and manoeuvres of defense, is indeed a *requirement* for the creative personality." In the foreword to Dr. Fried's book, Chaim Gross observes that many talented people feel tempted to quit their work when things go wrong in their personal lives: "Talent can get lost in unhappy marriages; or when love gets divided too drastically between work and children; or when the pressure to make a living becomes so great that it overshadows everything else. When talented people get confused in these complicated times in which we are living, they also frequently lose their ability to work."

Certainly, many of these factors were operative in Miss Porter's case. From the moment she ran away from home, she was engaged in a constant struggle to make a living, working as a low-paid reporter and ghost writer to augment her meager earnings as a serious writer of fiction, always existing on what she called "the barest of margins." She was also constantly moving, lecturing and teaching at various colleges and hating it because of the terrific psychic drain. Restless, insecure, unhappy and unlucky at love, she had liaisons with much younger men as she got older, but was unable to make any permanent commitments because of her basic mistrust of people. (It's interesting to note that she never wrote any of her best fiction while having an affair or while married to Pressley and Erskine.) Underlying much of this malaise was a lifelong insecurity dating back to the deaths of her mother and grandmother and the consequent fear of abandonment. Thus, the Miranda stories were essentially exercises in nostalgia, a wistful remembrance of the only secure home she ever knew.

Moreover, according to Erik Erikson's theories, her failure to commit herself to concrete affiliations, her inability to develop a sense of genuine intimacy with any of her lovers or husbands, inevitably led her to a deep sense of isolation and consequent self-absorption. Thus, she was unable to evolve into what Erikson calls "the stage of generativity," the bearing of children and the guidance of them. "Mature man needs to be needed," he says, "and maturity needs guidance as well as encouragement from what has been produced and must be taken care of. . . . Generativity thus is an essential stage on the psychosexual as well as on the psychological schedule. Where such enrichment fails altogether, regression to an obsessive need for pseudo-intimacy takes place, often with a pervading sense of stagnation and personal impoverishment."

There were many times when Miss Porter frankly admitted that she felt stagnant and depleted, and occasionally one of her friends would obliquely suggest that she seek psychiatric help to overcome her writer's block. But as Dr. Lawrence Kubie points out in *Neurotic Distortions of the Creative Process*, "Many psychologically ailing artists, including some individuals whose productivity may have been seriously injured by their neurosis, refuse therapy out of fear that in losing their illness they will lose their creative spark and zeal." Indeed, Miss Porter once told me that she totally agreed with Rilke when he said, "If you deprive me of my neurosis, you rob me of my genius," or words to that effect.

Having no inclination to let anyone tamper with her creative processes, she studiously avoided psychiatrists and simply decided to deal with her writer's block as best she could.

In 1951, at the age of sixty-one, she was a lecturer in American literature at the University of Chicago, where she wrote a brief essay on E. M. Forster, whose volume of essays called *Abinger Harvest* was one of her favorite books. She had also read and reread *A Passage to India*, which would always remind her of the first and only time she ever saw Forster — on a crowded, dusty evening (June 21, 1935) in Paris, where he spoke at the International Congress of Writers. ". . . Mr. Forster is an artist who lives in that constant state of grace which comes of knowing who he is, where he lives, what he feels and thinks about this world. Virginia Woolf once wrote: 'One advantage of having a settled code of morals is that you know exactly what to laugh at.' She knew, and so does Mr. Forster." (It's interesting to note that in her dedication to E. Barrett Prettyman, Jr., for *The Collected Essays*, Miss Porter observes, "Yet we can laugh together and we know what to laugh at.")

There is a hint of elite mockery in this attitude, a certain lack of compassion, which was probably true of Woolf but not of Forster. It certainly was not true of Willa Cather, about whom Miss Porter wrote an affectionate essay in 1952. Having noted a similarity in their backgrounds — both were reared in rural areas and were heavily influenced by domineering grandmothers — she further observed that "Miss Cather was a good artist, and all true art is provincial in the most realistic sense: of the very time and place of its making, out of human beings who are so particularly limited by their situation." In her opinion, Cather was as provincial as Hawthorne or Flaubert or Turgenev, and "as little concerned with aesthetics and as much with morals as Tolstoy."

Her unique and very positive definition of that usually pejorative word, "provincial," would have been an interesting theme for her opening speech at the 1952 Paris Conference on the International Exposition of the Arts, but she had other things in mind. As one of six American representatives — the others were James Farrell, William Faulkner, Allen Tate, Robert Penn Warren and Glenway Wescott — she argued against writers getting too much involved in politics, saying that an artist "can play the fool for the love of God, and he does, but he shouldn't play the fool for a political party." As for the general public neglect of artists in most countries, she said that American artists were being killed with kindness in "an immense nursery or cradle system for the fostering of artists," which had been created by various funds and grants from charitable foundations, whose selection committees were usually incompetent. ". . . I am afraid they (the artists) are being strangled with hot butter. We have a fearful, an unholy alliance between the professors, the universities, the faculties, the critics and the working artist."

While she was attending the conference, Miss Porter's French translator, Marcelle Sibon, urged her to see the pre-Columbian art exhibit in the Mexican pavilion. "It's the best thing in the show," she said with great enthusiasm.

"I've seen a Mexican show, Marcelle," she said, still bitter as gall about her long-ago unsuccessful attempt to import the controversial archaeological exhibit into the United States. "I don't want to see another."

"But I've never seen you behave this way before," said Miss Sibon, failing to understand the sudden bitterness. "You're just missing something that is truly wonderful."

Eventually, Miss Porter did go to the Mexican exhibit, alone, and she was just as impressed as her friend. She walked into the great hall, and there was the same show she had helped assemble thirty years before, the magnificent treasure of the Aztec, Mayan and Toltec civilizations. (The Mexican government had borrowed many of the objects from museums and private collectors who had purchased them in Los Angeles in 1922.) It was a heart-throbbing experience that brought tears to her eyes. "Everybody on the original committee was still alive then — Covarrubias, Enciso, Gamío, Lozano, Merida — and they had all worked on it again except me. They hadn't invited me again because I had gone into such a rampage the first time."

Shortly after her return from Paris, she published *The Days Before*, a collection of her occasional writings dating back to her early years in Mexico. Although most of the essays were of high quality, there was no particular enthusiasm from the critics, and the sales of the book were minimal.

The following summer (1953), while Miss Porter was fitfully working on her much-delayed novel in a small New York apartment at 117 East Seventeenth Street, she was jolted from her recurring ennui by the letter from Donald Sutherland, the professor who suddenly rekindled the Gertrude Stein controversy. Soon after their heated correspondence she applied for and was awarded a Fulbright grant designed to give her a chance to finish the novel. So once again she packed her belongings and took a ship to Belgium, where she was to be a sort of writer-in-residence at the University of Liège during the 1954–1955 academic year. But her work on *Ship of Fools* was sporadic and disconnected, and she would often leave a half-finished paragraph dangling for months at a time. Meanwhile, she wrote a trifling essay on writers' conferences, which she considered boring and useless. There was also a review of John Malcolm Brinnin's book *Dylan Thomas in America*, in which she remarked that Brinnin had discovered in his saddest days that a drunken poet was no more interesting than any other drunken man behaving like a fool. "His daily, personal life in fact was no better than that of tens of thousands of dull alcoholics who never wrote a line of poetry."

Aside from this book review, her most ambitious effort was an extended memoir on her traumatic introduction to bullfighting, "St. Augustine and the Bullfight," in which she expressed the horrifying realization that she actually enjoyed the bloody spectacle. She also described her involvement with the high-living, sexually liberated international rogues and millionaires who lived jaded expatriate lives in revolutionary Mexico, wistfully recalling that they took their fun where they found it. "I don't like gloomy sinners," she said, "but the merry ones charm me."

Although the "St. Augustine" piece was a brilliant commentary on bullfighting and rich expatriates in Mexico, it sharply underscored her failure to progress any further on her novel. In legal parlance, it was still *in medias res*, hanging in limbo, and remained at that stage long after she returned from Belgium in the latter part of 1955.

Now in her middle sixties and weary of moving from here to there, she would have liked to settle down in a quiet peaceful place where she could write at her own leisurely pace. She was hoping, of course, for another sudden and divine spark of creativity such as the one which helped her produce *Noon Wine, Old Mortality* and *Pale Horse, Pale Rider* in less than one month (seven days for each short novel); but that was almost twenty years before, and she was feeling much much older now — older and emotionally drained. Furthermore, her financial situation was bleak as ever.

There were numerous universities that would have gladly offered her a professorship, but she knew it would be impossible for her to write under such circumstances. So, after establishing a home base in Southbury, Connecticut, she once again started lecturing at various colleges and before certain literary clubs, "earning just enough money to keep myself together." And with a certain offhand discretion, she seemed to solicit writing assignments for additional income. In a chatty little letter to *The Village Voice* weekly newspaper, in 1956, she casually said, "Tell me some time if there is any little special thing you would like me to write about, how many words and all, and I'll be delighted to try."

There is no indication that the *Voice* ever accepted her offer (perhaps because she had made a slighting reference to Norman Mailer, who was a part-owner of the fledgling weekly), but the *Yale Review* did publish her brilliant autobiographical essay, "Noon Wine: the Sources," in its Autumn 1956 issue. (Much of the material included in it has been covered in earlier chapters of this book.) She also wrote a less than charitable review of Caitlin Thomas's book on her marriage to Dylan Thomas, *Leftover Life to Kill,* which Miss Porter found not too interesting or particularly unusual. "There are too many women with ambitions beyond their talents, experiences beyond their capacity, with romantic daydreams of glory and fame as the center of attention — we have too many of their sad histories." More specifically alluding to women who happen to marry gifted men or geniuses and "stubbornly refuse to play their natural role of second fiddle," she said that Caitlin Thomas has passed all bounds in her war against taking second place.

These essays and reviews were written while she was struggling to "get on" with her novel, but she was still having difficulty trying to find the proper ambience for her work. The situation was likely as that which she later described in a letter to Glenway Wescott: "... I need to keep submerged in the same mood and state of mind for *weeks* at a time, very hard to explain to people who need a change and recreation every day, and sometimes several times a day." She did, however, bake her own bread, water her plants, and take long walks in the meadow near the hilltop house she had rented. And, except for some of her favorite poetry, she read very little and had stopped listening to music. "I must keep silence," she insisted.

Nevertheless, she would frequently abandon her hermit life for periodic lecture tours, which she herself would arrange. And she would also spend a few weeks in New York, visiting friends and reassuring her editors that her novel would soon be finished. During one of her brief sojourns in Greenwich Village, she had several pleasant sessions with Edith Sitwell and brother Osbert, who came to visit her while she was staying in the half-basement apartment on Seventeenth Street. She subsequently described Miss Sitwell as "very tall, more than six feet, but slightly bowed over, with hair the color of day-old duck-fur and the face of Eleanor of Aquitaine, all dramatically accentuated by her strangely elegant clothes and huge dangling necklaces and bracelets."

One afternoon as she was having tea with Miss Sitwell, chatting and gossiping "in the most female way imaginable," Seymour Lawrence dropped in unexpectedly. (He had been urging Miss Porter to take her novel to the Atlantic Monthly Press.) "He nearly dropped dead when he saw Edith Sitwell sitting there with a cup in her hand, and then insisted we were probably tearing the living guts out of every writer in creation."

"That's pure fantasy, Seymour," said Miss Porter. "That's what you would like to think we were doing — but we weren't even talking about literature."

And when Lawrence asked how the novel was coming along, she said, "Now don't keep pressing me, Seymour. I'll finish it in my own good time. I've got a nice place to work in Southbury, but I've been torn away now and then by practical monetary considerations."*

Unfortunately, the lecture tours were yielding less and less money, because Miss Porter herself had shortened them in order to have more time to write. Consequently, she could no longer afford the house in Connecticut and ultimately decided to accept a long-standing offer to become writer-in-residence at the University of Virginia in the fall of 1958. During this period she wrote a review of *Dylan Thomas: Letters to Vernon Watkins* for *The New York Times Book Review,* in which she characterized the poet's correspondence as "fresh and reassuring as a spring of water — a very lively spring to be sure, bubbling and leaping and running sometimes through muddy flats and stones and rubbish. . . ." She also made a brief visit to Smith College to receive an honorary doctorate in Literature, sharing the platform with the handsome and very charming senator from Massachusetts, John F. Kennedy, who told her how much he admired all her stories.

The following year, 1959, Miss Porter once again packed her belongings and moved to Washington and Lee University, where she taught creative writing as the Glasgow Professor of Literature. Still unable to resume her work on the novel, she did little or no writing except for a short letter to the Washington *Post* and a brief accolade, which was published in the *Sewanee Review,* for her old friend Allen Tate on his sixtieth birthday. She also remembered one of her students asking her to comment on Malcolm Lowry's *Under the Volcano,* her answer being, "That was a sniveling, crybaby, feel-sorry-for-me drunken exercise if ever I saw one. . . ."

In 1960, now seventy years old but contentious as ever, she moved cross-country to Los Angeles to serve as Ewing Professor

---

* Lawrence, director of Atlantic Monthly Press, had been an intimate friend and confidant, and Miss Porter was godparent to one of Lawrence's children.

of Literature at U.C.L.A. While packing and unpacking her hoard of yellowing incomplete manuscripts, she found a copy of "The Fig Tree," the poignant story about Miranda and the chick she had buried, later thinking it was still alive. It had been written in 1934, and originally scheduled to be included in *The Leaning Tower* collection. She sent the rediscovered story to *Harper's* magazine, and it was published in June 1960.

Meanwhile, she wrote a scathing article for *Encounter* magazine on D. H. Lawrence's *Lady Chatterley's Lover*, which she had read thirty years before, thinking it was so sad and dreary that she had often wondered "at all the huzza and hullabaloo about suppressing it." Recalling that she herself had demonstrated and testified in defense of two books she actually disliked (*Memoirs of Hecate County* and *Tropic of Cancer*), she berated some of her fellow artists for recklessly championing "the most awful wormy little books we none of us would have given shelf room." As for the never-ending crusade for Lawrence's book, she called it a well-worn publicity device "calculated to rouse a salacious itch of curiosity in the prospective customer." Her quarrel with *Lady Chatterley's Lover* was that it was not genuinely pornographic but merely "obscenely sentimental." She particularly cited "the unbelievably grotesque episode of this besotted couple weaving flowers in each other's pubic hair, hanging bouquets and wreathes in other strategic bodily spots, making feeble dirty little jokes, inventing double-meaning nicknames for their sexual organs," which she characterized as "imbecilic harmlessness . . . meant in all solemn God's-earnestness." She also accused Lawrence of an utterly baleful ignorance of women, saying that he had no business writing about how females felt about sex or anything else.

It was a caustic, no-holds-barred attack on a writer much revered by two generations of readers and critics, some of whom were Miss Porter's colleagues at U.C.L.A. Three or four of them confronted her at a faculty party and accused her of female malice, an accusation that was becoming all too familiar and which she shrugged aside with feigned indifference. "There was no point arguing on *that* level," she later remarked.

Interestingly enough, one of her most vehement critics later praised her to the high heavens when "Holiday" was published in the December 1960 issue of *The Atlantic Monthly*. It was an indirectly autobiographical story told by an unnamed narrator whose sensibilities and background were similar to Miranda's. As a mature woman looking back at an incident which had taken place many years before, the narrator told of a visit she had made to an East Texas farm owned by the Müller family. She had gone there at the suggestion of a school friend, who had described the farm and the Müllers in rather romantic terms, but the forbidding farmhouse was actually located in a dry desolate area. She also quickly learned that her hosts were part of a conservative patriarchal society, in which Papa Müller and the other males were treated with submissive respect by silent wives standing behind their husbands at mealtimes, ever ready to replenish their plates, and thereafter eating the leftovers.

Carefully noting that the family formed its own extremely circumscribed society, she watched the taciturn elders and their disciplined children going through various phases of the life cycle — at a birth, at a wedding, and at a funeral. But all these events took on special meaning when she discovered that Ottilie, the crippled retarded servant girl, was actually one of the Müller children. Though immediately sympathizing with the hard-working cripple, the narrator soon realized that the Müllers had dealt with Ottilie "realistically," giving her an important function in the household while completely forgetting their blood ties and their spiritual obligations, their position being cruel but practical. Thus, when Mrs. Müller died, poor Ottilie stayed home as the rest of the family went to the funeral. Suddenly hearing Ottilie howl with grief in the kitchen, the narrator (who had also stayed home) hurriedly hitched a horse to a wagon to take her to the funeral. But they were too far behind. Then, in a moment of overwhelming pity, she had decided to take the cripple on a holiday outing, ironically musing that they would be home in time for Ottilie to prepare supper and that nobody need know about their holiday.

Recalling that she had gone to the Müller farm to escape some long-forgotten personal problem, the narrator inwardly reminded herself "that we do not run from the troubles and dangers that are truly ours, and it is better to learn what they are earlier than later. And if we don't run from the others, we are fools."

There were several interpretations of "Holiday," one of which came from John Hagopian, who felt that Miss Porter was saying that anyone's effort to shape his own life "is ultimately doomed since it will end with death and chaos. But while he is making the effort, he can be sustained by love — even love for a twisted, mute, half-beast of a human being like Ottilie. . . ." A somewhat less romantic view was expressed by Richard Poirier in his introduction to *Prize Stories 1962: The O. Henry Awards,* in which "Holiday" won first prize: "The story is about people whose communal labor has created relationships among them and between them and their natural environment, so close that literally nothing except death can disrupt them." But Professor George Hendrick read "Holiday" as a political parable, in which Miss Porter probed the German psyche: "She describes German clannishness, materialism, cruelty, love of animals and mistreatment of fellow human beings, and a willingness to put out of mind the unpleasantness of the past — characteristics she also has described in 'The Leaning Tower' and 'Ship of Fools'."

Some years later, Miss Porter wrote, " 'Holiday' represents one of my prolonged struggles, not with questions of form or style, but my own moral and emotional collision with a human situation I was too young to cope with at the time it occurred."

Haunted by the story for many years, she had written three separate versions, none of which measured up to her expectations. They all seemed to miss a particular point that kept troubling her. So she had set aside the manuscripts, forgetting them completely as she went on to other work. Then, suddenly, after a quarter of a century, the story "rose" from one of her boxes of paper, and she sat down to read all three versions with considerable excitement, and immediately knew that the first one was the right one. She changed one short paragraph and a line or two at the end, and mailed the finished manuscript to *The Atlantic Monthly*. As for the vexing problem which had forced her to reject all three versions back in 1935, "it had in the course of living settled itself so slowly and deeply and secretly I wondered why I had ever been distressed by it."

Though highly praised, "Holiday" yielded only minimal financial returns, and she was once again obligated to teach for a living, reluctantly accepting an appointment as the Regents Professor at the University of California at Riverside.* Before settling down in Riverside, she spent several months back East, at the end of which she told a *Time* magazine reporter (July 28, 1961) that she had wanted to write about "two wonderful old slaves who were my grandmother's companions, but someone is always giving a low name to good things, and I suppose the NAACP would say I was glorifying Uncle Tomism."

She had actually been engaged in a much more important project during that late spring and early summer: she had finally decided to finish writing *Ship of Fools* "come hell or high water." Taking three months off, she had gone up to Cape Ann and rented a room in a small inn.

"Now, don't let anyone come near my door," she told the manager. "Just give me my breakfast at eight o'clock in the morning, and I will leave the room for an hour for the maid to do it up. Otherwise, I'll come out when I'm hungry."

They did indeed leave her alone, and she finished the novel within the time span she had set for herself, working with the same trancelike absorption that had possessed her when she wrote *Noon Wine*, *Old Mortality* and *Pale Horse, Pale Rider*, steadily pulling together all the loose ends that had been dangling for twenty years. And when it was over, she graciously thanked the innkeeper and soon thereafter cheerfully delivered the hundred-sixty-thousand-word manuscript to the editors of Atlantic–Little, Brown and Company, some of whom had given up hope of ever receiving it.

---

* *Editor's note:* Mr. Lopez was appointed Regents Professor at U.C.R. ten years later.

"It feels like the end of a very prolonged pregnancy," she told a *Time* reporter.

Now she would have to wait another agonizing nine months for a second birth on the publication date, when the critics would get their chance to praise it or tear it apart.

14

The Ship Comes In

Miss Porter had written the last three pages of *Ship of Fools* about eighteen years before she actually finished the novel. "I have to know how it's going to end," she told a *Time* magazine reporter on July 28, 1961. "Beginnings are just like pulling straws."

She had written most of the book in "batches and binges" while living in Baton Rouge, Yaddo, Saratoga Springs, Santa Monica, Greenwich Village, Palo Alto and Roxbury, Connecticut, often stopping in the middle of a paragraph and not finishing it until a year or two later. The old inn on the far reaches of Cape Ann, Massachusetts, had been a propitious locale for the final phase. Her room had a glass-enclosed sun porch overlooking the harbor of Pigeon Cove, and she had occasionally paused to watch the waves tumbling toward the shore while the gray horizon remained motionless and remote. The rugged vitality of the sea and its enormous stability had somehow renewed her energies and strengthened her resolve to finish the much-delayed novel.

Knowing she was seventy-one years old and periodically plagued by poor health and financial pressures, most of her friends had long ago decided that her writing career was over and that soon she would be unable to lecture or teach. One of the oldest and dearest friends, Glenway Wescott, was convinced that her unfinished novel had become an albatross around her neck and was finally moved to write her a discreet letter suggesting that she abandon the book and turn her attention to shorter fiction. Fortunately, he never mailed it. "Thank goodness, I was persuaded by my closest friend to consign this melancholy suggestion to the wastebasket."

Had Wescott sent the letter, Miss Porter quite conceivably might have taken his advice and would have thus aborted the only financial success she ever had.

Although she freely alluded to the novel's twenty-year period of gestation in prepublication interviews in *Time* and *Newsweek*, Miss Porter made no mention of the chronic self-doubt which had concerned Wescott. Such negative talk would have vitiated the upbeat campaign planned by her publishers, who were already faced with the problem of gaining a broader public acceptance for a writer whose highly praised short stories had been read by comparatively few people. Needless to say, they breathed a deep sigh of relief when the Book-of-the-Month Club chose *Ship of Fools* as its April selection for 1962. In a brochure sent to its vast membership, the Club included an ecstatic review by Clifton Fadiman, who proclaimed the novel as Miss Porter's *magnum opus:* "Not only was it worth waiting for, but your judges would be derelict in their duty if they did not wholeheartedly urge it upon the attention of Club members."

Included in the same brochure was an even more breathless appreciation by Wescott in an essay subsequently published in *The Atlantic Monthly* and in his book *Images of Truth:*

Having delivered the entire final script of *Ship of Fools*, Katherine Anne confessed to her editor that she had scarcely been able to read it as reading matter; it remained work in progress for her even at that point. "Has it a form, a shape, as a whole?" she wanted to know.

"Yes," he answered, "it is like a great wave."

And so it is. It rises rather slowly and coldly at first, with an effect of distance, of remoteness from the reader's mind, indeed, of smallness of scale. Gradually one is impressed, gradually one is enthralled, then lifted higher and higher and submerged deeper and deeper, almost drowned. The wave breaks with, let us say, the burial at sea, and the procession of whales, fountaining in the distance. But by that time, our responsiveness, intentness, and ravishment are like a wide shelving shore, a flat and curving beach. And for almost two hundred pages after the breaking of

In the garden at Georgetown, 1959.
Photograph by Paul Schutzer

*In her elegant drawing room in Washington, D.C., February, 1960,
the year of* Ship of Fools. *Photograph by Carlo Maggi*

Portrait, at about seventy-five years, by Arthur B. Long

the wave, up it comes still, in long breakers or combers, some with sub-sidiary crests of great brilliance and violence.

One inevitably pictures Mr. Wescott lying on the beach, drenched and battered, waiting for the next tidal onslaught.

With huge sales guaranteed by Book-of-the-Month Club selection, aided by considerable literary speculation and advance publicity, the novel became number one on the best-seller list within a few weeks of its publication on April 12, 1962. On May 21, *Publishers Weekly* reported that Atlantic–Little, Brown had allocated over fifty thousand dollars for advertising the book, including full-page notices in the daily *New York Times* and other newspapers and magazines across the country. There were also 360 sixty-second commercials on FM stations in major metropolitan areas.

Though a shade less ecstatic than Wescott, most major reviewers were laudatory. In the lead article of the *New York Times Book Review*, Mark Schorer commented on the prolonged delay in publication but flatly declared that the novel would endure "for many literary generations." His exceedingly comprehensive and favorable review stressed the influence of Sebastian Brant's *Das Narrenschiff* (1494), which Miss Porter herself acknowledged in a prefatory note. He was also immensely impressed by her strongly developed *characters and by her subtle artistic techniques, finally concluding that Ship of Fools* could easily be compared with the greatest novels of the past century: "Call it for convenience, the 'Middlemarch' of a later day."

In another laudatory review in the New York *Herald-Tribune Books* (April 1, 1962), Louis Auchincloss, an acute observer of manners and morals, expressed great pleasure in what he called the novel's "Victorian qualities." The same supplement carried an interview by Maurice Dolbier, in which Miss Porter charmingly translated a Mexican drinking toast, introducing her own piquant variation ("Health and money, more power to your elbow, many secret love affairs and time to enjoy them"). Chatting about her ancestors, the difficulties of writing, and even greater difficulties with love, she sadly admitted, "I've had a very hard life, but it's not other people who have made it hard for me. I did that for myself. But I've had a good run for my money — a free field in the things that matter: the will to be an artist and to live as a human being."

On April 6, 1962, *Time* magazine's millions of readers were advised that *"Ship of Fools* is a study in despair. The despair is not relieved by the usual dilutions. . . . In fact there are no personal obtrusions, nothing of the gracious, 70-year-old Southern gentlewoman who in the 20 years since her last book has seemed to occupy herself chiefly with being a charming chatterer at literary gatherings. Her testament is objective and her verdict is unemotional: the world is a place of foulness and fools."

The review in *Newsweek* (April 2, 1962) was in a similar vein: "Among the lesser things to say about it is that it is the Book-of-the-Month for April. The main thing to declare is that in her full maturity, in a country where high-level fiction is scarce and likely to be fragile, Katherine Anne Porter has produced a work of rugged power and myriad insights, a book of the highest relevance to the bitterness and disruption of modern civilization."

With such rave reviews in the most prestigious newspapers and mass-circulation news magazines, Miss Porter and her friends were quite understandably euphoric. Some of them immediately predicted she would win the Pulitzer Prize and the National Book Award. Indeed, one went so far as to tell her in a private conversation that she might win the Nobel Prize for Literature. Although she outwardly dismissed the notion, she later told her most intimate acquaintances, "If I should ever get a Nobel award, I would charter a private yacht and take all my best friends on a long cruise through the Mediterranean."

But the general euphoria that swept over her was partially clouded by less favorable reviews. In the *Saturday Review* (March 31, 1962), Granville Hicks expressed certain reservations: "It is hard not to judge the book in relation to the extended period of gestation; the temptation is to proclaim that it is either the fulfilment of a great hope or a sorry disappointment. But if it is certainly not the latter, neither is it quite the former. It shows that Miss Porter is one of the finest writers of prose in America. It also shows that she has mastered the form — or one of the forms

— of the novel. On the other hand, it is something less than a masterpiece." Then, after commenting on several characters aboard the ship, he expressed concern about certain negative aspects in the general tenor of the book: "Miss Porter is saying something about the voyage of life, and what she is saying is somber indeed. Perhaps that is why the novel, for all its lucidity and all its insights, leaves the reader a little cold. There is in it, as far as I can see, no sense of human possibility. Although we have known her people uncommonly well, we watch unconcerned as, in the curiously muted ending, they drift away from us."

In an interview by Rochelle Girson, printed next to Hicks's review, Miss Porter declared that *Ship of Fools* was "the story of the criminal collusion of good people — people who are harmless — with evil. . . . It happens through inertia, lack of seeing what is going on before their eyes. I watched that happen in Germany and in Spain. I saw it with Mussolini. I wanted to write about people in these predicaments — really old predicaments with slightly new political and religious aspects."

When asked if she had altered her views as to present-day Germans, she answered with fierce conviction: "I believe that they are just as dangerous as they were then, and the moment they get back their power they are going to do it again. This complacency about Germany is simply horrifying."

Some of Granville Hicks's doubts were echoed by Howard Moss in *The New Yorker* for April 28, 1962, but he balanced his criticism with considerable praise. "Miss Porter is a moralist, but too good a writer to be one except by implication. Dogma in *Ship of Fools* is attached only to dogmatic characters. There is not an ounce of weighted sentiment in it. Its intelligence lies not in the profundity of its ideas but in the clarity of its viewpoint; we are impressed not by what Miss Porter says but by what she knows."

Voicing similar praise in his review for *The New Republic* (April 2, 1962), Stanley Kauffmann nonetheless had strong reservations regarding Miss Porter's characterization of some of her passengers. He particularly noted that the treatment of Lowenthal, the paranoid Jewish businessman, "gives too mean and sullen a picture."

Clearly disappointed in some aspects of the Moss and Kauffmann commentaries, Miss Porter was downright annoyed by
Peter De Vries's wicked satire in *The New Yorker* on June 11. As
one can assume from his title, "Nobody's Fool (A Character or
Two Overlooked in Katherine Anne Porter's Shipload)," De
Vries poked fun at Miss Porter's technique with his usual devastating humor. Perhaps forgetting her own witty parody of Gertrude Stein in 1927, Miss Porter was not amused. "It was one of
those vulgar smart-aleck pieces which no doubt delighted some of
my detractors," she subsequently declared.

But De Vries's needling wit was but a gentle harbinger of the
inevitable critical reaction that was led by Theodore Solotaroff*
in his scathing attack in *Commentary* for October 1962.

Noting that *Ship of Fools* had made its way to the top of the
best-seller lists in record time and that it had encountered little
opposition in taking its place "among the classics of literature,"
Solotaroff chided the critics for what he considered an excessive
reverence, which he attributed to Miss Porter's strong reputation
in the universities, "where she has taught off and on over the
years and where her stories have been studied with special zeal
and affection."

As if to prove that he himself was totally immune to such "reverence," Solotaroff criticized almost every aspect of her novel and
was particularly vehement in asserting that she had created a cast
of sick, mean, vicious, depraved caricatures who lacked even a
trace of human dignity. Further declaring it was "the most sour
and morbid indictment of humanity to appear in years," he
directly challenged the views of the *New York Times* critic:

One wonders which of those hapless or vicious grotesques Mark
Schorer (who said that "It will be a reader myopic to the point of
blindness who does not find his name on her passenger list") found to
represent himself, or what qualities Louis Auchincloss ("how easy it
would be for anyone to turn into even the most repellent of these incipient Nazis") would own up to that brings him so close to Herr Rieber

* Mr. Solotaroff was associate editor of *Commentary*, a journal financed by the American Jewish Congress.

with his clownish lust and serious wish to throw the steerage passengers into gas ovens."

In this apparent willingness of certain reviewers to see themselves in Miss Porter's characters, Solotaroff professed to see "a remarkable resemblance to the reaction of the American press to the disclosures of the Eichmann trial . . . where most editorial writers hastened to phrases like 'man's inhumanity to man.' . . . And in the mood of moral malaise that the trial seems mainly to have inspired, it apparently became increasingly easy to assert that we are all Adolf Eichmann, which immediately transformed Eichmann from a very special kind of 20th-century political figure into merely one more example of the imperfectibility of man."

To buttress this contention, he cited a sentence from *Newsweek's* highly favorable review of *Ship of Fools:* "To the author, anti-Semitism of any description is *only one form* of humanity's general failure to perceive the commonness of all humanity."

Then, quickly sliding over the fact that Miss Porter had been especially caustic in her portrayal of certain incipiently fascist German passengers — and using a sort of leapfrog logic — Solotaroff accused her of being a "proto-fascist" because one of her more sympathetic characters, Dr. Schumann, states that most people's "collusion with evil is only negative, consent by default," and that it is the "mere mass and weight of negative evil (which) threatened to rule the world."

Finally, after a mere passing reference to a couple of German characters whom Miss Porter had skillfully and intentionally portrayed as vile and loathsome creatures, Solotaroff came to the crux of his complaint:

This insistence upon a "general failure" of humanity creates not only a feeble portent of Hitler's Germany but in time a brutally indiscriminate one. *Among the Germans on board the "Vera," there is none more wretched and repulsive than the Jew Julius Lowenthal, with his whining, puny hatred of the goyim; with his lack of curiosity, much less passion, for anything in life save kosher cooking and the opportunities to make a killing off the Catholics; with his tendency to spit disgustedly into the wind. A caricature of Jewish vulgarity, Lowenthal is otherwise coldly reduced to an abstract tribal paranoia.* Thinking himself snubbed by Captain Thiele, he broods for hours:

> He wished for death, or thought he did. He retired into the dark and airless ghetto of his soul and lamented with all the grieving wailing company he found there; for he was never alone in that place. He ... mourned in one voice with his fated people, wordlessly he bewailed their nameless eternal wrongs and sorrows; then feeling somewhat soothed, the inspired core of his being began to search for its ancient justification and its means of revenge. But it should be slow and secret.

In brief, this successful peddler to the Catholics is the stage Jew of the modern literary tradition whom other Christian writers of sensibility (among them T. S. Eliot) have dragged out of the ghetto to represent the vulgar and menacing dislocations of traditional order. . . .

Far from exerting any understanding of or sympathy for Lowenthal — which he might have claimed if only because of the far from "nameless wrongs and sorrows" that he and his people will soon have to face in Germany — Miss Porter uses him in a situation whose implications are both historically misleading and morally vicious.

Citing still another passage from the book, Solotaroff openly attacked Miss Porter's motives in no uncertain terms: "And the trifling attitude that lies behind the treatment of Lowenthal is only one example of Miss Porter's compulsive tendency to simplify and close her characters and issues, to look down upon life from the perspective of a towering arrogance, contempt, and disgust."

On reading that accusation, *Commentary* subscribers must have wondered if Solotaroff had read the same book that prompted a completely contrary opinion from Mark Schorer, the *New York Times Book Review* critic, who wrote the following:

There is nothing (or almost nothing) harsh in her book. There is much that is comic, much even that is hilarious, and everything throughout always flashing into brilliance through the illumination of this great ironic style. At the same time, almost everything that is comic is simultaneously pathetic ... moving to the point of pain, nearly of heartbreak.

Needless to say, the Solotaroff article caused a considerable fuss in New York's somewhat incestuous literary community.

Quite a few social gatherings were disrupted by vehement arguments between Miss Porter's supporters and those who shared Solotaroff's views. Indeed, many of the disputants later felt compelled to write letters pro and con to the editors of *Commentary*. One of them was the distinguished poet and critic Robert Lowell:

TO THE EDITOR OF COMMENTARY:

A little sense on Katherine Anne Porter's *Ship of Fools!* (" 'Ship of Fools' & the Critics," October 1962) I don't see why Mr. Solotaroff's journalistic case for the prosecution was boxed off in white and featured on the cover of COMMENTARY. *Ship of Fools* should not be read after or placed beside the masterpieces of the ages, but rather with such a book as Edith Wharton's *Age of Innocence*. In such a context, its virtues, to me at least, are obvious: it is one of the very few American novels (almost unique in this lately) that deserves to be long; the writing is always alert, modest, and honest. As for its gloom and grayness, I find them in their way glorious. For what it is worth, *Ship of Fools* is in the American Liberal Tradition, a tradition that most of us follow in our non-fiction, but one that is hardly attempted any more in imaginative work. For the Liberal, 1931, just as now, is a time to look blue! I can't see that the fact that *Ship of Fools* doesn't include such opposite Germans as Einstein, Hitler, and Thomas Mann is an indictment. It would be easy to picture an idealistic prosecuting attorney, such as Mr. Solotaroff, reading *Macbeth* (I am making no comparison), and saying its perverse darkness has no room for Erasmus, Spinoza, and Sir Francis Bacon.

ROBERT LOWELL

New York City

On the other hand, there were numerous letters praising Solotaroff's views with varying degrees of fervor: ". . . It is salutary when an honest critic cuts through the reviewers' nonsense of equating pretension with importance, misanthropy with depth." (George Sklar) . . . "There should be room in a novel, which an author has shaped over a period of twenty years, to include at least one or two characters whose lives might add up to something more than unrelieved sordidness and degradation." (Beatrice Hirsch)

As one might expect, critics in Germany were almost unanimously opposed to the novel. Long before the German translation appeared in the fall of 1963, Norbert Muhlen reviewed *Ship of Fools* in the widely circulated *Der Monat* and accused Miss Porter of writing "a fashionable stereotyped image of humanity which affirms original sin but denies divine grace — an inevitable trade mark of 'sour kitsch' which no longer takes a rose-tinted but a murky view of the world." He further objected to Miss Porter portraying Germans in 1931 as talking of gas ovens or boycotting a German for marrying a Jew, claiming that about half of the Jewish marriages in 1931 were mixed marriages.

In another unfavorable review published in *Die Deutsche Zeitung* (October 13, 1962), Heinz Pächter partially adopted Solotaroff's thesis that Miss Porter's concept of an incipient Nazi was a much-too-easy symbol of human depravity. Indeed, he quoted from the *Commentary* article ("... out of her masochistic pessimism towards civilization, Miss Porter gives up every discrimination, and this attitude makes her unable to characterize even the real Nazis in their depravity ..."), but Herr Pächter significantly ignored Solotaroff's objections concerning her portrayal of Lowenthal, the Jew.

Perhaps the most dramatic and heated criticism of Miss Porter's novel appeared in *Die Welt* on June 9, 1962. The headline over a review written by Herbert von Borch clearly pinpointed his principal argument:

"The Germans are still cruel, evil and fanatic,"
Document of Hatred: K. A. Porter's *Ship of Fools*

Referring to the Porter interview in the *Saturday Review* for March 31, 1962, Borch pointedly quoted her current views on present-day Germans: "... They are just as dangerous as they were, and the moment they get back their power they are going to do it again. This complacency about Germany is simply horrifying. ... The Germans have taken the Jews as a kind of symbol, but they are against anybody and everybody, and they haven't changed a bit!"

Though understandably less passionate than the German critics, reviewers in England were generally negative in their appraisal of *Ship of Fools*. In a chillingly aloof critique for the influential *Observer*, Angus Wilson described it as "a thumbed-over, middlebrow formula for writing a novel." And the equally prestigious *Times Literary Supplement* referred to her passengers as "the pack of hysterics, alcoholics, thieves, hypocrites, and sex-starved weaklings assembled on the good ship *Vera* [who] stand for no larger truth. The claim of universality lies only in the outward symbolism."

Since she herself had written some equally caustic reviews on such writers as Gertrude Stein and D. H. Lawrence, Miss Porter had fully expected a few negative reactions to her novel, but the Solotaroff article went far beyond anything she had anticipated. "I deeply resented his attack on my personal motives and all that nonsense about my being a proto-fascist," she declared. "But I saw no point in answering that mean little man. After all, I had received some very generous praise from the critics who really mattered."

Unfortunately, the rave reviews in *The New York Times*, the *Herald-Tribune*, and various magazines such as *Time* and *Newsweek*, apparently failed to persuade the jurors who awarded the Pulitzer Prize and the National Book Award. Perhaps more bitter than Miss Porter herself, some of her friends felt that her failure to win either prize could be traced to Solotaroff's highly publicized accusations.

In any event, Miss Porter could console herself with the fact that *Ship of Fools* had given her an income of almost a million dollars from hard-cover royalties, motion picture rights, paperback sales, and other subsidiary income from translated editions in seventeen languages. She was also wined and dined in queenly style at a series of luncheons and cocktail parties given for the media by her publishers, who had rented her a fancy suite in a luxury hotel.

"It was all very frantic and somewhat exhausting," she later observed. "But I loved every minute of it."

Thus, at the age of seventy-two, she had finally achieved financial success, and as she sat in her suite sipping champagne and savoring some chilled caviar, she couldn't help remembering the many lean years when she hadn't earned a cent from her writing, when she had been forced to go on dreary lecture tours to earn enough money to buy a few months' freedom from her serious work. But now that she was economically secure, would she have enough energy to finish the rest of the yellowing manuscripts that she had been hauling around for years and years?

Such questions were left in abeyance in the euphoric aftermath of the publication date. There were more immediate problems to be dealt with, one of which was broached by a representative of her publishers, who wanted to know how she wanted her royalties paid.

"Why don't you just give me a check for $3,000 a month and bank all the rest for me?" she suggested.

Surprised that she was requesting such a small sum, considering the enormous sums she would be earning, the publishers asked, "Are you sure that's what you want?"

"Of course, I am," she said. "I'm tired of skimping — I want to splurge a little."

"I'm sorry," he said, somewhat flustered. "I guess you misunderstood me, Miss Porter. I was actually thinking you should allow yourself much more."

"Oh, no! That's plenty," she said. "In fact, that seems like an awful lot to me — much more than I'm used to."

Under the terms of her contract, apparently negotiated without any agent representing her, she had received twenty-seven thousand dollars upon delivery of the manuscript, and was to receive three thousand dollars per month for eight months and twenty-five hundred dollars per month thereafter, with a monthly deduction of three hundred dollars payable to her niece, Gaye Porter Holloway. She had never had access to that kind of money, but it didn't take long for her to get accustomed to her new wealth. A few weeks later she bought a beautiful ring with a large emerald surrounded with exquisitely matched small pearls. When she showed it to her good friend Mrs. Francis Biddle, who had also served on the Bollingen Prize committee, Mrs. Biddle simply shook her head.

"Now, Katherine Anne," she said. "After all the hard times you've been through, don't you think this is a bit extravagant?"

"Not at all, honey," said Miss Porter. "I've always said, 'First things first,' and this is what I've always wanted."

She had also wanted a house with plenty of room and a rose garden, preferably in Washington, D.C., where she had acquired several intimate friends while working at the Library of Congress. And with the conscientious help of a local real estate agent, she found a "quite suitable" house in a fine residential area, which she furnished with carefully chosen antiques that reflected the many years she had lived outside the United States. In her library, for example, there was a sixteenth-century cupboard from Avila, and a large refectory table of the early Renaissance period which had come from a convent in Fiesole; and Madame de Pompadour's dressing table now graced her bedroom.

As she gave me a tour through the house and garden on my first visit, Miss Porter told me that she had leased the house with an option to buy, then smilingly explained her reason for so doing: "A house is just like a man — you ought to live with it at least a year before deciding on anything permanent. And even then it's a big gamble."

In addition to the beautiful and costly antique furniture, she also bought three twentieth-century secondhand file cabinets, fully intending "to make an orderly appraisal" of thousands of pages of partially completed manuscripts and scribbled notes for projected stories or novels. But she never seemed to get around to that enormous, probably forbidding, task. Instead, she would go down to her basement now and then to browse through fifteen or twenty cardboard boxes stuffed with faded yellowing manuscripts, often sitting cross-legged (for she was still astonishingly limber in her mid-seventies) as she carefully read a few pages of something she had written thirty or forty years ago, forthwith promising herself to finish it right away. Clutching the few pages in her hand and leaving behind the still-disordered mass of manuscripts, she would hurry upstairs to her writing desk and try once more to recapture the zeal she had once felt for that particular story. And a few hours later, having scratched a sentence or two and added a phrase here and there, she would set aside the never-to-be-finished manuscript with a deep sigh of resignation.

At her suggestion, I once spent several hours browsing through that massive accumulation of papers, savoring a few pages in this box and that box as if it were an exquisite literary smorgasbord, a lump rising in my throat as I read passages of indescribable beauty, inevitably remembering how she must have felt when she read the never-to-be-published Hart Crane poem, the one he had pegged on nails protruding from the walls of his house in Mixcoac a few months before his suicide.

She knew that most of her manuscripts (probably all of them) would remain in that incomplete state for the rest of her life, and a deep sense of loss, of anguished frustration, would cloud her eyes as she wandered among the cardboard boxes in her basement, vainly trying to remember which box contained the fragment of a childhood memoir she had scribbed one rainy night in Paris.

"If I could only find it," she would say in a half whisper. "It must be somewhere in all this mess."

Seldom would she find what she was looking for, and what she did find would usually fail to evoke a compelling need to finish it. Then, as if to ease the ever-increasing frustration, she would write some nonfictional trifle about being snubbed by Hemingway, or about Jacqueline Kennedy's courage after the assassination, both of which were published in popular women's magazines such as *Mademoiselle* and *Ladies Home Journal*. Later on, she would be commissioned by *Playboy* magazine to write a serious piece about a much-publicized trip aboard the S. S. *Statendam* ("Voyage beyond Apollo"), where a group of artists and intellectuals conducted nine days of discussions on man's future in space. Norman Mailer, Isaac Asimov and several other "space freaks" were among the participants, all of whom had witnessed the launching of an Apollo spacecraft onn December 8, 1972. In an interview with a *New York Times* reporter, Miss Porter excitedly told him, "When I saw them take off, I wanted to be with them!" But in spite of her enthusiasm, she never submitted the article *Playboy* had asked her to write.

Ironically enough, her new wealth and celebrity status probably contributed to her failure to write any more stories. Always a witty and provocative conversationalist, she was a much-sought-after guest in Washington's elite society, especially among the high government officials, diplomats, Supreme Court justices and distinguished lawyers who gravitated around the extremely wealthy Mr. and Mrs. Francis Biddle, both of whom had been intimate friends of Miss Porter for many years. She enjoyed their fascinating company, "their good drinks and fine food," but after a while she decided to reduce her social activities and get back to work.

"I live like a hermit here," she told an interviewer in 1965. "I'm not going anywhere, not traveling any more. I have an income now, thank God, so I don't have to. But I'm getting one thousand dollars on October sixth for yapping at the Library of Congress, and this year I have refused seventeen thousand dollars' worth of speaking engagements — even though I have lived on as little as fifteen hundred dollars a year!"

Aside from invitations to speak at college campuses and before women's clubs throughout the country, she was also deluged with letters of all descriptions, most of which she couldn't possibly answer. "Now I get six or seven hundred requests a year to write an analysis for somebody's term paper," she once complained to a friend. "Because my letters are worth something now, I imagine. So they're like bloodsuckers trying to drain everything out of my veins. Well, I wouldn't have dared send a letter to Yeats or Hardy or James. I wouldn't have had the impudence." Using a slightly different figure of speech with respect to the hangers-on who inevitably plague celebrities, she once told Glenway Wescott, "They are as rapacious and hard to fight off as bluejays, but I have developed a great severity of rejection that I did not know I was capable of."

Part of the reason for her withdrawal from outside contacts was the increasingly precarious state of her health. She had suffered from a long series of illnesses and accidents throughout her life — several sieges of pneumonia, a rare form of tuberculosis that baffled specialists, thrombophlebitis, a fractured arm, a fractured leg, several fractured ribs at different times, a broken hip in her mid-seventies, and recurrent emphysema — but her spirits seemed indomitable. Wescott's comments on this are rather instructive: "All this balance of physiology in her case, strong constitution, poor health, has mystified those who care for her. Perhaps the physicians whom she happened on here and there — 'the pulse-takers, the stethoscope-wielders, the order-givers,' as she has called them — have been mystifiers in some measure." One of them, in upstate New York, told her that her trouble was all a matter of allergies, and when she inquired, "What allergies?" his answer was, "You're allergic to the air you breathe."

Whatever the reasons for her periodic ailments, she disliked having strange doctors poking around her body and often compared them to careless, untidy cleaning women: "They mess the place up; they don't know where things belong, or what goes with what." As for the medicines they prescribed, she once told a friend her bathroom cabinet was filled with "a fantastic row of apothecary's powders, pills, and potions, all of them in the most poisonously brilliant colors, amethyst and sapphire and emerald and purple. . . ."

Yet she managed to be cheerful and sometimes downright boastful about her poor health. At one memorable dinner party at the Biddles' mansion, she had a long conversation with Supreme Court Justice William Douglas about the various accidents they had suffered and the number of bones they had fractured, both of them finally becoming cheerfully competitive as to the battered condition of their respective rib cages. And a few months later, when Miss Porter fell on a stairway and fractured two ribs, she got an immediate hand-delivered message from the Supreme Court: "I guess you are the champ now, and get well soon. Fond regards — Bill."

While recovering from this accident, which occurred shortly after her seventy-sixth birthday, she learned that she was also suffering from emphysema. Suddenly the specter of old age and possible senility started fretting the outer edges of her consciousness, and she would stubbornly ignore even the slightest hint of the inevitable, refusing to discuss the problem of aging with anyone. "I don't want to talk about it," she would say. "There's nothing to be gained in brooding about it — and, besides, age is merely a relative thing."

Then, as if to stress its relativity, she would recall that when she was sixteen, a middle-aged neighbor had said, "Ha, that girl will never see eighteen again!" When she was less than thirty, someone had guessed she was at least forty. And when she was past fifty, her young lover was sure she was no more than forty. All of which would remind her of her favorite anecdote concerning the relative nature of anyone's age. This particular story actually took place while she was having lunch with Charles Brackett, the well-known screen writer, and two film directors. Margaret O'Brien, the famous child actress, was sitting at a nearby table with several adults, and suddenly Miss Porter's three companions turned and stared at Miss O'Brien as though she were a pony they were thinking of buying. "How old is she now?" asked one of the directors. "Six years old," said the other. And after a long pause, Brackett said, "She looks older than that."

Miss Porter herself was the object of the same kind of age-guessing when she won the Pulitzer Prize and the National Book Award for her *Collected Stories*, published by Harcourt, Brace & World in September 1965. When told she was seventy-five years old, several photographers refused to believe she was more than sixty or sixty-five.* And in the euphoria of winning the two prizes which had been denied her for *Ship of Fools*, she did indeed seem much younger than her years, even though she was slightly vexed by some of her old detractors (she called them "enemies") who felt it was unfair to award the highly coveted prize to a collection which contained no stories written within the designated year (1965). Two of the stories had been published five years before, and the rest were at least twenty years old. There were others who had no objection to this chronological disparity but would have preferred to have the two prizes awarded to Flannery O'Connor, who had died just before the publication of her collection *Everything That Rises Must Converge*. Indeed,

---

* Glenway Wescott once wrote that Miss Porter disliked photographers, but the numerous photographs in this book clearly show that she liked being photographed.

the citation honoring Miss Porter specifically noted that the judges "could not fail to pay special tribute to a writer lost to American literature by her death prior to the publication of her last book: Flannery O'Connor, whose work commands our memory with sensations of life conveyed with an intensity of pity and participation, love and redemption, rarely encountered."

In commending Miss Porter, the three judges (Paul Horgan, J. F. Powers and Glenway Wescott) praised her "tales of good and evil" and particularly cited "her unique gift: absolute prose with the poet's fire and light."

Several months later (December 1965) the *Yale Review* published a special supplement on the work of Miss Porter, with particular emphasis on *The Collected Stories.* In a thoughtful and penetrating analysis titled "Uncorrupted Consciousness: The Stories of Katherine Anne Porter," Robert Penn Warren referred to the five-hundred-page book as "the record of a life and the achievement of a rare, powerful, and subtle creative force. It is a beautiful and deeply satisfying book; and it promises to be a permanent and highly esteemed part of our literature."

In a companion essay, "The Eye of the Story," Eudora Welty observed that Miss Porter had written moral stories about "love and the hate that is love's twin, love's imposter and enemy and death. Rejection, betrayal, desertion, theft roam the pages of her stories as they roam the world. . . . 'If one is afraid of looking into a face one hits the face,' remarked W. B. Yeats, and I think we must conclude that to Katherine Anne Porter's characters this face is the challenging face of love itself. And I think it is the faces — the inner, secret faces — of her characters, in their self-delusion, their venom and pain, that their author herself is contemplating. More than either looking at her face or hitting it, she has made a story out of her anger."

There were accolades from several other sources and a new spate of invitations to speak on college campuses and television talk shows, most of which she graciously declined because of the uncertain state of her health. She was, in fact, unable to attend a commencement ceremony at the University of Maryland, where she was to receive an honorary doctorate in literature; so the university president brought the mountain to Mohammed. Accompanied by several deans and senior faculty, the president journeyed to Miss Porter's residence and awarded her the degree in what she called "a most delightful ceremony in my very own living room," after which she entertained the visitors with some very special champagne.

"I love impromptu parties like this," she told her guests. "But I hate parties that are too big and too well organized."

It was for this reason that she subsequently refused an invitation to Truman Capote's "party of the century" for several hundred of his most intimate friends. From certain preparty information, Miss Porter learned that she had been assigned to sit with a group of elderly writers and artists, an arrangement she found appalling. "Nothing could have been more deadly than getting together with a bunch of people as old as I am, so I simply informed one of his social secretaries — there must have been a whole battalion of them — that I was indisposed."

Even if she had been disposed to attend Capote's party at the elegant Plaza Hotel in New York, the effort of traveling back and forth from Washington and mingling with hundreds of alcoholically animated strangers would have been too exhausting, too jarring on her nerves. In fact, some much more modest social functions had left her "limp as a rag." Consequently, she began to limit her social life to cocktails and dinners with one or two friends (preferably men), with whom she could have meaningful conversations in depth rather than the much more taxing scattershot gossip one generally finds at larger gatherings.

"Lord knows, I've enjoyed some fairly elevated gossip with Edith Sitwell and people like that," she once admitted. "But it was all very witty and pointedly relevant — none of this dull, pointless and mean little chitchat that masquerades as conversation at some dinner parties I have been to."

Writing letters to old friends was a far more satisfactory form of social intercourse, but this, too, had certain drawbacks, particularly as she grew older and less energetic. A passage from Wescott's essay clearly pinpoints the problem: "I believe that her self-expressive and confidential first-person communication to her friends, freshly inspired or provoked each time, swiftly produced on the typewriter, and not rewritten, scarcely reread, has served to purify her mind of a good deal of that pride and willfulness and narcissism and excitability by which the life-work of most modern fiction writers has often been beclouded, enfeebled, blemished. *Of course her letter writing must have shortened her working days and used up incalculable energy, thus reducing the amount of her production of the more public forms of literature.*"

Two of the letters to her favorite nephew, Paul, were subsequently published in *Mademoiselle* magazine, and one can readily see that such extended and wide-ranging letters undoubtedly drained her energies. Significantly, in the second of these letters she wistfully comments that her loneliness was only that of a naturally lonely person. "I have never thought it a misfortune, but a part of my daily life most important to the work I do. Yet, there is no one I would call for in the hour of my death, and that I think is the final test of whether you are really alone or not. . . ." Several pages later she complained, "My mind is painfully distracted by all the hundreds of things irrelevant to anything I am doing, and it must end."

With the approach of death increasing her already desperate need to make the most of what little time remained, she tried to reduce her social obligations to an absolute minimum — but with all the additional free time, she still could not write the stories she had been promising to write, nor could she finish the long-delayed book on Cotton Mather. Yet she kept on trying, often sitting at her desk for hours, her fingers tentatively poised on the typewriter keys, until her back ached and forced her to give up.

Restless, moody, impatient with herself, she would occasionally fret about the distracting presence of her cleaning women, most of whom she dismissed after brief periods of employment. "They always want to talk about their personal problems," she once told me. "And I've enough of my own problems to worry about." Consequently, she firmly resisted the advice of well-meaning friends who wanted her to hire a live-in housekeeper, fearing it was dangerous for her to live alone in a two-story house with a cellar she frequently used. Aside from possible burglars, they worried about her having a dizzy spell and falling down the stairs, as she had in the past.

Unable to persuade her to employ full-time help, her friends were greatly relieved when she moved into a well-guarded skyscraper apartment building near the University of Maryland.* But they still worried about her deep frustration in no longer being able to write and her frequent references to "all the time I've wasted, when I should have been writing."

She talked frequently about death and occasionally hinted that suicide would be preferable to senility or a slow death. Having that in mind, she once told her nephew, "Now I don't have to have any more [doctors] until that day they round me up and try to put tubes in my nose and feed me in the veins, and on that day I want you or Ann to be present to say, 'Let my pore ole good ole aunt alone. Keep your busy hands off her!' "

It was during these conversations that we had the dialogues reported in the preface to this book, after which Miss Porter bought her own plain coffin.

---

* The university built a replica of her library, and the Katherine Anne Porter Room now houses all her manuscripts, including the unfinished portions of the Cotton Mather book.

15

IN the parlance of the cowhands she knew as a child in Indian Creek, Texas, she once told me, "I want to die with my boots on — I want to be working full tilt at my typewriter, so that I'll be in the middle of a sentence when the end comes."

There were, of course, many unfinished sentences when she died, but she was deprived of the kind of death she had always hoped for. Hers was a lingering end, with a series of debilitating illnesses that finally left her partially paralyzed. Yet she refused to lose hope. Shortly before her death, while bedridden at the Johns Hopkins Hospital, she stared at an old friend through eyes clouded by glaucoma and smilingly promised to "get out of this place and back to my work as soon as I can." But her voice was halting and weak, her face drawn and weary.

"It was heartrending to see her that way," the friend later told me, "and I knew she would never write a single line again — that she would die still feeling guilty for not having finished all those stories and novels she had planned to write."

Those unfinished manuscripts — some of which she had carried with her for several decades as she roamed restlessly from Mexico to Europe and back to the United States — are now safely deposited in the Katherine Anne Porter Room at the University of Maryland library, where future scholars will have a chance to catch a glimpse of what Robert Penn Warren called "the record of a life and the achievement of a rare, powerful, and subtle creative force."

Some critics, such as Theodore Solotaroff, may ultimately conclude that her "just cruelty" was more cruel than just, that she lacked compassion and human warmth — but even her most determined detractors will have to admit that she has left an indelible mark on the literature of this century. One can regret only that her constant wandering from one temporary "home" to another inevitably drained her creative energies. She had once described herself as "a refugee from Indian Creek forever searching for the right place to live, the right place to work." But as one contemplates the depth and range of her published work, characterized by Willie Morris as "her keen sense of the human condition," one could well say that she was always home, always in the right place, but somehow never knew it.

Miss Porter died on September 18, 1980, in the Carriage Hill Nursing Home in Silver Spring, Maryland, just a few months after her ninetieth birthday. And pursuant to her long-expressed plans, she was buried in the plain wooden coffin which she had purchased from the mail-order cabinet shop in Arizona.

Selected Bibliography

PRIMARY SOURCES

1. COLLECTED WORKS

The Days Before (New York: Harcourt, Brace and Co., 1952). Contents: "The Days Before," "On a Criticism of Thomas Hardy," "Gertrude Stein: Three Views," "Reflections on Willa Cather," " 'It is Hard to Stand in the Middle,' " "The Art of Katherine Mansfield," "Orpheus in Purgatory," " 'The Laughing Heat of the Sun,' " "Eudora Welty and 'A Curtain of Green,' " "Homage to Ford Madox Ford," "Virginia Woolf," "E. M. Forster," "Three Statements about Writing," "No Plot, My Dear, No Story," "The Flower of Flowers," "Portrait: Old South," "Audubon's Happy Land," "A House of My Own," "The Necessary Enemy," " 'Marriage Is Belonging,' " "American Statement: 4 July 1942," "The Future Is Now," "Notes on the Life and Death of a Hero," "Why I Write about Mexico," "Leaving the Petate," "The Mexican Trinity," "La Conquistadora," "Quetzalcoatl," "The Charmed Life"

Flowering Judas and Other Stories (New York: The Modern Library, 1940). Contents: "María Concepción," "Magic," "Rope," "He," "Theft," "That Tree," "The Jilting of Granny Weatherall," "Flowering Judas," "The Cracked Looking-Glass," "Hacienda"

The Leaning Tower and Other Stories (New York: Harcourt, Brace and Co., 1944). Contents: "The Source," "The Witness," "The Circus," "The Old Order," "The Last Leaf," "The Grave," "The Downward Path to Wisdom," "A Day's Work," "The Leaning Tower"

Pale Horse, Pale Rider: Three Short Novels (New York, The Modern Library, 1949). Contents: *Old Mortality, Noon Wine, Pale Horse, Pale Rider*

Ship of Fools (Boston: Atlantic–Little, Brown and Co., 1962).

The Collected Essays (New York: Delacorte Press, 1965).

The Never-Ending Wrong (Boston: Atlantic–Little, Brown and Co., 1977). This appeared first in its entirety in *The Atlantic Monthly*, 239(June 1977): 37–64.

2. WORKS NOT COLLECTED OR SUBSEQUENTLY INCLUDED IN *THE COLLECTED ESSAYS*

"Society Gossip of the Week" and "The Week at the Theaters," undated 1917 clippings from *The Critic*.

"The Adventures of Hadji: A Tale of a Turkish Coffee-House," retold by Katherine Anne Porter, *Asia*, 20(August 1920): 683–684.

"Where Presidents Have No Friends," *The Century Magazine*, 104(July 1922): 373–384.

"The Martyr," *The Century Magazine*, 106(July 1923): 410–413.

"Virgin Violeta," *The Century Magazine*, 109(December 1924): 261–268.

"Notes on Writing," *New Directions, 1940* (Norfolk, Conn.: New Directions, 1940), pp. 195–204.

For a biography of Cotton Mather: "Affectation of Praehiminincies," *Accent*, 2(Spring 1942): 131–138; (Summer 1942): 226–232. "A Bright Particular Faith A.D. 1700," *Hound and Horn*, 7(January 1934): 246–257. "A Goat for Azazel (A.D. 1688)," *Partisan Review*, 7(May–June 1940): 188–199.

" 'Noon Wine': The Sources," *Yale Review*, 46(September 1956): 22–39. Reprinted in Cleanth Brooks and Robert Penn Warren, *Understanding Fiction*, 2d ed. (New York: Appleton-Century-Crofts, Inc., 1963), pp. 610–620.

"A Wreath for the Gamekeeper," *Shenandoah*, 11(Autumn 1959): 3–12. This also appeared in *Encounter*, 14(February 1960): 69–77.

"The Fig Tree," *Harper's*, 220(June 1960): 55–59.

"Holiday," *The Atlantic Monthly*, 206(December 1960): 44–56. Reprinted in *Prize Stories 1962: The O. Henry Awards*, with an introduction by Richard Poirier (Greenwich, Conn.: Fawcett World Library, 1963).

"On First Meeting T. S. Eliot," *Shenandoah*, 12(Spring 1961): 25–26.

"A Country and Some People I Love," by Katherine Anne Porter and Hank Lopez, *Harper's*, vol. 231, no. 1384(September 1965): 58–69.

SECONDARY SOURCES

1. BIBLIOGRAPHY

SCHWARTZ, EDWARD. "Katherine Anne Porter: A Critical Bibliography." With an introduction by Robert Penn Warren. *Bulletin of the New York Public Library*, 57(May 1953): 211–247.

SYLVESTER, WILLIAM A. "Selected and Critical Bibliography of the Uncollected Works of Katherine Anne Porter," *Bulletin of Bibliography*, 19(January 1947): 36.

THURSTON, JARVIS, O. B. EMERSON, CARL HARTMAN, ELIZABETH V. WRIGHT. *Short Fiction Criticism* (Denver: Alan Swallow, 1960), pp. 176–180.

WALKER, WARREN S. *Twentieth-Century Short Story Explication* (Hamden, Conn.: The Shoe String Press, Inc., 1961), pp. 312–319.

WOODRESS, JAMES. *Dissertations in American Literature 1891–1955 with Supplement 1956–1961* (Durham: Duke University Press, 1962), pp. 181–185.

2. BIOGRAPHY

AARON, DANIEL. *Writers on the Left* (New York: Harcourt Brace & World, 1961).

BLOCK, MAXINE. *Current Biography* (New York: The H. W. Wilson Co., 1940).

JOSEPHSON, MATTHEW. *Life Among the Surrealists* (New York: Holt, Rinehart and Winston, 1962).

KUNITZ, STANLEY J. and HOWARD HAYCRAFT. *Twentieth Century Authors* (New York: The H. W. Wilson Co., 1942). For additional biographical information, see *Twentieth Century Authors, First Supplement*, edited by Stanley J. Kunitz and Vineta Colby (New York: The H. W. Wilson Co., 1955).

SEXTON, KATHRYN ADAMS. "Katherine Anne Porter's Years in Denver." Unpublished M.A. thesis, University of Colorado, 1961.

STALLING, DONALD. "Katherine Anne Porter: Life and the Literary Mirror." Unpublished M.A. thesis, Texas Christian University, 1951.

3. INTERVIEWS

"The Best Years," *Newsweek* (International edition), July 31, 1961, p. 39.

BODE, WINSTON. "Miss Porter on Writers and Writing," *Texas Observer*, October 31, 1958, pp. 6–7.

DOLBIER, MAURICE. "I've Had a Good Run for My Money," New York *Herald-Tribune Books*, April 1, 1962, pp. 3, 11.

"First Novel," *Time* (International edition), July 28, 1961, p. 65. A prepublication interview.

GIRSON, ROCHELLE. "The Author," *Saturday Review*, 45(March 31, 1962): 15.

JANEWAY, ELIZABETH. "For Katherine Anne Porter, 'Ship of Fools' Was a Lively

Twenty-Two Year Voyage," *The New York Times Book Review*, April 1, 1962, pp. 4–5.

"Some Important Authors Speak for Themselves," New York *Herald-Tribune Books*, October 12, 1952, p. 8.

THOMPSON, BARBARA. "The Art of Fiction XXIX — Katherine Anne Porter: An Interview," *Paris Review*, 29(Winter-Spring 1963): 87–114.

VAN GELDER, ROBERT. "Katherine Anne Porter at Work," *Writers and Writing* (New York: Charles Scribner's Sons, 1946).

WINSTEN, ARCHER. "Presenting the Portrait of an Artist," New York *Post*, May 6, 1937, p. 17.

"Writing a Prize Story Is Easy — To Miss Porter," New York *Herald-Tribune*, April 6, 1940, p. 9. Early comments on "Promised Land," an earlier title for *Ship of Fools*.

4. CRITICISM OF MISS PORTER'S WORK

ALLEN, CHARLES A. "Katherine Anne Porter: Psychology as Art," *Southwest Review*, 41(Summer 1956): 223–230.

BURNETT, WHIT, ed. "Why She Selected Flowering Judas," *This Is My Best* (New York: The Dial Press, 1942).

COWSER, ROBERT G. "Porter's 'The Jilting of Granny Weatherall'," *The Explicator*, 21(December 1962).

CRUME, PAUL. "Pale Horse, Pale Rider," *Southwest Review*, 25(January 1940): 213–218.

HAFLEY, JAMES. " 'Maria Concepcion': Life among the Ruins," *Four Quarters*, 12(November 1962): 11–17.

HAGOPIAN, JOHN V. "Katherine Anne Porter: Feeling, Form and Truth," *Four Quarters*, 12(November 1962): 1–10.

HAGOPIAN, JOHN V., and MARTIN DOLCH. *Insight I* (Frankfurt: Hirchgraben, 1962).

HENDRICK, GEORGE. "Katherine Anne Porter's 'Hacienda,' " *Four Quarters*, 12(November 1962): 24–29.

JOHNSON, JAMES WILLIAM. "Another Look at Katherine Anne Porter," *The Virginia Quarterly Review*, 36(Autumn 1960): 598–613.

KAPLAN, CHARLES. "True Witness: Katherine Anne Porter," *Colorado Quarterly*, 7(Winter 1959): 319–327.

KIELY, ROBERT. "The Craft of Despondency — The Traditional Novelists," *Daedalus*, 92(Spring 1963): 220–237.

MARSHALL, MARGARET. "Writers in the Wilderness: Katherine Anne Porter," *The Nation*, 150(April 13, 1940): 473–475.

MOONEY, HARRY JOHN, JR. *The Fiction and Criticism of Katherine Anne Porter.* (Pittsburgh: University of Pittsburgh Press, 1957).

NANCE, WILLIAM L. *Katherine Anne Porter & the Art of Rejection* (Chapel Hill: University of North Carolina Press, 1964).

PIERCE, MARVIN. "Point of View: Katherine Anne Porter's *Noon Wine*," *The Ohio University Review*, 3(1961): 95–113.

POSS, S. H. "Variations on a Theme in Four Stories of Katherine Anne Porter," *Twentieth Century Literature*, 4(April–July 1958): 21–29.

PRAGER, LEONARD. "Getting and Spending: Porter's 'Theft,' " *Perspective*, 11(Winter 1960): 230–234.

RYAN, MARJORIE. "*Dubliners* and the Stories of Katherine Anne Porter," *American Literature*, 31(January 1960): 464–473.

SCHWARTZ, EDWARD GREENFIELD. "The Fictions of Memory," *Southwest Review*, 45(Summer 1960): 204–215.

STEIN, WILLIAM BYSSHE. " 'Theft': Porter's Politics of Modern Love," *Perspective*, 11(Winter 1960): 223–228.

WARREN, ROBERT PENN. "Irony with a Center: Katherine Anne Porter," *Selected Essays* (New York: Random House, 1958).

―――. "Uncorrupted Consciousness: The Stories of Katherine Anne Porter," *Yale Review* (December 1965): 280–290.

WELTY, EUDORA. "The Eye of the Story," *Yale Review* (December 1965): 265–274.

WEST, RAY B., JR. "Katherine Anne Porter: Symbol and Theme in 'Flowering Judas,'" *Accent*, 7(Spring 1947): 182–187.

WIESENFARTH, BROTHER JOSEPH. "Illusion and Allusion: Reflections in 'The Cracked Looking-Glass,'" *Four Quarters*, 12(November 1962): 30–37.

WILSON, EDMUND. "Katherine Anne Porter," *Classics and Commercials* (New York: Farrar, Straus and Co., 1950). Reprinted from *The New Yorker*, 20(September 30, 1944): 72–75.

YOUNG, VERNON A. "The Art of Katherine Anne Porter," *American Thought — 1947* (New York: The Gresham Press, 1947), pp. 223–238. Reprinted from *The New Mexico Quarterly*, 15(Autumn 1945): 326–341.

YOUNGBLOOD, SARAH. "Structure and Imagery in Katherine Anne Porter's 'Pale Horse, Pale Rider,'" *Modern Fiction Studies*, 5(Winter 1959): 344–352.

5. CRITICISM OF *SHIP OF FOOLS*

AUCHINCLOSS, LOUIS. "Bound for Bremerhaven — and Eternity," New York *Herald-Tribune Books*, April 1, 1962, pp. 3, 11.

BEDFORD, SYBILLE. "Voyage to Everywhere," *The Spectator*, November 16, 1962, pp. 763–764.

BORCH, HERBERT VON. "'Die Deutschen sind allzumal grausam, böse und fanatisch'/Dokument des Hasses: K. A. Porters 'Narrenschiff,'" *Die Welt*, June 9, 1962.

BRANT, SEBASTIAN. *The Ship of Fools*. Translated and with introduction and commentary by Edwin H. Zeydel (New York: Dover Publications, Inc., 1962).

DE VRIES, PETER. "Nobody's Fool (A Character or Two Overlooked in Miss Katherine Anne Porter's Shipload)," *The New Yorker*, 37(June 16, 1962): 28–29.

FADIMAN, CLIFTON. "Ship of Fools," *Book-of-the-Month Club News* (April 1962), pp. 2–4.

HEILMAN, ROBERT B. "Ship of Fools: Notes on Style," *Four Quarters*, 12(November 1962): 46–55.

HENDRICK, GEORGE. "Hart Crane Aboard the Ship of Fools: Some Speculations," *Twentieth Century Literature*, 9(April 1963): 3–9.

HICKS, GRANVILLE. "Voyage of Life," *Saturday Review*, 45(March 31, 1962): 15–16.

HORTON, PHILIP. *Hart Crane: The Life of an American Poet* (New York: The Viking Press, 1957), pp. 283–287.

KAUFFMANN, STANLEY. "Katherine Anne Porter's Crowning Work," *The New Republic*, April 2, 1962, pp. 23–25.

LEVITAS, GLORIA. "Katherine Anne Porter at the 'Y': 'I Wrote the Book I Meant To,'" New York *Herald-Tribune*, October 11, 1962 (Rowalt clipping book).

"The Longest Journey," *Newsweek* (International edition), April 2, 1962, pp. 58–59.

MOSS, HOWARD. "No Safe Harbor," *The New Yorker*, 38(April 28, 1962): 165–173.

MUHLEN, NORBERT. "Deutsche, wie sie im Buche stehen," *Der Monat* (December 1962): 38–45.

"On the Good Ship Vera," *The Times Literary Supplement*, November 2, 1962, p. 837.

PÄCHTER, HEINZ. "Miss Porters neue Kleider/Missverständnisse um einen amerikanischen Bestseller," *Deutsche Zeitung*, October 13–14, 1962.

SCHORER, MARK. "We're All on the Passenger List," *The New York Times Book Review*, April 1, 1962, pp. 1, 5.

SOLOTAROFF, THEODORE. "'Ship of Fools' & the Critics," *Commentary*, 34(October 1962): 277–286.

SOUTHERN, TERRY. "Recent Fiction, Part I: 'When Film Gets Good ...,'" *The Nation* 195(November 17, 1962): 330.

"Speech After Long Silence," *Time* (International edition), April 6, 1962, p. 67.

TAUBMAN, ROBERT. "A First-Class Passenger," *The Statesman*, November 11, 1962 (Rowalt clipping book).

WESCOTT, GLENWAY. "Katherine Anne Porter," *Book-of-the-Month Club News*

(April 1962), pp. 5–7. Appeared in an expanded version in "Katherine Anne Porter: The Making of a Novel," *The Atlantic Monthly*, 209(April 1962): 43–49; appeared also in "Katherine Anne Porter Personally," *Images of Truth* (New York: Harper & Row, 1962), pp. 25–58.

WILSON, ANGUS. "The Middle-Class Passenger," *The Observer*, October 28, 1962, p. 27.

Index